A CONTEMPORARY HISTORY OF SOCIAL WORK
Learning from the past

Terry Bamford

First published in Great Britain in 2015 by

Policy Press
University of Bristol
1-9 Old Park Hill
Bristol BS2 8BB
UK
t: +44 (0)117 954 5940
e: pp-info@bristol.ac.uk
www.policypress.co.uk

North American office:
Policy Press
c/o The University of Chicago Press
1427 East 60th Street
Chicago, IL 60637, USA
t: +1 773 702 7700
f: +1 773-702-9756
e:sales@press.uchicago.edu
www.press.uchicago.edu

© Policy Press 2015

British Library Cataloguing in Publication Data
A catalogue record for this book is available from the British Library.

Library of Congress Cataloging-in-Publication Data
A catalog record for this book has been requested.

ISBN 978 1 44732 216 0 paperback
ISBN 978 1 44732 215 3 hardcover

Cover design by Andy Bamford
Printed and bound in Great Britain by by CPI Group (UK) Ltd,
Croydon, CR0 4YY
Policy Press uses environmentally responsible print partners

Contents

Acknowledgements

Social work has provided me with a rich variety of experiences. Being deloused after a visit from a 'man of the road' in my early days in probation, sharing a boat with social work's doyenne Dame Eileen Younghusband in Puerto Rico, being electrified by an address entitled 'Clients are fellow citizens' by a man in a white suit, academic Bill Jordan, at a British Association of Social Workers (BASW) conference, spending 12 hours talking shop with academic and former social worker Professor Ray Jones in Moscow airport, and countless other memories flood in when looking back.

I could not begin to list the many people who have helped to shape my thinking often without them knowing it. I am grateful to all my colleagues in probation, in BASW, in social services departments in the London Borough of Harrow and the Royal Borough of Kensington and Chelsea, and in the Southern Health and Social Services Board in Northern Ireland. They all contributed to what has been a rich experience of social work.

In writing this book, there are some people to whom I owe particular thanks. The staff at the British Library, where much of the book was written, have been unfailingly helpful in tracking down references. Fortunately, the Library's Newsroom, which offers access to newspapers from the past hundred years, opened too late to distract me from the task, but it is a wonderful resource nonetheless.

Isobel Bainton has been a helpful and supportive editor, responding swiftly to any queries. Jo Morton and her colleagues at Policy Press have helped to produce the book as speedily and efficiently as I could have hoped.

My thinking has been helped by discussions – usually over a glass of wine – with Marianne Griffiths, John Dixon, Ray Jones and June Thoburn. Richard Hugman, Rhiann Huws Williams, David Jones, Ruth Stark and Anne James have also given me helpful guidance.

Sally Trench has helped me greatly with proofreading and has been an invaluable adviser on style, although I suspect there may be a deficit of commas for her liking. Her interest in the book has been a real help in keeping me to the discipline of writing.

My special thanks go to my family. Andrew has helped with the cover design. Sarah and Rupert have been subjected to testing out my ideas. My wife Margaret has been a patient source of encouragement, gentle criticism and constant support in writing the book. I thank her for that and for so many other things.

Preface

The past is never dead. It's not even past.

William Faulkner, *Requiem for a Nun*, 1951

Writing contemporary history is a risky business. Hindsight may be a great teacher, but, looking back, what seems obvious now was rarely so clear at the time. Anybody purporting to write a history of the past 50 years has immediately to acknowledge that what follows can only be a partial and imperfect summary of the influences that have affected social work.

The reasons for attempting a contemporary history are part personal and part professional. It is personal because the story of the past 50 years is the story of my life in social work. I qualified in 1965 and worked in probation before the Seebohm Committee had been appointed and at a time when social work was fragmented between different occupational settings. It is professional because many of the issues facing social work today are those that have been around for many years. While learning lessons has become a cliché of serious case reviews, I believe that we can learn from the mistakes of the past and put into practice some of those lessons. Social work should be playing a leading role in delivering high-quality care and in helping to drive social policy change. Yet the story of the past 50 years is one of its declining influence.

My credentials for writing this book are not those of an academic. Despite having done many things in a social work career, I have never taught social work from an academic base. I did run a student unit and from that came to appreciate the risk of too wide a gap between theory and practice. The challenge of integrating theory and practice makes demands on practice educators whose role is undervalued and underfunded.

Some of the topics discussed in the book – the failure of BASW, the growth of managerialism, the regulation of the profession, the challenge of integrating health and social care, and the development of the College of Social Work – are those in which I have had some personal involvement. So let me declare my prejudices at the outset so that readers can bear those in mind.

Prejudices

BASW is – to borrow from the Conservative politician Rab Butler's famous remark about Harold Macmillan being the 'best prime minister we have' – 'the best professional association we've got'. It has faltered along the way, it has taken some wrong directions and at times its leadership has been erratic. But it is the only substantial democratic association in the field of social work and will only be strengthened if social workers join and work to make it better.

Management is necessary in large-scale organisations. Social workers should be naturally good managers with their skills in relationship building and understanding human behaviour. Management tilts into managerialism when it becomes enmeshed in bureaucratic procedures, checklists and processes, and strips out the creativity of good social work. The way in which the employer voice and management voice have become dominant in discussions with government has been to the detriment of social work as a profession.

The demise of the General Social Care Council (GSCC) in 2012 was politically driven. The council gave an identity to social work now lost in its successor, the Health and Care Professions Council. The dismissal of the GSCC chief executive was a tawdry process. The reforms of social work education may provide an opportunity to reinvent a social work-driven regulatory body, which will be even more important if social workers are to become more engaged in social enterprises and small-scale practices.

The dream of integrated health and social care is beloved of politicians. Its complexity is not fully appreciated. The evidence base for improved services is thin. The different financial contexts pose almost insuperable difficulties. Even 40 years' experience of integration in Northern Ireland has failed to deliver improved outcomes. To present it as the way to deliver improved quality and cost savings is the ultimate triumph of hope over experience.

The College of Social Work has had a rocky start. Its falling out with BASW was unedifying. It incurs reputational damage by its dependence on government funding and corporate membership. It has, however, some excellent social workers and academics supporting it and can develop its role in driving up social work standards in education and practice. It will, however, need to establish a rapprochement with BASW if it is to achieve its full potential.

Pattern of book

The book uses the recent history of social work to pick up those issues that have relevance for contemporary debates. The genericism-specialism argument is again being rehearsed but this time in the context of training rather than practice. Have we got the right balance in social work programmes or should we move towards a specialist basic qualification?

The concern of social workers with social justice and anti-oppressive practice is under challenge from the Narey review (Narey, 2014). The label of political correctness is still used to stereotype social work. How can we best hold on to social work values when under pressure?

The search for integrated health and social care continues as it has done since 1974. The territory that is exclusively that of social work is narrowing. With the continuing pressure on local authority budgets, is it time to look at alternative structures, and what can we learn from pilot studies and alternative models of delivery?

One of the advantages of writing a book is that it gives a chance to review the literature on social work generated in recent years. Undoubtedly the most influential works have been those taking a critical stance on the neoliberal trends in social work. The word neoliberalism contains almost as many different meanings as the word integration, but it captures the shared belief systems of the main political parties in favouring the introduction of market disciplines into the public sector. At first this was achieved through financial mechanisms like the Special Transitional Grant following the introduction of community care. Subsequently, it has been extended to outsourcing swathes of social welfare provision. Those who seek a smaller role for the state have a deep hostility towards the public sector. They are hostile to public expenditure on welfare provision, believing, as did the Victorians, that this fosters dependency and rewards idleness.

Thirty-five years ago, a delegation from BASW, of which I was a member, met Margaret Thatcher, then leader of the Opposition. She opined that children's social work should be handed over to the NSPCC, the children's welfare charity (Mrs T did not ask – she stated). The idea has not gone away. The belief that the voluntary and community sector will step up to fill the gaps left by the hollowing out of public services has been around since the Barclay report (Barclay, 1982), with its reference to 'a vast untapped reservoir of volunteers' – a reservoir yet to be discovered, although the mirage is periodically cited by politicians.

Radical social work has been a hugely beneficial influence on social work in general. Its critique has helped to drive the recognition of the factors leading to social exclusion and the marginalisation of many of the people with whom social workers come into contact each day. It offers a potent challenge to the neoliberal trends of public policy and to the 'depersonalisation' of the social work role in an age of managerialism. It has some brilliant thinkers and writers. One of the weaknesses is that some of those prominent in the 'New Left social work' (described by Gray and Webb, 2013) prefer to muse on moral philosophy than to offer insights into practice. I may be accused of anti-intellectualism, but I prefer writing that has a bias to understanding rather than the opposite.

Not all social workers share the rosy view of state socialism held by the critical social work school. Nor are they likely to respond to the call to join in the overthrow of capitalism, a somewhat hyperbolic call for a small profession. But they do want to find the answer to the question posed by Ferguson (2008, p 21): 'How can social work rediscover its humanity as well as its radicalism?'

This book suggests that it can indeed do both once it accepts that radicalism does not demand a particular world view, class analysis or the denial of the importance of personal relationships. Radicalism requires a challenge to the established order, a conviction that society should be fairer and more equal, and that those with whom we work deserve support and assistance in their quest for a better life. It does mean questioning current policies and gathering the data to demonstrate where policies are wrong and unfair. Feeding such information into the Joint Strategic Needs Assessment may sound hopelessly bureaucratic, but it may be the most effective way of influencing policy at local level.

Social work at its best is a combination of 'heart and head', in Olive Stevenson's words: 'heart' because emotional intelligence, sensitivity, empathy and warmth are essential elements in the process of building relationships with those using services (while I may occasionally use the word client in the text, I accept the criticism that it denotes a relationship that is not one of equals but one in which services are provided to or for rather than *with* the service user); and 'head' because a warm heart is not enough. It needs to be accompanied by the ability to locate service users in their environment and to understand the pressures that imposes on them, and then to mobilise various forms of social support including practical support to assist.

The contention in the book that social work should accept the challenges of the market will not be acceptable to many. My fear is that if we do not accept that challenge because of our hostility to competition, we will leave the field open to the corporate predators with their exaggerated claims of success. Learning lessons from what works – in particular from social work practices and the systemic model – can help to restore social work as the leading profession in delivering high-quality and sensitive care.

Terry Bamford
December 2014

ONE

A brave new world: social work at its zenith

KEY LEARNING POINTS

» The enduring influence of the Poor Law on social policy
» The threat of pauperism
» The role of Victorian philanthropy
» The different philosophical approaches of the Charity Organisation Society and the settlement movement
» The impact of the Royal Commission on the Poor Laws
» The development of social insurance
» Beveridge and the post-war welfare state
» Universalism and the Seebohm report
» The creation of local authority personal social services

In 1970 social work was in a position of power and influence greater than at any time in its history. The passage of the Local Authority Social Services Act promised a new dawn in the creation of a large and powerful department in local government meeting the needs of vulnerable people in the community – children, those with disabilities, those with mental health problems and older people. The vision of the Beveridge report of care from the cradle to the grave was to be realised with social care services for all matching the national insurance-based scheme of financial support to those in need and the National Health Service. Social work was to be the lead profession running the new departments, having seen off a rearguard action by Medical Officers of Health backed by the British Medical Association to retain control of community services.

Parallel with this legislative development, the social work profession, previously fragmented between a number of separate professional bodies, came together in one single association – the British Association of Social Workers. The path to unity had not been untroubled. The National Association of Probation Officers decided not to join the new organisation after a ballot of its members.

The ambitions for the new department and the new association were huge but were never to be fully realised. The period since 1970 has seen a gradual decline in the reputation and the reach of public sector social welfare services. Understanding why this has happened and why the professional association failed to establish itself as the unchallenged voice of social work requires an examination of the period preceding 1970, for many of the issues that were to bedevil social work can be traced back to the genesis of social work itself.

The purpose of the Poor Law

Anxiety about the cost of social welfare is not a new phenomenon, nor is the stigmatisation of those claiming welfare.

In early Tudor times, the Church played a central role in the distribution of help to the poor. With the dissolution of the monasteries in 1536–40 followed by the dissolution of religious guilds, fraternities, almshouses and hospitals in 1545–49, a key source of charitable support to the poor was removed.

Placing the responsibility for assistance to the poor at a local level was the necessary consequence in order to address the threat of potential social disorder. The parish was the only effective source of administration and had been the basic unit of local government since the 14th century. There were 15,000 parishes in England alone so there were wide variations in administration. The postcode lottery is not a new concept.

The 1563 Poor Law was the first to place the poor in different categories:

- the deserving poor – the old, the sick and young children – were given outdoor relief of assistance with clothing, food or money;
- the deserving unemployed, who were willing to work but unable to find a job, were given indoor relief in workhouses or orphanages;
- the undeserving poor, who had become beggars or become involved in crime, received harsh treatment and no material assistance.

The Poor Law has cast a long shadow. The categorisation of deserving and undeserving remains with us, although no longer expressed in exactly those terms. Punitive sanctions against those claimants who are unable or unwilling to comply with the requirements of the Department for Work and Pensions are the contemporary equivalent.

Each parish was required to levy a rate to support the deserving poor. A succession of laws followed before being consolidated in the 1601 Poor Law, which provided a national system of poor rates in every parish with the provision of working materials and support for the deserving poor.

The provision of support was motivated in part by a sense of obligation to the poor. More powerful, however, was the fear of social unrest. Social pressures had built during the second half of the reign of Elizabeth I. Between 1595 and 1598 there were four poor harvests. Coupled with the rise in enclosures reducing the demand for agricultural labourers, this accentuated the migration from the countryside into the towns. The 1601 Act led to the appointment of overseers of the poor to be responsible for setting and levying the rate and for supervision of the parish poorhouse. While the first to derive income from supervising a rudimentary system of social welfare, they were far removed from anything recognisable as social work. The punishment of those classed as undeserving was brutal, with either whipping or boring through the ear as the usual punishment for a first offence and for a second offence they could be hung. This exemplary punishment was intended to deter beggars and encourage them to return to their place of birth.

The parish officers' handbook (Handbook, 1601) stated that overseers were responsible for 'employing by worke, releeving by money, and ordering by discretion the defects of the poor'. The system worked well as a 'system of income maintenance for well defined groups of people, especially the young, the recently married and the elderly' (Hindle, 2004, p 297). Alongside the system of parish relief, there was a growth of endowments from bequests for the provision of specific forms of relief – sometimes workhouses and sometime cash sums available to the parish for specific purposes like the apprenticeship of pauper children.

Containing costs

One consistent theme as relevant now as then was the importance of restraining expenditure on social welfare. The 1662 Act of Settlement set limits on expenditure by limiting eligibility to those ordinarily resident (a term in use four centuries on to determine eligibility for assistance) in the parish and authorising justices of the peace to remove newcomers to the parish who were likely to be chargeable to the parish: 'Migrants had to give notice of their arrival, parishes to keep bundles of settlement certificates, and justices to respond to requests for removal orders for a century or more' (Hindle, 2004, p 195).

The Workhouse Test Act of 1723 empowered parishes to refuse relief to all those who refused to enter a workhouse. The austere and disciplinarian regime of workhouses was not designed to make a profit from the labour of the poor but to reduce the numbers on outdoor relief by acting as a deterrent. Their success is questionable. The provision of employment often added to parish costs and the scale of expenditure on relief continued to grow.

Boyer (1990) describes the various ways in which relief for the able-bodied was provided. The most important of these were: allowances-in-aid of wages (the so-called Speenhamland system), child allowances for labourers with large families, and payments to seasonally unemployed agricultural labourers (Boyer, 1990, pp 10-23).

The Speenhamland system offered a guaranteed weekly income to the head of the household determined by the price of bread and the size of the family. The payment was made to the household head whether employed or unemployed.

Cost control and the perverse incentives within the system of supplementing low wages led to attacks on the Poor Law, with allegations of corruption and abuse. Driver (1993) noted that in particular the Speenhamland system was regarded as undermining both the self-discipline of labourers and a free labour market. This critique of the Poor Laws contained a strong moral element in the belief that the availability of wage supplementation was promoting pauperism by its erosion of self-reliance. It is important to see this moral judgement in the social and political context of the time.

Adam Smith wrote of the 'invisible hand' that led the individual seeking to better himself to promote the public good. Ricardo saw the operation of laws of supply and demand as inexorable and any attempt by the state to influence them as doomed to failure. Bentham's utilitarian pursuit of the greatest happiness of the greatest number was interpreted as support for the laissez-faire principles driving the rapid expansion of the industrial north in the wake of the Industrial Revolution. It was wholly consistent with this philosophical position therefore to argue for self-reliance and self-improvement as the goals of public policy. Conversely, interference by the state with the operation of the free market was justified only by utilitarian principles.

Dealing with abuse of the system

The Royal Commission was appointed in 1832 to examine the operation of the Poor Law. Its deliberations were influenced by Edwin Chadwick's utilitarian beliefs. Chadwick, who was to become the first secretary of the Poor Law Commission, had a view that all outdoor relief should be abolished as it discouraged self-reliance. The remedy proposed by the Royal Commission in its report was based on the principle of 'less eligibility', ensuring that nobody in receipt of relief should receive more than 'the independent labourer of the lowest class' (Her Majesty's Commissioners, 1834). The Poor Law Amendment Act of 1834 adopted the majority of the Commission's recommendations. Parishes were grouped into Poor Law unions with the aim of abolishing outdoor relief to the able-bodied and their families. A centralised Poor Law Commission was established to ensure consistency of administration, with assistant commissioners responsible for a region and independent of local interests charged with delivering that consistency.

Young (1936, p 40) provides a vivid picture of the time:

> The Poor Law filled the whole horizon in 1834. And here there and everywhere were Chadwick's young crusaders, the assistant commissioners, scouring the country in stage-coaches or post-chaises, or beating up against the storm on the Weald, returning to London, their wallets stuffed with the tabular data so dear to Philosophical Radicals, to draft their sovereign's decrees declaring the union and stating his austere principles of administration, and then back to see they were carried out.

There was a sharp decrease in spending of 43% in the decade following the legislation. The numbers of paupers on relief fell from an estimated 8.8% of the population in 1834 to 5.7% in 1850 (Rose, 1972, Appendix A, p 53). Although not all unions, particularly those in the north of England, ceased the provision of outdoor relief, in most areas the workhouse became the main instrument for helping the poor. Wages were paid to the able-bodied but at a lower level than any wages in paid work. Families were separated, with husbands and wives in separate sections of the workhouse. With inmates forced to dress in workhouse uniform and with a restricted diet, conditions in the workhouse were designed to increase the stigma of pauperism.

The original report recommended different types of workhouses for different categories: able-bodied males over 15, able-bodied females over 15, aged and infirm males, aged and infirm females, boys between 7 and 15, girls between 7 and 15, and young children (Her Majesty's Commissioners, 1834, Appendix A3). This more enlightened approach proved too expensive for most boards and it was less costly to provide one large workhouse albeit with different sections. This categorisation was intended to reinforce the deterrent to pauperism, to prevent contagion between the groups and to allow separate regimes to be developed. The design of the workhouse was large and forbidding, with a deliberate similarity to prisons.

The harshness of the regime in the workhouse was criticised not least by Charles Dickens in *Oliver Twist* (1839) and *A Christmas Carol* (1843). Workhouse scandals in the late 1840s attracted national attention. Those placed in the Andover workhouse were so hungry that they were eating the marrow from the bones that they were required to crush. The ensuing coverage in press and Parliament led to the establishment of a Select Committee on the scandal, which established that the inmates were served less food than the inadequate diet prescribed. The authoritarian rule of the workhouse master meant that it was difficult to challenge his authority. The report in 1846 (Select Committee of the House of Commons, 1846) eventually led to the replacement of the Poor Law Commission by a new Poor Law Board.

This was not a move to a more liberal regime. The board tightened restrictions on outdoor relief by making the work as unpleasant as possible, largely consisting of stone breaking, but there remained wide local variations. Despite the pressure from the National Poor Law Board, local boards often found it more economical to provide outdoor relief at a low level than to meet the cost of accommodating the family in the workhouse. There were, however, two arguments deployed by opponents of outdoor relief: the destructive impact on individuals of dependency on welfare provision, sapping their will to provide for themselves, and the laxness of those administering the system as shown by the variations in provision.

The role of charity and philanthropy

There were paid staff supervising workhouses and administering outdoor relief, but this was not a welfare role. A very different approach to the relief of poverty was developed in Scotland by Thomas Chalmers, a Glasgow churchman. He visited and recorded information on every family in his parish and found that a large proportion were living hand to mouth on poor relief. With the approval of the town council, he devised a scheme to divide his parish into 25 units, each having around 400 people and supervised by a deacon. The deacons had to investigate the circumstances of each individual seeking help. They were expected to encourage applicants into employment, to look at their patterns of spending to see if economies could be made, to encourage family support and only as a last resort to use the resources of the parish fund.

Chalmers stressed what he called the Four Fountains – self-help, help from relatives, help of the poor for each other, and help from the rich as an option only if all else had been explored. His approach had characteristics that were subsequently consolidated by the Charity Organisation Society – individualised assessment, hostility to sentimental giving, understanding the needs of applicants, recourse to financial help as a last resort, and guidance and advice to those carrying out the home visits.

Visiting societies, usually linked to churches, adopted the principles of Chalmers' work. This involved fortnightly visits and a discussion of both moral improvement – whether the family had a Bible or went to a place of worship – and material circumstances. The Metropolitan Visiting and Relief Association established in 1843 drew together their work.

> Keeping records of cases seems to have been a prominent part of the scheme, each visitor being expected to keep two documents. One was his own journal, where he noted the facts of a family's situation, his impressions, and the general help given, and the other was a report to the local committee. It was clear, said Pringle (the Rev J.C. Pringle was later to be Secretary of the Charity Organisation Society), that this was family case work. (Young and Ashton, 1956, p 90)

The Jewish Metropolitan Board of Guardians was established in 1859. Its approach differed significantly from the attitudes adopted both by boards of guardians overseeing the Poor Law and the charities working with the poor. The Metropolitan Board believed in what today we would call early intervention, giving help to prevent the decline into pauperism. It investigated every case and kept a full record. Refusals of assistance were as low as 5% in marked contrast to other organisations.

The mid-Victorian years saw a profusion of charities – denominationally based charities and visiting societies, charity schools, dispensaries for the sick, asylums, orphanages, reformatories and penitential homes for fallen women. Derek Fraser suggests that charity was a response to 'four types of motivation: a fear of social revolution, a humanitarian concern for suffering, a satisfaction of some psychological or social need and a desire to improve the moral tone of the recipients' (Fraser, 1973, p 117).

The last of these – the moral purpose of charity – led to a belief in what was to become a founding principle of social work – self-help. Pauperism was seen as disastrous because it eroded self-reliance. Despite the extraordinary level of involvement in charitable activity of various kinds, there was no systematic organisation with a resultant overlap and duplication. The president of the Poor Law Board, George Goschen, issued a minute in 1869 calling for a clear separation between charitable work and those administering the statutory system. 'It would seem to follow that charitable organisations, whose alms could in no case be claimed as a right, would find their most appropriate sphere in assisting those who have some, but insufficient, means ... leaving to the operation of the general laws the provision for the totally destitute' (Goschen, cited in Rose,1971, p 225).

The Charity Organisation Society

Two important pamphlets preceded the establishment of the Charity Organisation Society: Henry Solly's paper, *A few suggestions on how to deal with the unemployed poor of London, and with its 'rough' and criminal classes* (Solly, 1868) and Henry Hawksley's *Charities of London and some errors in their administration* (Hawksley, 1869). They reflected a wish to apply a more rigorous and systematic approach to tackling the problems of the poor. As a result of the interest stimulated and the variety of schemes proposed, a conference of charities was called in February 1869, which led to the establishment of the Society for Organising Charitable Relief and Repressing Mendacity. The full title illustrates part of the declared purpose, but the Charity Organisation Society (COS) swiftly became the working title.

Two important strands can be identified from these early days. First, COS had a profoundly moral approach, with its emphasis on self-help and self-improvement with support to families struggling to keep themselves from destitution. Second, it believed that begging should be repressed and indiscriminate alms giving discouraged. Help of a deeper kind involving social or physical rehabilitation or spiritual care was necessary if effective intervention was to take place.

The initial plan of COS was explicit: 'Confirmed beggars and vagrants will be sent to the Poor Law guardians or prosecuted before the magistrates as circumstances demand' and 'the Public are therefore earnestly requested not, under any circumstances, to give direct relief to applicants in the streets, but to offer them the tickets provided by the District Committees' (Rooff, 1972, p 30). The tickets would be the basis for registering the poor and establishing a pattern of home visits. Within a year there were 17 district committees in London and by 1872 there were 36, each supported by volunteers.

The strength of COS lay in its systematic approach to the distribution of charity, its administrative systems and record keeping, its organisation and training of volunteers, and its success in sharing effective techniques of intervention. It had weaknesses too. In its determined pursuit of self-reliance, it was actively hostile to collective solutions to the problems of poverty. Its first annual report dismissed the concept of state pensions for the elderly, preferring charitable pensions 'for such of the poor as can show that they have practised some degree of providence, and are receiving all the help they can from friends and relations' (COS, 1879, p16). It was also, as its full title implies, concerned with the prevention of begging and the detection of impostors. Its zeal in this direction meant that early reports from districts gave more attention to 'detailed and lively stories of attempted fraud and imposture' than to 'the more prosaic case histories of the widow provided with a mangle, or the workman enabled to get his tools out of pawn, or the costermonger helped to restock his barrow' (Rooff, 1972, p 56). One reason for the hostility engendered by COS was its inappropriate enthusiasm for investigating other charities for unsound methods and lax investigations. Both Barnardo's and the Salvation Army came under the critical gaze of COS (Rooff, 1972, p 90).

Its stance on pensions and later on other social reforms made COS a controversial charity, admired and criticised in equal measure. Overall, the gains clearly outweigh the liabilities. Social casework started with the records of visits made by those working for COS. Its records were meticulous. Its support for the principle of inquiry preceding assessment remains fundamental to social work practice today. The 1895 annual report summed up its approach:

> Investigation has four-fold value. It enables us to decide whether a case is one for help or not. It helps us to decide the form that assistance should take to give the most permanent results. It enables us to find means of assistance apart from cash, and it helps us to give the best advice for the future welfare of the client. (COS, 1895)

COS's approach to visiting too differed from that taken by Chalmers and the visiting societies. Visiting was not to be house to house but for a specific purpose and by 1908 with the agreement of the client (COS, 1908). The visits were then the source material for the case paper containing details of the family, income and expenditure, and the nature of the help requested.

COS was also a pioneer in the use of paid staff. Its first general secretary, Charles Bosanquet, was paid. By 1883, five paid officers were attached to the districts to advise and to help to train volunteers. This was not without controversy, as some active members feared that it would weaken the spirit of voluntarism and discourage volunteers (a tension that has been experienced by many voluntary organisations in the ensuing years).

The development of training was an important function of the paid district staff. The subject assumed increasing importance in the annual reports of COS, with animated debates about the most effective form of training. Octavia Hill, who had been active in the early days of COS and remained a supporter, was an advocate of apprenticeship training and worked closely with the settlement movement. Jointly with Margaret Sewell, warden of the Women's University Settlement, she established a combined course of theory and practice for both volunteers and paid workers. A pioneering paper in 1895 by Mrs Dunn Gardner was published as a COS Occasional Paper (COS, 1895b) and continues to be relevant. It asserted the importance of seeing individuals in relation to their family and neighbourhood, matching resources to need, and stressed the importance of supervision.

COS swiftly became a key source of information on social problems and an effective campaigning voice. It was active in promoting the interest of minority groups. Blind people were supported by a central commission of charities for the blind and successful passage of legislation; those with learning disabilities by the pressure for a central committee to promote the education and welfare of this group; and the Invalid Children's Aid Association, established a year before COS, was a ready partner in developing children's welfare.

The welfare of children

The deterrent principles of the Poor Law meant that 'children, lunatics, incorrigible, innocent, old and disabled were all mixed together' (Webb, 1910) in the workhouse. The poor conditions led to a range of experiments with different approaches. District schools specifically for pauper children were developed by some boards of guardians. Dr Thomas Barnardo opened his first orphanage in 1866, applying the principle 'no destitute child refused admittance'. He also boarded out some children with private families and pioneered cottage homes for young girls. In 1869, George Stephenson opened his first home in what was to become National Children's Home, a Methodist foundation. Cottage homes with a mother and father in each developed as a means of providing substitute family care.

Florence Hill led a campaign to establish fostering as a means of providing care for children. She argued that this was a far more natural life for a child compared with district schools and workhouses where 'the vices of the slave, lack of self-control, indifference to the value of property, and absolute dependence on others, are painfully apparent' (Hill, 1894, p 15). By 1870, a Boarding Out Order empowered all boards to place children and over time regulations were developed to govern the boarding-out process. The 1889 guide to boards of guardians prescribed that the foster parents must not be related to the child and should not be receiving relief themselves, that the father should not be employed on night work and that there should be no more than two children placed per family. There were also specific rules about sleeping accommodation.

The responsibility for supervision of boarding out rested with the relieving officer. Inspectors from the Local Government Board were able to inspect homes outside the parish. In the reports of Miss Mason, who inspected female children boarded out, we see again a contemporary echo in her emphasis on children being seen for a physical examination: 'Bruising is generally on the upper parts of the arms ... where this is the case I undress the child as much further as is necessary. I have thus now and then found a child covered with bruises' (Local Government Board, 1895). Scotland went further and faster in promoting boarding out. By 1894, 84% of orphans and deserted children in Scotland were boarded out. The Superintendent viewed this 'as the means by which thousands of children have been raised from the pauper class into the higher grade of self-supporting and independent workers' (Board of Supervision, 1893).

A society for the prevention of cruelty to children was established in Liverpool in 1883 and swiftly followed by London and other towns. The national body was established in 1889 and granted a Royal Charter in 1895. From the outset, the NSPCC had twin objectives: securing legislation to improve the protection of children and the deployment of staff to take action against cruelty. The Prevention of Cruelty to and Protection of Children Act came in the year of the society's foundation and was popularly known as the children's charter. It made criminal offences of ill treatment, abandonment and neglect, and gave the court powers to remove children to a place of safety. The investigation of reported cruelty or neglect was carried out usually with admonitions and warnings – a rather more traditional approach to wrongdoing than that promoted by COS. Its approach to record keeping was inconsistent and the rich body of knowledge captured through visits went largely unrecorded.

The outlines of the system of child welfare in force throughout the 20th century can thus be seen as being established in the last quarter of the 19th century. The development of family casework driven by COS, the provision of residential care for children in need, the development of fostering and a strong legislative framework to address abuse and neglect constituted an enduring legacy.

Probation

Just as we can recognise the foundations of childcare in the latter half of the 19th century, so too were the foundations being laid of the work of the probation service.

The reforming efforts of Elizabeth Fry in prisons helped to focus attention on the needs of discharged prisoners. A number of Discharged Prisoners Aid Societies were established to try to find lodgings and employment for those released from prison. A payment of up to £2 per prisoner could be made to help with a return to employment and stability. In practice, expenditure was much lower than this and the quality of work done extremely variable. Some societies worked only with first-time prisoners, some visited in prison prior to discharge while others relied on information from prison officers, and some would work with short-sentence prisoners while others favoured the prisoner with a long-term sentence.

A major problem then as now was that of alcohol. Temperance societies were particularly active in work with prisoners. A member of the Church of England Temperance Society, Frederick Rainer, donated a postal order of five shillings to promote rescue work in the courts. This led the society to appoint a special agent to work in courts. Within 20 years there were a hundred court missioners, all employed by charitable agencies and predominantly by temperance societies. The 1886 Probation of First Time Offenders Act authorised the nationwide extension of court missions.

Medical social work and the beginning of a profession

As early as 1870, concern was expressed about the pressures on outpatient departments in hospitals and the potential for abuse of free treatment as a result of the proliferation of medical charities. In a paper to the British Medical Association titled 'The medical aspects of pauperism' (Moberly Bell, 1961), Fairlie Clarke, a surgeon at Charing Cross Hospital, criticised the demoralising effect on patients of receiving free treatment when they might have been able to pay. Similar to COS's philosophy, he argued that the ready availability of free services did not promote the self-supporting and self-respecting citizens needed to drive social progress. The COS established a sub-committee to look at the medical charities and Fairlie Clarke became the secretary. District committees continued to report on the problems of overwhelmed outpatients departments in London. COS pressure was instrumental in the establishment of a House of Lords Select Committee in 1890 to examine the treatment of the sick poor in hospitals and whether the system was being abused.

In its evidence COS expressed concern about the poor conditions in outpatient departments of hospitals and their use by people who were not entitled to charitable relief. The recommendations of the Select Committee for a London Board to supervise the hospitals and establish a common system of accounts were not implemented immediately, but the spotlight shone by the Select Committee on the problems in outpatient departments helped to create a momentum for change. COS seconded one of its able district secretaries, Mary Stewart, to the Royal Free Hospital in 1895. Her role as defined by the hospital board was to interview 'patients who could afford to pay for treatment elsewhere or who dressed down in order to appear to be more destitute and thus receive free treatment' (Cullen, 2013, p 552). COS funded the initial appointment and went on to recruit and train almoners appointed in other London hospitals and major hospitals outside London.

Stewart's initial role was consistent with the philosophy of COS being concerned with the means testing of patients to ensure that only those deemed appropriate received free hospital treatment and to ensure that those able to contribute towards their care did so. This involved visiting and classifying patients. In her four years at the Royal Free, Mary Stewart maintained the detailed records to be expected of one trained in the COS approach. In 1895/96, 13% outpatients were interviewed and classified but within three years this had risen to 39%. Of these, over 95% were either referred to Provident dispensaries or given charitable assistance. Only 3% were referred to the Poor Law authorities. The fears and fantasies about widespread abuse are not borne out by these statistics. The great majority of those seen as outpatients were in genuine need and unable to afford hospital treatment.

The settlement movement

Samuel Barnett was an early supporter of COS, but felt that its approach was too limited. He established the first university settlement at Toynbee Hall in 1885 with a view to enabling Oxford and Cambridge University students to live among the working poor and to understand the problems of poverty. Settlements provided a range of educational and social services to impoverished neighbourhoods. The students were male, thus immediately distinguishing them from previous charity workers who had been predominantly female. The settlements had a strong commitment to the local community and sought to promote neighbourliness. And they eschewed the moralistic approach of COS by working with all sorts and conditions without seeking a sense of moral purpose.

The educational aspect was a crucial part of the settlement philosophy. In his biography of William Beveridge, Harris (1997, p 80) describes:

> ... a centre for experiments in education, philosophy and social investigation. Toynbee residents organised local clubs and societies, conferences on social problems, University Extension lectures and many other forms of recreation and education. They served on local school boards, vestries and boards of guardians and helped to promote local trade union organisation. They gave free legal advice, pressed for the improvement of local amenities, and conducted pioneering studies of homelessness and unemployment.

The Toynbee Hall 1889 annual report described the roles of the resident members of the settlement: six were school managers, six were committee members promoting evening classes, four were COS committee members, two were almoners of the Society for the Relief of Distress, one was a guardian of the poor, five organised children's holiday funds and nine organised boys' clubs.

Within 15 years of the establishment of Toynbee Hall, over 30 other settlements had been started. There was no standard model. Much depended on the personality of the warden. In Manchester, 'settlement work extended into readings to the blind, penny banks, social evenings, poor man's lawyers, clubs for boys, for girls, for cripples and for the casuals from the common lodging houses' (Young and Ashton, 1956, p 231) .

What was significant in the approach pioneered by Barnett was the belief in 'starting where the client is'. Only by living and working with those living in poverty could a true understanding be gleaned of the nature and impact of poverty on the human spirit. And only through that understanding could one begin to build on the strengths of the community.

The settlement movement has contributed two important dimensions of modern social work. First, we see the emphasis on building a sense of community and neighbourliness. Second, we see the beginnings of what today would be termed a strengths-based approach, building resilience by a focus on the positive elements in the social situation rather than one based on the deficits of individuals

The contribution of COS to training was the insistence on assessment, rigour in taking a social history and record keeping. The settlement movement contributed the importance of understanding the needs of the local community and building on strengths.

The birth of social welfare

By the turn of the century, the foundations of social work were laid in a form recognisable over a century on. While training remained rudimentary, its basic elements were in place. Great strides had been made in the care of the vulnerable. There were developments in organisation and the appointment of paid staff in a number of branches of social work. The rapid growth of both COS and the settlement movement showed the increasing concern of the middle classes with the inadequacy of the system of social welfare.

Social work had moved on, in Clement Attlee's telling phrase, from being undertaken by 'persons of a superior position in society engaged in the endeavour to ameliorate the lot of the poor' (Attlee, 1920, p 2) to a concern with social justice.

That concern was reinforced by the accumulating evidence of the prevalence and persistence of poverty. Charles Booth's epic study, *Life and labour of the people in London*, published between 1892 and 1897 (Booth, 1903), documented the scale and distribution of poverty. It showed that up to 35% of the population was living in abject poverty. Seebohm Rowntree's study of poverty in York (Rowntree, 1901) demonstrated that these findings were not peculiar to London. They had a huge impact at a time when there was a ferment of ideas for social development. The old laissez-faire policies were being challenged by a different approach moving away from individualism and towards collective solutions.

The work of Booth and Rowntree had a profound impact by suggesting that more radical reform was needed to address the social inequities revealed by their work. The Boer War had also had an impact on the military establishment by revealing the poor physical condition of recruits, with nearly 40% being classified as unfit for military service, suffering from rickets and other poverty-related illnesses (Winter, 1980).

Traditional laissez-faire Liberalism was also challenged by the rise of the trades union movement and the political threat posed in the areas of traditional Liberal support. The Fabian Society founded in 1884 was an intellectual forcing house for a more radical reconstruction of society. Bernard Shaw and Sidney Webb were early members, contributing to a flood of publications and pamphlets with over 200 published in the first 40 years. One of their continuing concerns was the need for reform of the Poor Laws. The Poplar Guardians, located in the same geographical area as Toynbee Hall, challenged the traditional basis of Poor Law administration. In evidence to an inquiry conducted by the Local Government Board, W.G. Martley, the secretary of the Poplar branch of COS, had the following to say:

> The first principle of the Poplar policy as I understood it is that Society has a duty to its weaker members, which is not fulfilled by throwing them back on themselves, but requires social action to be taken on their behalf, and the second is that those who seek or need relief are

neither better nor worse than men and women in general and are to be regarded for the most part as victims of an unfair social system. (Local Government Board, 1906, p 216)

Royal Commission on the Poor Laws

Into this febrile political atmosphere came the Royal Commission on the Poor Laws. The commission was established in 1905 following concerns about high unemployment in London and took a huge volume of evidence. It swiftly became clear that there were deep political and philosophical divisions, which were expressed in the publication in 1909 of two reports, the majority and minority reports.

The majority report sought to reform the system of Poor Law administration. It was signed by 16 of the 20 commissioners, including C.S. Loch, Helen Bosanquet and Octavia Hill as well as a number of those with experience through the Poor Law division of the Local Government Board. It embraced the principles of deterrence set down in 1834 and retained the workhouse, but sought to modify some of the harshness in the system. The chief inspector for the Poor Law division of the Local Government Board, James Davy, was not a commissioner, but in his evidence set out his consistent belief in the principles laid down in 1834: 'first, the loss of personal reputation (which is understood by the stigma of pauperism; secondly the loss of personal freedom which is secured by detention in a workhouse; and third the loss of political freedom by suffering disenfranchisement' (Royal Commission, 1909, Appendix, vol 1, question 2230).

Despite this, the majority report sought a significant shift in emphasis, recognising that 'the name Poor Law has gathered about it associations of harshness and still more of hopelessness, which we fear will seriously obstruct the reforms we desire to see initiated' (Royal Commission, 1909, part IV, p 96). Consequently, it proposed a change of name to Public Assistance, the establishment of labour exchanges, unemployment insurance and the separation of provision for children and the mentally ill. The emphasis was in future to be geared to more differential treatment, with 'specialist public institutions for children, the aged and the sick; and industrial and agricultural institutions, labour colonies, and detention colonies for the various categories of the able-bodied' (de Schweinitz, 1943, p191). Influenced by the substantial body of COS representation on the Commission, it wanted to keep the primary role in social administration for charitable organisations, with a first application for assistance being made to a voluntary aid committee.

Octavia Hill produced a memorandum to the majority report, setting out starkly her position. She objected to medical help 'because it opens the door too widely to free medical relief', disapproved of the extension of the suffrage to those dependent on public funds and reiterated the COS position that people should provide for themselves by foresight, insurance or savings' (*The Times*, 1912, cited in Darley, 1990, p x). Her biographer notes that 'the weakness of her small scale individualist approach when applied to problems perceived and investigated on a national scale was cruelly revealed' (Darley, 1990, p 292).

By contrast, the minority report, largely drafted by Beatrice Webb, was not a minor disagreement but a fundamental challenge to the principles of the 1834 Poor Law and the less eligibility philosophy. It saw poverty in structural terms dependent on factors beyond the control of the individual, such as changes in demand for labour or personal factors such as sickness or the need to care for a loved one. It wanted to move from relief – essentially the prevention of starvation – to a systematic framework of prevention that recognised different circumstances and tailored assistance to meet those needs. It argued that the principle of deterrence and less eligibility had helped to create dependency by breaking down self-respect and initiative. It saw the state as having a responsibility of providing a 'national minimum' for those in work and adequate benefits for those out of work. Local authorities, through health education and asylum services, should provide for the needs of children, the sick, the elderly and the mentally ill.

These ideas were to become public policy two generations later when a young researcher for the Royal Commission, William Beveridge, wrote a report in 1942 setting the framework for the welfare state.

Despite the polarisation of majority and minority reports in 1909 there was a wider degree of consensus than is immediately apparent. The strong deterrent element of the 1834 Commission was replaced in public policy by a more positive emphasis on assistance. Both reports envisaged a substantial extension of the role of government, local and national, in administering the system, recognising that the patchwork quilt of voluntary endeavour led to unacceptable variations in the nature of provision.

The 1906 election had seen a huge shift to the Liberals and the election of 51 MPs representing Labour. The language of political leaders was radical. Three years before the 1909/10 People's Budget, the Liberal politician David Lloyd George said: 'There is plenty of wealth in this country to provide for all and to spare. What is wanted is a fairer distribution' (Lloyd George, 1929, p 8).

Many of the reforms instituted by the government in advance of the report of the Royal Commission trespassed on the territory of the Poor Law. Free school meals were introduced outside the control of the boards of guardians and without the stigma of pauperism by the 1906 Provision of Meals Act. Medical inspections of children in primary schools stemmed from concern about the poor physical condition of many children living in poverty and were introduced by the 1907 Education Act. Old age pensions were introduced by the 1909 Old Age Pensions Act, although the residue of Poor Law thinking remained in the provision that an applicant would not qualify if he 'habitually failed to work according to his ability for the maintenance or benefit of himself and those legally dependent on him'. The pensions were means tested, but had a dramatic impact on the work of the guardians, with the numbers of those over 70 in receipt of outdoor relief dropping by over 90% between 1910 and 1913.

The rift between COS and the Fabians over the Poor Law reforms is neatly captured by Eileen Younghusband (1960, p 2):

> The mistake they [COS] made was in thinking that financial or other aid was in its nature calculated to undermine independence so that few should receive it and those few be subject to individual diagnosis and personal supervision. This was why the COS disliked the Fabians because they fell into the opposite error of thinking that to cure economic ills and to offer certain universal services would of itself cure most individual problems of social maladjustment.

The publication of two reports from the Royal Commission enabled the Liberal government to pick and mix ideas from both. The 1909 Labour Exchanges Act pre-empted one element of the commission's recommendations, but the government was preoccupied with a more far-reaching reform with the introduction of unemployment and health insurance (incidentally opposed by Beatrice and Sidney Webb – leading protagonists of the minority report in 1909).

The 1911 National Insurance Act, drawing on models in Germany, was based on a tripartite model of contributions by employer, employee and the state. The principle has remained intact for a century. The impact was huge because it emphasised the receipt of benefits as a right. While elements of the basic structure of the Poor Law remained, the ferment of discussion created by the minority report and the subsequent campaign to break up the Poor Law meant that the delivery of social welfare was on the political agenda. It was clear that staff with expertise in social work would be required to operate the system, whether the delivery was through charitable bodies or through a publicly run structure. The Lady Bountiful image of social work was being replaced by skilled and trained staff.

Councils of Social Welfare began to develop to coordinate the delivery of local services, bridging the area between the work of Poor Law guardians and the proliferation of voluntary agencies.

There was a major shift in 1929 with the abolition of the boards of guardians and the transfer of their function to local government. Instead of the principle of less eligibility and the deterrent effect of the workhouse, councils were urged to provide assistance to people living in their own homes.

The Depression of the 1930s and large-scale unemployment that followed posed a huge challenge to the system of social insurance, which had not been designed to cater for such large numbers. The Unemployment Assistance Board was established in 1934, becoming the Assistance Board in 1941 and the National Assistance Board in 1948, to provide support for those outside the ambit of social insurance. It had a single test of eligibility and a standardised level of payments. A national system had replaced a myriad of local systems.

Beveridge and beyond

The unifying characteristic of these developments was the reduction of local discretion in favour of government-led responses to need. It was in this context that an interdepartmental committee was established in 1941 chaired by Sir William Beveridge to review the future of social insurance and allied services. The committee reported in 1942 in a report bearing the name of its chairman that was an instant, if unlikely, bestseller, with over 100,000 copies sold within a month of publication along with 600,000 copies of the summary report. Its promise of an end to the five 'giant evils' in society – squalor, ignorance, want, idleness and disease – resonated with the public struggling with the privations of wartime Britain. It held out a promise of a better future, echoing Lloyd George's First World War promise of a 'land fit for heroes to live in'.

Beveridge proposed a 'national minimum' and called for reforms to establish a national health service and reforms in housing and education. The report's recommendations were swiftly adopted by all parties, although ironically the Labour Party was the slowest to grasp the recommendations, with many in the trades union movement seeing higher wages as a better solution than compulsory universal insurance.

The 1945 Attlee government embarked on implementing Beveridge's recommendations, introducing family allowances, pensions, the National Health Service, the national minimum through the National Assistance Board and a framework that remained essentially for a further 60 years. With the establishment of children's departments through the 1948 Children Act, social workers could be found across social welfare working as mental welfare officers, welfare officers with the elderly, child guidance workers, medical social workers and probation officers. The welfare state established by the post-war Attlee government was to remain unchallenged as a model of service organisation for half a century, but the organisation of social work was to undergo fundamental change.

The majority of social workers remained untrained. Services had grown to meet the needs of particular groups, leading to administrative responses to need, but Younghusband concluded that the existing patchwork of services no longer made sense (Younghusband, 1959). Her report went on to propose a 'general purpose social worker' (a proposal that was to resurface in the Seebohm report in 1968), a National Council for Social Work Training and an expansion of training courses, both qualifying courses and in-service training.

Gradually, the proportion of social workers who were trained grew, although continuing to lag behind the demand for trained staff in all settings. All the social work professions were expanding rapidly, but the generic base to training that had developed in universities became a driving force towards unity in the professions. The Standing Conference of Organisations of Social Workers (SCOSW) was established in 1963 to give effect to that sense of unity.

While there was recognition within the professional associations of the need for unity, there was a parallel discussion within central government about the best organisational model for the delivery of social welfare. Within the Home Office, there was strong support for the concept of a family service, building on the work of the children's department. This had been articulated in a Fabian pamphlet in 1965 (Hastings and Jay,1965), but challenged among others by Richard Titmuss, who argued that 'a large number of needs are not essentially "family needs"; mentally ill migrants, elderly widows and widowers, the isolates and childless ... who might well hesitate before turning to a Family Department' (Titmuss, 1966). He argued for the creation of a department that would meet all needs and not those of specific groups.

This debate was played out in submissions to the Seebohm Committee, which was appointed in 1965 and reported in 1968. Phoebe Hall notes that juvenile crime was used by proponents of both viewpoints (Hall, 1976). The Longford report (Longford, 1964) and the Kilbrandon report (Scottish Home and Health Department/Scottish Education Department 1984), which examined the issue in the Scottish context, both emphasised the importance of prevention, seeing the family service as the instrument to improve the health, happiness and wellbeing of the whole family. By contrast, a small group building on the ideas of Titmuss produced a memorandum setting out the argument for a much broader reconstruction of welfare services and bringing together social work services in children's and welfare departments and social work functions in health, education and housing. The effective lobbying of that group is described by Hall (1976) and was reflected in the terms of reference eventually agreed for the Seebohm Committee, although they included reference to a family service.

In its report, the committee set out clearly the rationale for change to:

a) meet needs on the basis of the overall requirements of the individual or family rather than on the basis of a limited set of symptoms;
b) provide a clear and comprehensive pattern of responsibility and accountability;
c) attract more resources;
d) use these resources more effectively;
e) generate adequate recruitment and training of the staff skills which are or may become necessary;
f) meet needs which are at present being neglected;
g) adapt to changing conditions;
h) provide an organisation for collecting and disseminating information relevant to the development of the social services;
i) be more accessible and comprehensible to those who need to use them. (Seebohm, 1968, p 37)

The report concluded that a comprehensive service meeting the needs of all those requiring care from young children through to the elderly and infirm was best equipped to achieve a coordinated response and to use resources most effectively.

There were two other important themes in the report. The first was its unequivocal focus on prevention. Before cost-benefit analysis became fashionable, it compared the cost of a social worker with residential childcare, concluding that 'if an additional social worker can remove the need for even two children coming into residential care the benefit to the community in terms of money alone is obvious' (Seebohm, 1968, p 16). The argument was repeated in the context of older people: 'If the use of one home help on a full time basis could avoid the need for a family of three to be taken into public care, public money would be saved' (Seebohm, 1968, p 16).

The second was the focus on community development. The report recognised that work with individuals was 'bound to be of limited effect in an area where the community environment itself is a major impediment to healthy individual development' (Seebohm, 1968, p 148). It recommended a focus on deprived areas and developing citizen participation to reduce the gap between givers and receivers of social services.

Recommendations of Royal Commissions and committees are not necessarily implemented. Social services were not a priority for the 1966–70 Labour government. The Local Authority Social Services Bill is mentioned only five times in the third volume of Crossman's 1,039-page diaries, detailing his time as Secretary of State for Social Services (Crossman, 1977) (perhaps because Crossman himself was opposed to the recommendations). The introduction of a Bill owed much to the lobbying of the Seebohm Implementation Action Group, which was established specifically to campaign for legislative action.

The activities of the group, based on SCOSW but including leading voluntary organisations, included meetings with MPs in all the major regional centres, the publication of leaflets and pamphlets, a mass lobby of Parliament and the exploitation of key contacts in Parliament.

There were two divisive issues in Cabinet. First, the Home Office wanted to ensure that probation remained independent of local authority control. Second, the British Medical Association fought a rearguard action to retain the primacy of the Medical Officer of Health as the natural person to coordinate services. These issues became intertwined with the reform of local government. The Maud Committee, which was reviewing the structure of local government, was attracted to the idea that health provision at local level should come under local authority control.

The lobbying of the Seebohm Implementation Action Group succeeded in building a cross-party consensus in favour of legislation. Even then the Bill was under threat because of the decision to call an election in June 1970. It was passed in the last days of the preceding parliament because it was uncontroversial, unlike the rival candidate for legislative time – Barbara Castle's Equal Pay Bill (Crossman, 1977).

1 April 1971 was the momentous day on which social services departments came into being and they were to dominate the provision of social welfare for

all care groups for 35 years. Looking back, however, one can see the genesis of some of the problems that were to bedevil the departments.

First, in the optimism of the era it was assumed that resources would be matched to meet needs. The Seebohm report itself was largely silent on the cost implications of the changes. Second, the concept of need was static. The National Health Service was built on the heroic assumption that once the backlog of ill health that had not been treated was addressed, the costs of the service would stabilise and even decrease. So too in social welfare no account was taken of hitherto unidentified need – domestic abuse and child abuse are two examples where the prevalence and consequences were unrecognised at the time. Third, there was no attempt to rein back expectations. Pinker acidly remarked 'it was a time when expectations raced ahead of available resources and the Babel of universalist aspirations overwhelmed the language of priorities' (Pinker, 1990, p 88). Fourth, there was no consistently trained workforce available to meet the demand for services and specialisms were downplayed or ignored altogether in the search for generic social work. The consequences for professionalism and for training are examined in following chapters.

AREAS FOR DISCUSSION

Why has the Poor Law continued to influence social policy for nearly 500 years? Can you identify current policies that resemble aspects of Poor Law philosophy?

Which of the two major Victorian influences on the development of social work – the Charity Organisation Society and the settlement movement – has had the greatest influence on social work as practised today?

In what way was the establishment of social services departments following the 1970 Local Authority Social Services Act the completion of the post-war welfare state?

FURTHER READING

Pierson, J. (2011) *Understanding social work: History and context*, Maidenhead: McGraw Hill/Open University Press, has excellent material on the early days of the Charity Organisation Society and the settlement movement.

Rogowski, S. (2010) *Social work: The rise and fall of a profession*, Bristol: Policy Press, has an excellent chapter covering the same period but also including references to the New Left and counterculture.

Hall, P. (1976) *Reforming the welfare: The politics of change in the personal social services*, London: Heinemann Educational, gives a vivid insight into the deliberations of the Seebohm Committee and what shaped the 1970 Local Authority Social Services Act.

TWO

Social work's ambivalence about professionalism

KEY LEARNING POINTS

- » Growth of social work training in the 1960s
- » 'Generic' courses and their influence
- » Drive to a unified profession
- » Establishment of the British Association of Social Workers and its subsequent failure to consolidate
- » The impact of the social workers' strike
- » Failure of 'generic' social work and the move to specialisation
- » The Barclay Report and the long road to the General Social Services Council
- » The Social Work Task Force and the Social Work Reform Board
- » Troubled birth of the College of Social Work

Social work after the Second World War still had few trained staff. One of the pioneers of social work training was Eileen Younghusband, author of two reports funded by the Carnegie Trust. Her first in 1947 argued for the establishment of an independent but university-affiliated school of social work that would combine research with a 15-month diploma course. The initial proposal was not for a wholly generic course but one in which certain core subjects would be studied together – the basic social science subjects, principles and practice of social work, administration of social agencies and research methods in social work. There would be options dependent on the interests and professional orientation of the students (Younghusband, 1947).

The second Carnegie report (Younghusband, 1951) fleshed out the earlier proposals and went further in its advocacy of employing general case workers to counter 'the disease of over-specialisation'. With support from Richard Titmuss, head of the Department of Social Science and Administration, Younghusband established the first applied social studies course at the London School of Economics and Political Science (LSE), initially known as a Carnegie course because of its funding origins.

Younghusband was not herself a qualified social worker, although she was an early supporter of more joint training and eventually a generic base to all social work practice. Her prominence in speaking for social work made her the subject of some bitter professional jealousy. This denied her the role of leading the generic course at LSE that followed the pilot Carnegie course. Nevertheless her position made her the obvious choice for the government to lead a working party examining the role of social workers in local government.

Where did social workers work in local government?

Research for the report on social work in local government (Younghusband, 1959) had found 89% of social workers to be untrained. Although the major reforms following the Beveridge report were designed to address need in all its manifestations, those actually providing the services relied on common sense, compassion and their personal experience to offer assistance. The report has a curious list of those staff regarded as social workers by local authorities:

- officers responsible to the council for welfare services or their administration;
- officers employed as welfare officers or mental welfare officers;
- administrative officers with some social work functions, many of whom were visiting officers;
- workers with the blind;
- workers with the deaf;
- workers with the general classes of handicapped persons including occupational therapists and craft instructors;
- psychiatric social workers;
- almoners registered with the Institute of Almoners;
- workers with families including 'problem' families;
- home help organisers and deputies;
- staff of residential accommodation;
- visitors to residential accommodation;
- occupation centre staff;
- nursing staff including health visitors;
- some staff who could not be grouped under these headings. (Younghusband, 1959, para 320)

Like all surveys, the degree of knowledge held by the respondent can skew the response, but it is startling to find such a diverse grouping regarded as social workers. That confusion endured for many years until the title 'social worker' achieved statutory protection 45 years after the working party reported. Significantly, the work of the Children's Officer and childcare officers, albeit located within local authorities, was not covered by the terms of reference of the working party.

Services had grown to meet the needs of particular groups, leading to administrative responses to need, but Younghusband proposed a 'general purpose social worker', a National Council for Social Work Training and a major expansion of training.

The Younghusband report led to the establishment of two-year courses in further education colleges leading to a professional qualification. There was inevitably a trade-off between quality and quantity. Many existing social workers had reservations about the dilution of standards. The Institute of Medical Social Workers and the Association of Psychiatric Social Workers were firmly allied to this position but the demand for trained staff was such that the new courses found a ready market.

What did social workers learn?

Social casework became the core content for courses encouraging reflection and analysis of individuals in their social and environmental context. This was not 'a kind of second best psychotherapy' (Younghusband, 1978), but an approach rooted in reality. American textbooks by authors like Perlman (1957), Hollis (1964), Biestek (1961) and Bartlett (1970) were influential in helping a generation discover the doubtful joys of process recording (a method of recording interviews in detail that analyses motivation and significant interpersonal transactions between interviewer and interviewee). But this emphasis on the interpersonal was balanced by increased awareness of social and environmental factors. The studies *Family and kinship in East London* (Young and Willmott, 1959) and *Growing up in the city* (Mays, 1959) helped students to locate problems in their social context. The work of Peter Townsend on the elderly (Townsend, 1959; Townsend and Wedderburn, 1965) and later on poverty exposed the all-embracing welfare state as something of a myth by demonstrating the grim conditions in which many older people lived their last days, with the legacy of the workhouse still present in both buildings and attitudes.

The distinguished sociologist Barbara Wootton contributed to a more rounded view of social work in a trenchant critique (Wootton, 1959) in which she laid into the pretensions of social casework, the fuzziness of its language and the lack of evidence for its efficacy. The quest for rigour and demonstrable outcomes has been a consistent theme over the past 40 years but evidence of effectiveness remains limited.

The great growth in social work training courses began in the 1960s. One-year applied social studies courses based on the Carnegie model developed in the early years of the decade, but these were only available for graduates in social studies. Others with non-relevant degrees had to take one-year diploma in social administration before going on the applied course. The two were eventually integrated in 17-month courses (later extended to two years) combining professional training with academic studies. Only the placements differentiated the professional settings for which the graduates from these programmes would be qualified.

What was the core content of these evolving courses? Academically, the parameters were fairly clear – an understanding of social administration and social policy, sociology , psychology, human growth and development including health, disease and disability, and the legal framework, with only cursory attention to substance misuse and domestic violence, which were viewed as fringe issues.

Sadly, this list excludes research and social work has been held back by the lack of a research orientation among its practitioners compared with health professions.

The fieldwork element of the programmes evolved from the early days of learning by 'sitting with Nelly' and thus picking up an understanding of the administrative requirements of the agency coupled with sterile visits of observation. It was based on the recognition that, as the Younghusband report said, 'we regard field teaching, based upon actual responsibility for a small case load as of equal importance with theoretical study in all forms of training for social work' (Younghusband, 1959, p 251). Then, as now, resources were stretched and it was difficult to persuade agencies under pressure to free up time for good-quality supervision. Student units were created in many agencies as a partial solution.

Expansion and the drive to unity

Gradually, the proportion of social workers who were trained grew, albeit continuing to lag behind the demand for trained staff in all settings. All the social work professions were expanding rapidly, but the generic base to training that had resulted from the earlier Carnegie courses became a driving force towards unity in the professions. The Standing Conference of Organisations of Social Workers (SCOSW) was established in 1963 to give effect to that sense of unity and achieved a quick win in today's management language.

Entry into social work required prospective students to know which profession they wanted to join. Younghusband comments:

> People sought information from university appointments officers, individual staff members, the training councils, National or local Councils of Social Services, local probation services, children's departments, CABs, social workers and anyone else who seemed able to give it. (Younghusband, 1978, p 91)

In 1963, soon after SCOSW came into being, a joint working party was established with the National Institute for Social Work Training, itself only two years old, to tackle the wasteful confusion and proliferation of advice. All major interests were consulted and four years later the Social Work Advisory Service (SWAS) was established in London. It acted as a clearing house for all enquiries about training and career prospects, produced information leaflets, and collated information about every aspect of social work and training. After an initial grant from the Gulbenkian Foundation, SWAS was publicly financed by 1970 until its functions were absorbed into the Central Council for Education and Training in Social Work in 1974.

Despite the establishment of SCOSW and its early success in securing the unified advice service SWAS, the road to unity proved tortuous. The constituent associations were in very different places. The Institute of Medical Social Workers (IMSW) had in 1964 recognised the base of its work in its title, abandoning the historic and universally recognised title Almoner. It was relatively well endowed and it controlled its own training course. The Association of Psychiatric Social Workers (APSW), while not itself training students, exercised considerable control over training and in particular the quality of fieldwork placements. The Association of Child Care Officers was the most politically attuned of the associations, owing much to the leadership of Tom White, who chaired its Parliamentary and Public Relations Committee. The Association of Social Workers, the Association of Moral Welfare Workers, the Society of Mental Welfare Officers and the Association of Family Caseworkers were smaller associations within SCOSW. The National Association of Probation Officers was also an active member of SCOSW.

The initial discussion paper produced by SCOSW canvassed two options – a federation that would take over common interests but leave the constituent bodies to carry on their specialist function, or the formation of a new national association for social workers. It swiftly became clear that the momentum lay with the more radical option of a new national association.

There were many obstacles to be overcome. Many of the older members in both IMSW and APSW were reluctant to give up their privileged position and tortuous negotiations took place. As Terry Cooper writes, 'some members of SCOSW were very reluctant, as they saw it, to give up access to the accumulated knowledge and sources of support they possessed, for an uncertain future in a large amorphous body' (Cooper, 2012). But of the members of SCOSW, only one, the National Association of Probation Officers (NAPO), decided not to join the new association.

At the time, I was working as a probation officer and voted with the minority in the ballot in 1970 that decided that NAPO would remain independent. There were two factors in the decision – one explicit and one implicit. Explicitly, probation officers shared the fear of loss of identity within a larger body, a fear accentuated by developments in Scotland where the White Paper *Social work in the community* (Scottish Home and Health Department/Scottish Education Department, 1966) proposed the integration of probation in generic social work departments – a recommendation clearly supported by the Seebohm Committee (Seebohm, 1968) albeit excluded from its terms of reference. The implicit issue was one of gender. Alone among the associations, NAPO was predominantly male. Probation officers' self-image was one of decisiveness and working in an environment where the control functions were as important as care. The long-term consequences of probation's assertion of independence are explored in Chapter Seven. But without NAPO, the British Association of Social Workers (BASW) came into being in 1971.

A professional association without a profession?

Despite the establishment of a strong professional association, had social work truly become a profession at this time? The hallmarks of a profession are expert and specialised knowledge, tested and recognised education prior to practice, integrity and impartiality, high standards of conduct, behaviour and attitudes to those using the service of the professional, and a code of ethics or professional conduct.

Social work had a code of ethics. BASW may have had only a minority of social workers in membership, but its code was widely accepted as the basis for professional practice. There was a recognised qualification prior to practice, although many in practice remained unqualified for several years. There were clear standards of integrity and impartiality, although the latter was subsequently redefined in terms of anti-discriminatory practice and anti-oppressive practice.

Even BASW's code of ethics inadvertently acknowledged the weakest element of the criteria for a profession by using the word growing: 'social work has developed methods of practice which rely on a growing body of systematic knowledge and experience' (BASW, 1975).

Certainly, knowledge derived from psychology and sociology had increased in relevance and application, but the existence of a systematic body of knowledge was itself challenged. In its evidence to the Barclay Committee reviewing the role and tasks of social workers, the National Association of Local Government Officers (NALGO) asserted that there was no generally recognised body of skill and knowledge that distinguished social work from other occupations.

There is a recognisable and shared body of knowledge, but it is predominantly secondary knowledge from studies carried out for other disciplines. Only in the past decade has social work begun to develop a strong research culture. That lack of rigorous testing of knowledge and its application has contributed to the problem of defining social work and its boundaries. This was reflected in the problems of the newly established social services departments in the lack of any boundaries to the needs they attempted to meet.

If social services departments were struggling to deal with the pace of change, their struggle was mirrored in the professional association. Under the leadership of Kenneth Brill, an experienced and successful Children's Officer (Bamford, 1997), BASW early in its life took the fateful decision to move its headquarters from London to Birmingham. This was motivated by considerations of cost, as London weighting had been payable to staff in the capital, and the move meant substantial savings both on salaries and other staff costs. Finance was an early concern as membership of the association had not increased as rapidly as anticipated. The move, however, meant that the association was physically distant from government ministries, the Central Council for Education and Training in Social Work and the national press. While it endeavoured to keep a high profile, it was adversely affected by the move.

Why did BASW's membership fail to expand at a time of unprecedented growth in the numbers of social workers? First, those with affiliations to the former constituent organisations felt that the new body was muted in the expression of the concerns and issues it had previously discussed. BASW attempted to address this issue through sections on general health, mental health, child and family care and treatment of offenders, but without ever achieving the clear sense of identity it had enjoyed formerly in specialist associations. Second, the turmoil in the new departments meant that organisational issues rather than professional concerns were paramount considerations for staff. Third, BASW had no real influence on salaries and conditions of service, despite having a strong committee with that title (with a future Labour chief whip, a future local authority chief executive and two future directors of social services in its membership). Its relationship with NALGO was tenuous, with NALGO reluctant to concede any special relationship to BASW. Fourth, BASW itself was attacked as an elitist, professional closed-shop organisation catering only to the narrow group of qualified social workers.

To understand this last strand, it is important to recall the political context of the time. Britain was experiencing unprecedented levels of inflation, with five years in the 1970s recording double-figure increases. The three-day week imposed to combat the miners' strike in 1973 led to austerity and hardship. The Heath government narrowly lost the general election called on the 'who rules Britain' platform, to be succeeded by a weak minority government led by Harold Wilson. And with a ballooning balance of payments deficit, the International Monetary Fund imposed strict conditions on public spending. Anthony Crosland told a local government conference in 1975 'the party's over', and this heralded a period of severe constraint on public expenditure that hit social services particularly heavily after their rapid growth.

Social work was divided between those who saw their task as to minimise the impact of the social stress and financial pressures on clients and those who saw a wider political role for social work in campaigning for change, forging alliances with trade unions and user groups, and using their direct experience to bring about change. The latter group saw social work itself as reinforcing the status quo by operating as a form of social control.

Chapter Six considers the development of radical social work and its impact on current practice, but this chapter is geared to noting the professional arguments raging in the 1970s.

The multi-purpose social worker

Achieving the vision set out by Seebohm required leadership of a high order. Those newly appointed as directors had to shed their previous allegiance to a particular service or client group and take a broader strategic view. Not all were able to do so. Their problems were exacerbated by a number of factors.

The hectic growth referred to earlier meant major increases in staffing and new developments each year. Growth would normally be welcome, but, coupled with the scale of the reorganisation task, it proved difficult to manage. New jobs appeared each month with the result that competent (sometimes half-competent) managers moved swiftly on to another appointment without consolidating anything in their previous post.

Workload, too, increased dramatically as the determined attempt to implement and publicise an open-door policy fuelled demand for services. There were new legislative requirements in relation to children in trouble, the chronically sick and disabled persons, playgroups, childminding and adoption, which added to the demand pressures.

The strategic role envisaged by Seebohm for social services in leading social planning for the community meant that the department was required to forge closer relationships with housing, education and health than had existed previously.

But the greatest confusion stemmed from the attempt to match a single department with a single all-purpose social worker. This faithfully reflected the recommendation of the Seebohm report that one social worker dealing with the problems of one family would replace the fragmentation by age and client group that prevailed in the 1960s. The single worker was expected not only to span all the needs in the family, but to use a diversity of methods:

> Different divisions between methods of social work are as artificial as the difference between different forms of social casework ... in his daily work the social worker needs all these methods to enable him to respond appropriately to social problems which involve individual, family group and community aspects. (Seebohm, 1968, p 172)

This was too great a step for social workers, many of whom were untrained, who found themselves grappling with unknown legislation and unfamiliar groups of clients. The bold vision and unbounded ambition outran the reality of daily practice. There was a recurrent debate about the respective claims of, on the one hand, a geographically defined local service meeting all needs presented within that locality, and, on the other hand, a specialist service meeting similar needs across a much wider geographical area.

Specialisation was often the result of pressure from frontline staff. As early as 1978, the BASW annual general meeting passed a resolution expressing dissatisfaction with the management and organisation of local authority social service structures. The range of knowledge and skills required was too great for any individual practitioner. Dealing with a mental health emergency required detailed knowledge of the legislation as did a childcare emergency, but the statutory provisions were very different. Keeping up to date with research findings and changes in laws and regulations was demanding. It can be argued that GPs manage a similarly broad spread of knowledge, but they are at an advantage in that their training is much longer and academically more rigorous. In addition, their salaries are three times greater and they have ready access to the specialist knowledge of consultants.

Child protection was the forerunner of specialism, building on a model of specialist teams developed by the NSPCC. It was swiftly followed by other developments within the childcare field, with adoption and fostering teams and intermediate treatment teams working with children at risk.

Challis and Ferlie (1987) carried out a major national study of fieldwork in the mid-1980s that showed that nearly 29% of fieldworkers were in specialist roles. When changes in progress or planned were included, the trend was more marked, with significant shifts to formal specialisation. Informal specialisation was also evident, with 70% of fieldworkers showing over three quarters of their caseload drawn from a single care group – children, old people and disabled people or mental health.

The other tension in discussion about how fieldwork teams should be organised was about the role of social work assistants or social services officers – those working in social care who did not have a professional qualification. In truth, only one in seven of the staff of social services departments was a social worker, although they were regarded as the dominant profession and the majority of directors came from a social work background.

In their analysis of fieldwork teams, Parsloe and Stevenson (1977) found that what distinguished the qualified from the unqualified was less evident in relation to the tasks performed than it was in relation to the client groups served. Social work assistants frequently carried a caseload of elderly and disabled clients. Work with elderly people was seen as more straightforward and practical (an ageist assumption that, although it can be challenged, still reflects the reality of everyday practice in social care).

This split was mirrored in professional training, with the development from 1977 of the Certificate in Social Service designed to provide a qualification for those working other than in social work roles. Social work education is considered in Chapter Five, but its development has mirrored the tensions within the profession both about its role and its status.

The social work strike of 1979

The tensions within social work about its role were demonstrated by the social workers' strike in 1979. The strike was not a coordinated national stoppage. Its genesis lay in discontent with the derisory levels of pay for night and weekend cover, a task that had been rendered far more difficult by the proliferating responsibilities of the social worker in the social services departments. NALGO and the National Union of Public Employees (NUPE) – the two largest public sector unions – were pressing for improvements in these out-of-hours arrangements but also for salary increases and regrading. In total, only 15 out of 143 local authorities in England went on strike, but the impact on social work and its standing was profound. The strike itself was divisive, rarely attracting 100% support even in those areas that had called a strike. It raised ethical issues about the impact of the strike on vulnerable individuals. In most areas, some exceptions were made for cases where inaction might threaten the safety of clients even if this lessened the immediate impact of the stoppage. NALGO nationally supported the strikes with strike pay, but even in the 'winter of discontent' when other public service workers (predominantly members of NUPE, NALGO's rival) were on strike, the official trade union attitude was less than whole-hearted in its support.

Eventually, a settlement was reached, with some improvements in standby allowances, a commitment to improved training and the introduction of a grading system for social workers that was presented as the beginnings of a career grade to keep good workers in practice. Those social workers who had not been on strike benefited from these changes.

The strike changed public perception of social work. First, social workers who hitherto had been generally regarded positively (although the Colwell case, dealt with in Chapter Three, showed the level of anger that could be generated by perceived incompetence) had become just another group of public service workers using the same tactics as other groups. Second, by putting vulnerable people potentially at risk, they were viewed as betraying their ethical responsibilities. Third and most damaging of all was the lack of any visible impact from the strike, inevitably raising the issue of whether social workers fulfilled any useful function in society.

An official report into the impact of the strike (DHSS, 1980) in one London borough, Tower Hamlets, where the strike lasted for nine months, concluded that 'the weight of opinion presented to us indicated that many did suffer, and in the main these were the most vulnerable and less articulate members of the community'. This latter comment may help to explain the lack of visible impact. Beasley's personal account of the strike and the divisions it generated within NALGO, the local government union, pointed the finger at 'the social workers ... in the forefront of the strike are supporters of the extreme left i.e. the Marxist wing of the Labour Party, Communist Party, International Marxist Group, Socialist Workers Party and the Workers Revolutionary Party' (Beasley, 1986, p 19).

The strike was damaging to social work and full-scale industrial action has rarely been used in the field since 1979. With the 'winter of discontent', it played into the hands of those wanting to stereotype social work as linked to the Socialist Workers Party. Tapping into this rich vein of attack, Brewer and Lait (1980) asked *Can social work survive?* in a polemic attacking social workers' practice of casework and arguing for subsuming social services within health. Their call struck a chord with certain elements of the Conservative Party and with the right-wing press. This questioning of social work led to the establishment of the Barclay Committee to examine the role and tasks of social workers.

The Barclay Committee

It is important to note that the Barclay report (Barclay, 1982) was not the only review into the workings of professions under way at the time. In its introduction, the report noted the questions being raised about the legitimacy of current arrangements that had led 'to the setting up of a Royal Commission on the Legal Profession and to widespread debate on teaching and on policing' (Barclay, 1982, p viii). But social work did not have the solid foundations of those other professions and the publication of the report was awaited with some anxiety.

In practice, the report was very positive about social work, concluding that 'social workers are needed as never before' (Barclay, 1982, p xi). It identified two strands in social work practice – counselling and social care planning. The former was direct relationship-based work with clients, helping them to deal with the problems they were confronting. The latter role was partly coordination of the various services and assistance needed by the individual or family; and partly the indirect work needed to prevent social problems by working with communities and groups.

This aspect of practice was termed community social work in the report, which explicitly endorsed the concept of working on a neighbourhood basis and going beyond individual help. This was an important endorsement of 'patchwork' and was the most controversial aspect of the report. The first dissenting note was by three members of the committee and was drafted by Roger Hadley. This argued for a more wholehearted embrace of a different structure for social services delivery. It argued for neighbourhood work to be delivered by community-oriented social workers, with specialist workers being called in to deal with problems beyond the capacity of generalists.

Professor Robert Pinker's second dissenting note challenged the underlying concepts of the ambitious role sketched out for social work. He wrote:

> Social work should be explicitly selective rather than universalist in focus, reactive rather than preventive in approach and modest in its objectives. Social work should be preventive with respect to the needs which come to its attention; it has neither the capacity, the resources nor the mandate to go looking for needs in the community at large. (Barclay, 1982, p 237)

This was a direct challenge to the broad concept of need envisaged in the Seebohm report.

Pinker went on to attack the loose concept of community used in the report and for good measure the looseness of the concept used in the Seebohm report 'when it failed to discover a specific definition of "the family" and immediately proceeded to extol the virtues of "the community" which, for the purposes of the Committee, came to mean everybody and everything' (Barclay, 1982, p 242). Pinker argued for more specialist workers within teams and available as consultants outside teams.

While the committee was sceptical about the continuing relevance of social casework, redefining it as counselling, Webb and Wistow suggested that Pinker's note of dissent 'partly reflected the casework traditions of child care and of psychiatric and medical social work' (Webb and Wistow, 1987, p 207). In doing so, it reflected the area of practice that was recognisably social work and to which other professions laid no claim. As the counselling aspect of practice became pushed to the perimeter of social services practice, it became vulnerable to absorption by other groups. Counselling itself has grown exponentially, with the recognition of its central role in dealing with disasters and with helping troubled people who do not have a recognisable psychiatric disorder, but most of this growth has been outside social care services.

In practice, Barclay did not provide a national prescription for action. Some local authorities embraced the patch approach with enthusiasm, but the majority began to move towards greater specialisation as a means of improving quality in social work practice. The pressure from the press in relation to childcare scandals was an important factor driving this change, with the development of teams specialising in work with children. The establishment of area child protection committees by the 1975 Children Act to coordinate child protection work through a multidisciplinary approach was a direct response to the Colwell case, discussed in Chapter Three, but subsequent cases drove the further development of specialist teams and informal specialisation within teams.

The long struggle for professional recognition

As early as 1975, the BASW annual general meeting passed a resolution calling for the accreditation of social workers based on competence in practice and qualification. In its evidence to the Barclay Committee, BASW argued for the setting up of a new body with associated accreditation machinery to maintain, develop and enforce standards of training and professional behaviour in social work. It based its case on the need to protect the interests of clients by assuring standards of practice.

Barclay devoted a chapter to the issue of maintaining standards, beginning with a discussion of the vexed question of whether social work was a profession at all. It noted that 'whereas other activities in the welfare field (such as nursing) have always been reasonably clear, reasonably stable and well understood by the public, social work practice does not have such clearly defined, coherent or readily understood task or set of tasks' (Barclay, 1982, p 179). It went on to question the tensions between employment in large bureaucracies like social services departments and the demands of professional codes and ethics. It suggested 'community action and community involvement in services may be seen as part of a growing assault on professionalism itself' (Barclay, 1982, p 180). The development of self-help and community action was thus presented as a threat to the exclusive knowledge of the social worker – a view consonant with Brake and Bailey's advocacy of radical social work and others – but one that ignored the rich history of social work with its emphasis on self-help and the pioneering settlement work in community development.

Counter to BASW's advocacy of a General Social Work Council was the evidence of NALGO, the largest public sector trade union, which challenged the claim to professionalism and a special status for social work. A number of submissions cited the danger of a professional group acting in a self-protecting and distancing manner often at the expense of rather than for the benefit of the clients. The Barclay report noted that the case for a council was flawed by the lack of any pressure from frontline staff for such a development.

The Barclay Committee was divided on the merits of change, but concluded that the time was not yet ripe for a development of this kind. But the issue did not die. Every time there was sustained criticism of the competence of social workers, usually in the context of childcare, the call for better training and better regulation was repeated.

Roy Parker's (1990) report, *Safeguarding standards*, noted that there had been a significant change in context. There had been especially in adult services a major growth in the independent sector as a result of the transfer of residential day and domiciliary services to independent sector providers. While the majority of social workers continued to be public sector employees, the balance was fast shifting. A working group was established to develop the case for the council and after some false starts the Labour Party in opposition committed itself to the establishment of a council.

The General Social Care Council (GSCC; the change of nomenclature was significant) was established in 2001 following the Care Standards Act 2000. I was a member of the council and of the advisory group, which did some detailed work before the council came into being. It provided a rare moment of euphoria, as it seemed to promise a leap forward in the long struggle to become a recognised profession.

The GSCC was charged with protection of the public and with raising the standards of practice. One of its early achievements was the promulgation, after extensive consultation, of codes of practice for social care workers and for employers. Tellingly, only the former code was enforceable. It is interesting to note that in its final annual report the chief executive of GSCC suggested that 'on reflection more specific standards for social workers may have been beneficial' (GSCC, 2012). The designation as a council for social care meant that it was not possible to devise separate codes of conduct for different occupational groups, but differentiation was required when it came to the process of registration. The government had always indicated that social workers should be the first occupational group to be registered. The register was opened in 2003, at first on a voluntary basis. The slow stream of registrants turned into a flood only when protection of title was agreed by government, meaning that only those registered could use the designation 'social worker'. By March 2012, over 105,000 social workers were registered.

The registration of other occupational groups in social care was a less satisfactory process. Successive ministers had different ideas about priorities for registration – often influenced by the latest press headlines. Managers of children's homes, managers of care homes and domiciliary care workers were all favoured priorities at one time. The vain task of working out how to register three quarters of a million home care workers, many of them unqualified, the majority part-time and many in only short-term employment, wasted a lot of management time for the GSCC.

The GSCC survived the arm's-length review of non-departmental public bodies initiated by the 2005–10 Labour government but foundered when the incoming Conservative government in 2010 decided to pursue a populist war on quangos. The credibility of the GSCC had been severely damaged by a backlog of regulatory hearings that eventually resulted in the dismissal of the chief executive.

The episode was an interesting illustration of the forked tongue with which central government speaks when dealing with non-departmental public bodies (popularly known as quangos). Even before the financial crisis of 2008 there were severe restrictions on public expenditure and by autumn 2007 the council had overspent its planned budget on conduct hearings. The GSCC was told by the Department of Health that the absolute priority was to live within its budget. The chief executive informed the council with the knowledge of the department that conduct hearings were being suspended in order to meet that financial priority. A similar problem occurred the following year, with only the most serious cases of severe risk involving violence or sexual abuse being referred to conduct hearings. A backlog built up of over 200 cases. A subsequent review was severely critical of the council for having no overarching system of risk assessment; inadequate performance management; poor-quality investigations, record keeping and decision making; and differences in procedures because of teams being spilt between Rugby and London. As this geographical spilt had been imposed by central government pressure to move staff out of London, this last criticism was particularly ironic.

The result was that a cost-containment policy introduced with the full knowledge of the Department of Health and a geographical split introduced at the specific behest of the department were used to criticise the GSCC and led to its eventual demise.

The responsibilities of GSCC were handed over in 2012 to the Health and Care Professions Council despite sustained opposition from within social work to the move. The shift symbolises the marginalisation of social work, which is a consistent theme running through this book, as it removed a distinctive and separate identity for social work.

The Social Work Task Force

In parallel with the travails of GSCC, the government established a Social Work Task Force in 2009. Its terms of reference were 'to undertake a comprehensive review of frontline social work practice, and to make recommendations for improvement and reform of the whole profession across adult and children's services'.

The task force, chaired by Moira Gibb, reported in December 2009 (DCSF, 2009b) and recommended a major overhaul of social work education and training. It sought improvements in the calibre of social work students and in the content and delivery of social work education. It called for an assessed and supported year in employment. It wanted national standards for employers and for supervisors of social work students. It argued for a coherent system of Continuous Professional Development and the establishment of a National College for social work.

The report was widely welcomed and in January 2010 – four months before the general election that defeated the Labour government – the government announced the creation of the Social Work Reform Board, also chaired by Moira Gibb. This developed the recommendations of the task force into firm proposals set out in its interim report (DfE, 2010). It set out a Professional Capabilities Framework (PCF) that aimed to show how a social worker's skills and knowledge should develop over a professional career. It covered nine different stages of a career from student to senior manager and contained nine domains – professionalism; values and ethics; diversity; rights justice and economic wellbeing; knowledge; critical reflection and analysis; intervention and skills; contexts and organisation; and professional leadership.

The PCF has been widely welcomed, but its implementation has been confused somewhat by the production by the Health and Care Professions Council standards of proficiency for social workers (HCPC, 2012a). These standards cover 15 areas, according to which social workers should:

1. be able to practise safely and effectively within their scope of practice;
2. be able to practise within the legal and ethical boundaries of their profession;
3. be able to maintain fitness to practise;
4. be able to practise as an autonomous professional, exercising their own professional judgement;
5. be aware of the impact of culture, equality and diversity on practice;
6. be able to practise in a non-discriminatory manner;
7. be able to maintain confidentiality;
8. be able to communicate effectively;
9. be able to work appropriately with others;
10. be able to maintain records appropriately;
11. be able to reflect on and review practice;
12. be able to assure the quality of their practice;
13. understand the key concepts of the knowledge base relevant to their profession;
14. be able to draw on appropriate knowledge and skills to inform practice;
15. be able to establish and maintain a safe practice environment.

The reform board's proposals were more wide-ranging, setting out development across a career, whereas the standards of proficiency were designed as minimum standards for registered social workers. The confusion meant that a separate paper had to be produced mapping the two documents against one another (HCPC, 2012b).

The reform of social work education initiated by the reform board was hardly under way before two further reviews were announced in 2013. Professor David Croisdale-Appleby, chair of Skills for Care, was asked to review social work education and specifically the case for a generic qualifying course and scope for increased specialisation within the degree. Almost simultaneously, Sir Martin Narey was asked to review social work training for children's services.

There are two interesting elements here. First, the latter review was announced by the Department for Education and was limited to children's services in contrast to the unified approach to social work education promoted by the reform board and reflected in Croisdale-Appleby's terms of reference. Second, the 'Frontline' scheme, designed to fast track academic high flyers with at least 2:1 degrees from Russell Group universities and beloved of the then Secretary of State, Michael Gove, was also geared to children's services.

The agenda for the Narey review seemed to be set by a speech of Gove, who commissioned the review. He said:

> In too many cases, social work training involves idealistic students being told that the individuals with whom they will work have been disempowered by society.... They will be encouraged to see these people as victims of social injustice.... It risks explaining away substance misuse, domestic violence and personal irresponsibility rather than doing away with them. (Gove, 2013)

Coupled with a separate chief social worker for children's services and for adult services, the division introduced by the 2004 Children Act now threatens to undermine the unity of social work educationally, with long-term consequences for social work in England and transferability throughout the UK, Europe and globally.

The College of Social Work

The Social Work Task Force was clear in its recommendation for an independent national College of Social Work, developed and led by social workers, which would include the following in its remit:

- promoting the public understanding of social work as a public service and as a profession;
- providing an independent voice for social work in public and media debate and reporting publicly on the state of social work in England;
- representing the interests of effective social work and the views of the social work profession in relation to the development of changes to policy, legislation, education and regulation;
- bringing to light excellent practice in social work and promoting its wider adoption;
- agreeing and articulating high standards for the profession and working with employers, educators, government and the public to ensure that all parties have the same expectation of what makes high quality social work practice;
- relations with other professions and similar professional bodies (Social Work Task Force, 2009b, ch 4)

The recommendation was warmly received by central government and by social workers. It promised a fresh start for a profession still reeling from cumulative press criticism of social work failings. Central government funding was made available to support the establishment of the college and it was at this stage that very different approaches to the development of the profession became evident.

The college in advance of its formal constitution was hosted by the Social Care Institute for Excellence (SCIE). Its initial funding of £5 million over two years meant that early attention had to be given to securing a funding base for the organisation at the end of the two years. As it became clear that the college intended to establish itself as a separate organisation, relations with BASW cooled. BASW had welcomed the task force report, including the recommendation of the college, and saw a congruence between the remit of the college as set out in the task force report and its own role as prescribed in its constitution. It favoured folding BASW and the college into a new body and thus creating a strengthened voice for the profession.

A number of obstacles emerged early in the discussion. First, the BASW was a UK-wide organisation. The college was specifically for England and the devolved parliaments and assemblies showed no great desire to follow the same route. Second, SCIE, charged with the responsibility of bring the college into being, sought to apply a governance model akin to a non-departmental public body establishing a board without elections. Not until 2016, seven years after the college coming into being, will there be a full directly elected board. Third, in its quest for funding, the nascent college proposed a joint membership deal with trade union UNISON, offering college membership at a heavily discounted rate to UNISON members. BASW, which had an uneasy relationship with UNISON after its own exploration of joint membership had come to naught reacted angrily. Its combative chief executive, Hilton Dawson, a former MP, registered the trade name 'BASW – the College of Social Work' and used that in all BASW publicity.

The bilious nature of the relationship was laid bare in a public hearing before the Education Select Committee, which in its report criticised the college's proposed deal with UNISON as akin to a closed shop. A further round of negotiations between the two bodies ensued following the appointment of two mediators – David Jones, former president of the International Federation of Social Workers, and Penny Thompson, chief executive of the General Social Care Council – leading to a detailed draft agreement. Then, quite unexpectedly, the college withdrew from discussions, citing the role of BASW as representing its members through the Advice and Representation Service as irreconcilable with the college's role in raising standards of the profession. That potential conflict of interest was present in 2010. Much time, money and ire could have been saved at an earlier stage. From the BASW perspective, the association has always argued that it can represent and support its members without condoning bad practice. This has been its position since its inception. Access to the Advice and Representation Service has been an attractive benefit to members. The recent surge in BASW membership to 16,000 is in large measure attributable to the comfort that access to that service offers at a time of great insecurity in the employment market.

Profession or occupation?

Fifty years on from the creation of a unified professional association, social work remains in disarray. The divisions between BASW and the college remain, despite some tentative steps to re-establish dialogue. The different visions of social work offered by Narey (2014) and Croisdale-Appleby (2014) in their respective reports on social work education epitomise the continuing debate about its role and status. While Croisdale-Appleby sets a challenging agenda, it is based on a clear recognition of social work as a valid profession. By contrast, Narey wants to equip social work students for an occupational role in children's services and one devoid of any challenging political content or concern for social justice.

Social work does not have many friends in the political arena. Viewed from the outside, its internal dispute has added to the sense of disorganisation and division within the profession. This disunity at a time of crisis is deeply damaging. It does not help social work to protect itself well against challenges from reductions in spending, scepticism from ministers, and the growing interest of the private sector in social work and social care provision.

AREAS FOR DISCUSSION

After the long struggle to secure professional unity, why did the British Association of Social Workers fail to consolidate its membership?

What factors in the 1970s precipitated the social worker strike and what was the impact of the strike on social work?

Has the establishment of a regulatory council fulfilled the hopes of its advocates? Does the College of Social Work represent an advance towards professionalism?

Does the Professional Capabilities Framework offer a clear framework for social work?

FURTHER READING

Rogowski, S. (2010) *Social work: The rise and fall of a profession*, Bristol: Policy Press, discusses the decline of social work from a critical perspective but accurately reflects the ambivalence of many radicals about the trappings of professionalism.

Brewer, C. and Lait, J. (1980) *Can social work survive?*, London: Temple Smith, is worth reading, albeit very dated. Many of its arguments are those still repeated by right-wing commentators today.

DCSF (2009b) *Building a Safe, Confident Future, Social Work Task Force report*, London: DCSF, is an excellent summary of the ills of the profession and a brave attempt to restore professionalism. It contains a good description (not a definition) of social work.

THREE

Childcare and the loss of trust

KEY LEARNING POINTS

» The enduring role of scandal in shaping policy on children
» The repeated pendulum shifts between:
  - rescue (early removal and adoption) and rehabilitation in work with vulnerable children
  - welfare and punishment in juvenile offending
  - the universalism of Every Child Matters and the narrow focus on child protection
» The marginalisation of social work in the Troubled Families initiative

In Chapter One, we noted the importance of campaigners against slavery, poverty and child exploitation in shaping first, public opinion, and second, legislation in the Victorian era. Those campaigns often followed scandals first picked up in the press and then succeeded by a public inquiry. The death in 1945 of 12-year-old Dennis O'Neill at the hands of his foster parents and the Monckton Report (Monckton, 1945) that followed led to the wide-ranging review into the care of children by the Curtis Committee (Curtis, 1946). Its recommendations were translated into the 1948 Children Act. Successive iterations of legislation about children and young people have followed a similar trajectory: tragedy, inquiry, recommendations to government, legislation.

The 1948 Act was aimed at improving the 'boarding out' of children, but those working with children in the 1950s appreciated that more needed to be done to support families and prevent the admission of children into care. Mounting concern, especially among the magistracy, about the sharp increase in juvenile crime led to a review of juvenile delinquency by the Ingleby Committee. The committee reasserted the emphasis on prevention and family support and recommended the provision included in the 1963 Children and Young Persons Act, and subsequently retained in successive legislation, to provide advice, guidance and assistance, including, where necessary, cash assistance to prevent the need to place children in care.

The 1969 Children and Young Persons Act and its impact

The perceived value in a family-oriented preventive service led to the 1969 Children and Young Persons Act. Despite the powerful lobby led by the Fabian Society, this legislation was not the precursor of a family service as some had hoped. Instead, it was followed by the all-purpose, all-age social services departments introduced by the 1970 Local Authority Social Services Act. Childcare was one of the many responsibilities to be carried by the new departments.

It is important to look in more detail at the 1969 Act because it 'proved to be the highwater mark of the welfare model, committed to providing various forms of treatment rather than punishment for all children in trouble whether abused, neglected or delinquent' (Pierson, 2011, p 170). *Children in trouble* was the title of the 1968 White Paper that preceded the Act and neatly captures the focus on the needs of children that characterised contemporary thinking. Children were to be treated differently, with a raising of the age of criminal responsibility from 10 to 14. This change was not implemented by the incoming Conservative government and the age of criminal responsibility remains disputed political territory 45 years on. Criminal proceedings for juveniles were replaced by care proceedings. Supervision by the local authority replaced probation for juvenile offenders. Intermediate treatment – activities designed to divert potential offenders – was introduced.

The Act was a source of controversy from its inception. For some in the magistracy and police, it seemed like an abdication of society's responsibility to deal effectively with juvenile delinquency. The right-leaning press reported on an increase in the number of crimes committed by 10- and 11-year-olds, which the courts were unable to deal with. This was, of course, false. The youngsters could have been brought before the court using care proceedings. The impression was left of the role of the courts being displaced in favour of the discretion of social workers.

The tug of war between the welfare-based approach to juvenile offending and that of punishment has continued. Similarly, in child protection the pendulum has swung between rescue (removing children swiftly from abusive or neglectful parents) and rehabilitation (family support to safeguard children). And the competing elements have been heavily influenced by the press and the consequent pressure on politicians to 'do something'.

Maria Colwell

The death of Maria Colwell in 1973 was a tragedy. She died at the hands of her stepfather after a sustained period of neglect and physical abuse while subject to supervision by the local authority. She had been returned to her natural mother after a period in foster care. The trial and subsequent inquiry led to a firestorm of media coverage dominated by a search for scapegoats. As in so many subsequent cases, this almost bypassed the perpetrator to focus on the social worker concerned.

The 'tug of love' between the caring foster parents and uncaring natural family gave the story resonance. The degree of reliance on the blood tie relationship between natural parents and their offspring was much debated.

At the time, I was working for the British Association of Social Workers (BASW) and was responsible for press and public relations. Every day, I had patiently to explain the powers social workers had, the legislative framework within which they operated, and the number of other families for which the social worker would have been responsible. In a minority report to the subsequent inquiry (Colwell Report, 1974) committee member Olive Stevenson bravely asserted 'there, but for the grace of God, go I', explaining that many social workers encountered difficult and obstructive parents and that hard evidence was necessary to justify removal from the parental home. The press, however, were unanimous in their criticism of the inadequacies of the supervision given to the family and the failings of the social worker.

Chris Andrews, general secretary of BASW, describing the inquiry said:

> Apart from the individuals who have been pilloried social work itself has at times appeared to be on trial. Basic assumptions have been questioned as has the legal and judicial framework within which much social work is practised. (Andrews, 1974)

The committee of inquiry was critical of the lack of communication between the various agencies working with the family. It was concerned at the lack of specialist training for work in child protection. And these criticisms drew a prompt response from the Department of Health and Social Security in terms of procedural actions in its circular *Non-accidental injury to children* (DHSS,1974). This was designed to minimise risk in future by promoting inter-agency communication and collaboration. Actions included the establishment of area review committees to coordinate procedures, a child protection register to identify those children at risk, a system of multi-agency case conferences to ensure communication of concerns and agree actions, and the designation of social services as the lead agency in the system. That framework still essentially governs practice today, although there have been many subsequent changes in administrative arrangements.

The political response to the Colwell inquiry was the 1975 Children Act, which improved adoption law and gave greater powers to adoption agencies. It was presented by David Owen, then a minister at the Department of Health and Social Security, as a response to Colwell by introducing the concept of 'custodianship', thus buttressing long-term fostering as a legitimate outcome for children. The rights of natural parents were reduced, as it was felt that too much weight had been attached to the 'blood tie' between Maria Colwell and her mother. The focus overall had moved from the family to the child, with a new emphasis on security and permanence. This shift was influenced by research (Rowe and Lambert, 1973) that had identified the large numbers of children in care waiting for substitute families but for whom no clear plan existed. The overall effect 'meant the removal of children seen to be at risk more rapidly from their birth families, the severing of parental links while in residential or foster care with the explicit goal of establishing permanent placements, and ultimately the adoption of the child' (Horner, 2003, p 39).

It is worth remembering that all this was within the first years of operation of social services departments when most were still pursuing the vision of the 'generic' social worker and when residential care was often the poor relation within children's services with many untrained staff. The legacy of those days is still experienced today as historic abuse cases come to light.

The 1980 Child Care Act was predominantly a consolidation of previous legislation dealing with children. It did, however, contain a clause allowing local authorities to assume parental rights where the parent 'is of such habits and mode of life as to be unfit to have care of the child', further emphasising the shift in thinking to the welfare of the child. This was interpreted by some departments as justifying early removal of children and termination of access rights for parents in the name of permanency planning.

The call for more specialist training in child protection triggered by the Colwell inquiry was part of the drive to greater specialisation within social services departments, first as informal and then formal specialisms, as discussed in Chapter Two. But the protective network seemed to fail repeatedly as other child deaths were reported and highly publicised. The Jasmine Beckford (Blom-Cooper, 1984), Tyra Henry (LB Lambeth, 1987) and Kimberley Carlile (LB Greenwich, 1987) inquiries showed a repeated pattern of poor communication between agencies, missed warning signals and inadequate supervision. The Beckford report contained a robust defence: 'Social workers have become the butt of every unthinking journalist's pen whenever a scapegoat was needed to explain a fatality or serious injury' ((Blom-Cooper, 1984, p 13). Nevertheless, the report criticised social workers as losing sight of the child and treating the parents of the child in care as if they were the clients.

A more assertive response in social work practice seems to be indicated by the sharp subsequent increase in the numbers placed on child protection registers or made subject to place of safety orders from 17,000 in 1985 to 41,000 four years later.

Despite this, the public perception of social workers had shifted dramatically from well-meaning do-gooders to incompetent, ineffective workers who ignored obvious warning signs. Satirist Alexei Sayle captured the public mood, saying 'save a child … kill a social worker' and mocked the limp apologies forthcoming after each inquiry (Sayle, 1985). Procedures were tightened and departments were urged by the press to be more assertive in removing children where there was a risk of neglect.

The cost of assertiveness

The consequences of that assertiveness were seen in Rochdale and the Orkney islands. In Rochdale, 20 children were removed from their parents because of suspicions of satanic ritual abuse. In South Ronaldsay in Orkney, nine children were removed on suspicion of being subject to sexual abuse within their families and of suggested links to satanic ritual abuse. In both cases, the children were eventually returned home and subsequent inquiries found no evidence to justify the allegations of satanic ritual abuse.

The most publicised example of swift intervention came in Cleveland where 121 cases of suspected child sexual abuse were diagnosed by two paediatricians. Seventy per cent of the children were separated from their parents using a place of safety order that allowed social services to remove children for up to 28 days. The large numbers of children involved led to a media frenzy. Ninety-six of the cases were subsequently dismissed by the courts. Nevertheless, abuse was confirmed in a number of cases, and 'opinion swiftly polarised between those who thought a kind of hysteria was under way (including the local MP) and those who thought at last the enormity and prevalence of (male perpetrated) sexual abuse of children had been unmasked' (Pierson, 2011, p 176). In the media, the parents of the children were presented sympathetically compared with the paediatricians and social workers, who were accused of acting precipitately with little evidence. Parental rights had been overruled by the discretion and wide powers invested in social workers. This in turn had been exacerbated by the failure to keep parents informed about what was happening to their children.

Lord Justice Butler-Sloss led the subsequent inquiry (Butler-Sloss, 1988). The issues she examined were at the heart of social work practice – risk, multi-agency working, the exercise of discretion and the relationship with parents who were subject to suspicion. The inquiry found that at times the children themselves had been overlooked in the pursuit of potential abuse and the investigation process had been seriously flawed.

Social workers found themselves 'damned if they do and damned if they don't', criticised both for acting too swiftly on suspicions and for taking too long to remove neglected children from failing parents. The criticism reflected the ambivalence within society about the right balance between parental rights and child rights. It was in this context that the major reform of childcare law was launched.

The 1989 Children Act

The 1989 Children Act tilted the balance decisively in favour of parents. This landmark legislation was not in itself a direct response to the childcare scandals of the 1980s. It drew on a departmental review of childcare law and a Law Commission report on guardianship and custody. Nevertheless, the legislative changes reflected many of the issues that had emerged from the inquiries.

The Children Act stated explicitly the primacy of the welfare of the child. It introduced a single test for a care order – that a child had or was likely to suffer significant harm – to replace the various grounds for a care order set out in the 1969 legislation. It replaced the 28-day place of safety order with a 72-hour emergency protection order. It introduced the 'no order' principle, which meant that an order would not be made unless the court was satisfied that doing so would be better for the child than making no order at all. It produced a checklist of factors to be taken into account in adjudicating on a child's welfare. It set limits on the local authority's freedom to act without reference to the parents, even when the children were in care, by introducing the concept of shared parental responsibility. The ethos of the Act was around supporting parents in bringing up their own children.

In this way, the Act mirrored the 1969 legislation in terms of its focus on rehabilitation within the family, but it also set in place safeguards for parents to ensure that they received the information and support they needed. The emphasis placed was on securing support for families where there were 'children in need'. Unfortunately, resource limitations meant that local authorities did not take an expansive view of their responsibilities and tended to restrict their involvement to those where child protection was an issue. The bold vision of the drafters was never fully realised as no additional resources were made available for implementation. Local authorities could define for themselves who were children in need and tended to apply as restrictive a definition as possible. Arrangements for care leavers and educational support were non-statutory and there were wide variations in provision.

One of the driving forces for family rehabilitation was the emerging evidence about the deficiencies of residential childcare. The weaknesses in practice identified in the well-publicised reviews of child deaths were confirmed by research findings. Care leavers were found to have multiple problems and little support (Stein and Carey, 1986), while their educational attainment lagged far behind that of their contemporaries (Jackson, 1987).

The vulnerability of children in residential care became evident as details emerged of a repressive and harsh regime operated in the name of behavioural modification in Staffordshire. The pindown regime led to a report on the abuse (Levy and Kahan, 1991) and to two reports by the government's Chief Inspector of Social Work (Utting, 1991, 1997). Allegations about widespread abuse including sexual abuse in residential care grew in intensity throughout the 1990s, leading eventually to the Waterhouse report into abuse in North Wales children's homes (Waterhouse, 2000).

Following the second Utting report, the government launched Quality Protects, an ambitious and wide-ranging programme to improve the life chances of children in care. It set specific targets to narrow the gap between children in care and others in the school system and tightened responsibilities for the health of children in care. Local authorities were corporate parents responsible for the progress of children in their care. The Quality Protects programme was backed by additional resources and focused attention on the whole cohort of looked after children and not only the youngest for whom adoption might be possible. But another childcare tragedy switched the focus back to the shortcomings of child protection.

The Climbié legacy

The pendulum was to shift again as a result of a tragic death. Victoria Climbié died at the hands of her aunt and her aunt's boyfriend with whom she had been placed by her parents, who lived in Sierra Leone. The inquiry, led by Lord Laming, was scathing about the numerous failures to protect Victoria. He identified a number of familiar themes from earlier inquiry reports into child deaths: a lack of coordination; a failure to share information; the absence of anyone with a strong sense of accountability; and frontline workers trying to cope with staff vacancies, poor management and a lack of training.

In his evidence to the House of Commons Health Committee shortly after the publication of his report, Laming criticised the confusion between children in need and children in need of protection. In the report he said: 'many of those from social services who gave evidence seemed to spend a lot of time and energy devising ways of limiting access to services, and adopting mechanisms designed to reduce service demand' (Laming, 2003, para 1.52).

The inquiry was highly critical of the poor performance of most of the agencies involved with Victoria and scathing about the quality of management, with 'too many examples of those in senior positions attempting to justify their work in terms of bureaucratic activity rather than in outcomes for people' (Laming, 2003, para 1.28).

Butler and Drakeford (2005) draw attention to the racial context of Climbié – a black girl killed by two black carers, and a black social worker with black managers (a very unusual combination even in multicultural London). In the wake of the Lawrence inquiry's findings of institutional racism in the Metropolitan Police Service (Macpherson, 1988), Laming commented that 'cultural heritage cannot take precedence over standards of child care embodied in law' (Laming, 2003, para 16.10), but there may be a reluctance of social workers to interfere in family situations where there are linguistic or cultural issues.

Garrett (2009, pp 54-6) traces the degree to which decision making in the case was influenced by a desire to repatriate Victoria and her aunt to France in order to save costs for the local authority, which drew on the test of habitual residence, itself little changed since the 1834 Poor Law.

The emphasis placed by Laming on accountability is also part of what Butler and Drakeford see as a managerial response rather than one that looked at the gross underfunding, low staffing and poor morale in the agencies under scrutiny.

Laming's recommendations were well received. The government indicated a general willingness to follow them through, although it did not immediately respond to his recommendation for clear lines of accountability for children's services. He proposed a ministerial Children and Families Board and a National Agency for Children and Families reporting to the board. At local authority level, Laming sought a Committee for Children and Families and an inter-agency management board to ensure proper coordination of services, with a director appointed to lead the development of services. This cumbersome structure was the one aspect of Laming's recommendations that was criticised as a bureaucratic solution to a problem of poor practice. In his report, Laming omitted any reference to social services departments except to criticise their practice. He must, however, have recognised that implementation of his recommendations would be the death knell of these departments, which had survived for over 30 years following the Seebohm report.

The government's response was arguably even more radical. It published a Green Paper (Chief Secretary, 2003) followed by a White Paper in 2004 (DfES, 2004) under the strapline *Every Child Matters*. This set out a radical programme of reform subsequently implemented in the 2004 Children Act.

It established a local authority children's service separate from adult services that would incorporate education and social care support. It replaced area child protection committees by local safeguarding children boards on a statutory basis to oversee child protection. It planned to enhance data sharing by a nationwide database of children – Contactpoint. It established children's trusts. A children's commissioner was appointed. It wanted to gear services to the five outcomes of the Every Child Matters initiative – being healthy, staying safe, enjoy and achieve, making a positive contribution, achieving economic wellbeing.

This programme reflected both the strengths and weaknesses of the policy initiatives under New Labour. It was hugely ambitious, covering all aspects of a child's life from diet and nutrition through to transition into employment. It placed exaggerated faith in electronic databases to resolve communication problems – Contactpoint did not survive the change of government in 2010. It also had an exaggerated faith in the virtue of multi-agency partnerships, which, both in children's trusts and in local safeguarding children boards, were seen as offering a guarantee of coordinated effort. It underestimated the difficulty involved in establishing new structures and making them work effectively. It overlooked the importance of transition, particularly for those with disabilities moving from childhood to adult services.

Local government duly established the new departments and recruited to the post of director of children's services. The majority of those appointed came from an education background. Some had an oversimplified view of how to organise children's social services with various different models being tried. One county established a multi-purpose family service based on localities recruiting managers from day nurseries, family support services or education. As a consequence, many former social services staff left and the number of unallocated children on the register soared to over 200 – partly as a result of staffing problems but partly too because the absolute priority of child protection work was not sufficiently appreciated. There were, too, inevitable tensions between the universalist approach of education with its remit to provide for all children and the more narrow focus of social services on children in need and children in need of safeguarding.

Family support services including the flagship Sure Start centres were largely the province of the voluntary sector. Statutory resources went predominantly on child protection and permanence, preferably through adoption for children in care (Thoburn, 2013).

Children's trusts had the responsibility of producing a children and young persons' strategic plan. Beyond that, it was left to local discretion to work out a role for the trust. Many failed to find a coherent role and were reduced to annual meetings to agree the plan rather than engaging in meaningful debate. Where they did have an impact was in securing a high degree of participation from children and young people in the process. The change of government in 2010 led to the abandonment of statutory guidance and the requirement to produce an annual strategic plan. The requirement to have children's trusts was left in place, with the duty to cooperate with health and wellbeing boards and with Healthwatch – a new consumer champion.

Local authorities responded in different ways to the removal of statutory guidance. Some used it as an opportunity to fold children's trusts into other partnership groups concerned with children, while others streamlined the membership but kept the board in existence. All saw the Joint Strategic Needs Assessment and the relationship with the new health and wellbeing boards as critical in securing a strategic approach (Easton et al, 2012).

Baby P

Before the change of government in 2010 another case attracted media coverage of a savagery not seen since the Colwell case. It concerned the death of Peter Connelly, known as Baby P, a 17-month-old boy who suffered neglect and severe injuries at the hands of his mother, her boyfriend and a lodger at a time when health and social work services were involved with the family.

The trial of the two men – the mother had pleaded guilty – for 'causing or allowing the death of a child or vulnerable person' brought huge press coverage. The trial had all the elements of a cause célèbre. First, it was Haringey Council, which had borne the brunt of the criticism in Lord Laming's earlier Climbié report, that was again the centre of attention. Second, the victim was an attractive, blond-haired young boy and virtually every media report was illustrated with his photo. Third, this was a case in which there had been egregious failings by police and paediatricians as well as children's services staff.

A consistent theme of the reportage was the identification in the press of a feral underclass – 'these are people who have sponged off the welfare state their whole lives and who believe that nothing is their responsibility, their fault or their problem' – and of social workers who 'just left him there while they went off to fill in their forms, tick their boxes and cover their cowardly backsides' (Malone, 2008). The *Daily Mail* columnist, Melanie Phillips, attacked social workers for 'bending over backwards not to pass judgements on those who were demonstrably incapable of looking after a child' and commented that 'social work is plagued by low calibre recruits, whose training is more akin to indoctrination in political correctness, working in a culture which intimidates any dissent and turns morality and common sense inside out' (Phillips, 2008).

The director of children's services was dismissed by Haringey following intervention by Secretary of State for Education Ed Balls, an intervention that was unjustified and unlawful and for which the taxpayer has ultimately had to pick up the bill.

Lord Laming was asked to review his previous recommendations and identify what further action was needed in light of the Baby P case. His report (Laming, 2009) called for the establishment of a national safeguarding delivery unit to achieve effective coordination of safeguarding services across all the relevant government departments, the development of targets and performance indicators for child protection in health, schools and social work, improvements in training for children's services, and improvements in serious case review procedures to ensure the independence of review chairs.

As in his first report, Laming adopted a managerial response rather than addressing the issues of pressurised staff and inadequate resources that continued to characterise work in Haringey four years on from the Victoria Climbié case.

The government responded swiftly (DCSF, 2009). It accepted all Laming's recommendations and appointed a chief safeguarding adviser, Sir Roger Singleton, who had formerly been chief executive of the children's charity Barnardo's. It set out the remit of the delivery unit as: identifying and promoting good practice and bringing greater coordination, coverage and complementarity to existing advice on good practice; undertaking gap analysis of where more support was needed and commissioning work to fill any gaps; and developing practice reports, for example on thresholds, to assist frontline staff. While restating its commitment to Contactpoint (which did not survive the change of government in 2010), the response accepted the need for changes in the integrated children's system to simplify processes for frontline workers. It also identified problems in the recruitment and retention of social workers and the need for improving specialist training for workers in children's services, including the development of specialist post-qualification training.

Established in 2009, the safeguarding delivery unit was abolished within a year. The chief safeguarding adviser resigned at the same time and was not replaced. The change of government brought a new approach, with safeguarding replaced by child protection in the lexicon of the Department for Education.

The problems within social work had already been recognised by government by the appointment of the Social Work Task Force early in 2009. The task force was established jointly by the Department of Health and the Department for Children, Schools and Families to undertake a comprehensive review of frontline social work and to make recommendations for improvement and reform across both adult and children's services.

Its interim report (DCSF, 2009a) was a damning indictment of the state of social work. It concluded that:

• widespread staffing shortages were compromising the ability of social work to be a durable, attractive public sector profession;
• practical and professional support to frontline social workers was inconsistent and sometimes inadequate;

- current arrangements for education, training and career progression were not producing or retaining enough social workers equipped for the demands of frontline practice;
- social work had no single body responsible for representing the profession, and for driving up standards and spreading best practice;
- social work needed a clearer account of how its effectiveness should be judged;
- the distinctive role of social work in public service was unclear. (DCSF, 2009a)

The final report (DCSF, 2009b) published later that year set out how these issues should be addressed. It recommended major changes in education and training, including higher-calibre entrants, an overhaul of the content and delivery of degree programmes, high-quality practice placements and an assessed and supported first year in employment. It sought national standards for employers, covering the supervision and support available to social workers. Recommendations for a programme of continuous professional development and a national career structure for social work sat alongside specific training for frontline managers. The report called for a National College of Social Work and a national reform programme. Progress with these recommendations is discussed in the chapter on education and training (Chapter Five).

In relation to children's social work there were other forces for change resulting from the advent of the Coalition government in 2010 and the changed economic climate it inherited. Titles have significance. The Department for Children, Schools and Families – an accurate measure of its wide responsibilities – became the Department for Education. Safeguarding became child protection. The five outcomes of Every Child Matters ceased to be the language of choice within the renamed department. A series of reviews were initiated, including Professor Eileen Munro's review of child protection, a review of adoption and a review of family justice.

The Munro review (Munro, 2011) criticised the tendency of the many reviews into child deaths to focus on professional error rather than the whole system of child protection. Munro noted that the focus on performance indicators and targets valued processes above quality and effectiveness. Doing the right thing was more important than doing things right. Her report was refreshing for many social workers in its proposals to reduce prescription and its focus on evidence-based decisions and developing the expertise of practitioners. She called for the appointment of a chief social worker to advise the government on social work practice (a recommendation implemented with two chiefs – one for adults, reporting through the Department of Health, and one for children, reporting through the Department for Education). In addition, she urged local authorities to designate a principal social worker for families and children who would be in touch with frontline practice.

Munro's report and the wide-ranging work of the reform board cloaked the discontinuance of the much trumpeted national safeguarding delivery unit and chief safeguarding adviser. Implementation of Munro's recommendation for a chief social worker was delayed by interdepartmental struggles between health and education before a chief social worker for children was finally appointed. Despite all the changes, do we have a better and safer system now than existed previously?

The response to childcare tragedies has been a repeating cycle of media storm, public inquiry, accepted recommendations, legislative change and tightened procedures, followed by progress reviews by the inquiry chairs (Laming, Gibb, Munro) that inevitably find the pace of progress disappointingly slow and lead to the progressive dismantling of some recommendations. Then the cycle starts again.

It is important to note how influential the media is in driving policy. One of the most trenchant critics of social workers over the past 20 years has been Richard Littlejohn, writing in the *Sun* and latterly the *Daily Mail*. Recently he wrote:

> We hear every week of children being removed from their parents on the flimsiest of excuses by social workers who hide behind secret courts to conceal the full facts. Something like 25000 children a year are taken into care, half of them against their parents [sic] wishes. Social workers target decent families but shy away from anyone who may be violent or may scream 'racism'. As a result the most vulnerable children are abandoned to their fate. (Littlejohn, 2013)

The tragedy is that many *Daily Mail* readers will believe this to be an accurate representation of social work practice rather than a travesty of the truth.

The deafness of the Coalition government to the irrefutable evidence that more children are living in poverty and that these numbers are likely to increase further is illustrative of the failure of policymakers to grasp the negative correlation between child safety and poverty. In a literature review Griggs and Walker wrote in 2008: 'Low income, material deprivation, disadvantaged neighbourhoods and schools, parental stress and social exclusion, all recognised attributes of poverty, seem individually and possibly cumulatively negatively to shape the lives of children with short and long term consequences' (Griggs with Walker, 2008, p 24). While the language of prevention is often heard from those in government, translating it into practice is more difficult. It requires the whole-system approach advocated by Munro, addressing income, housing, poor schools and struggling neighbourhoods. Instead, we have a polarised debate about hard-working families versus shirkers and scroungers, although many of the children living in poverty come from those hard-working families in receipt of poverty wages.

Family intervention projects and troubled families

The initiatives to address these issues did not come from children's services but from family intervention projects (FIPs), established under the Labour government's Respect Action Plan in 2006. They were designed to tackle the problem of antisocial behaviour and to address the five outcomes of Every Child

Matters using assertive and persistent styles of working. Typically, FIPS worked with families for between six and 12 months.

The early evaluation of FIPs was positive (White et al, 2008). Families engaged in the project showed a reduction in antisocial behaviour, reduced risk of eviction and improvements for children across the five outcomes. The evaluation identified a number of factors critical to the success of projects. These were small caseloads, recruitment and retention of key staff, a dedicated key worker working intensively with the family, creative use of resources, using sanctions with support, staying involved with the family as long as necessary and effective multi-agency relationships.

Looking at the content of the work with families, there are two distinctive features of FIPs – the assertiveness and persistence mentioned earlier and the availability of support on a seven-day-a-week basis. With those exceptions, however, the work undertaken looks very much like social work – emotional support, financial support, behaviour management, organising family leisure-based activities, household management and guidance, financial advice and guidance, health advice and guidance, helping children get back to school, parenting advice, and guidance and onward referrals to other agencies.

The relative success of FIPs was confirmed by a later evaluation (DfE, 2011) showing improvements in over half of the families receiving an intervention in relation to parenting, school attendance, substance misuse, diet, domestic violence and antisocial behaviour. The two areas that proved most intractable were mental health and worklessness.

Building on this evidence, the government launched in November 2011 its Troubled Families initiative with the target of 'turning around' the lives of 120,000 families by 2015. Turning around was defined as: achieving more than 85% attendance at school and less than three exclusions for each child, a 60% reduction in antisocial behaviour across the whole family and a 33% reduction in youth offending, and progress towards work by enrolment in the Work Programme or European Social Fund programme or one adult in the family moving off benefits and into work.

The initiative was supported on a payment-by-results basis, with local authorities receiving £4,000 for each family meeting these targets with a proportion of that sum paid up front to establish the local service. While the scheme has been criticised because of the element of 'gaming' as local authorities self-assess their performance and the uncertain evidence of the sustainability of improvements after the period of intensive intervention, it has many positives. It uses a community budget, drawing in resources from different agencies. It recognises the high cost to society of failing families. It stresses the importance of consistency and the positive use of sanctions.

The head of the programme, Louise Casey, is herself assertive mirroring the qualities of the initiative. She told the Local Government Association that too many social workers colluded with parents to make excuses for their children's behaviour and called on social workers to be more authoritative and challenging in their dealings with families (Casey, 2013).

In looking at the evolution of social policy and social work in children's services, we can see how the focus has shifted from rescue to rehabilitation through to the current focus on 'tough love', with conditional support to families if they meet certain objectives. But the Troubled Families initiative is one strand of policy. The other is articulated by the government's adviser on adoption, Sir Martin Narey, who in his previous role as head of Barnardo's called for more children to be taken into care and criticised the emphasis on 'fixing families'. He argued that more use should be made of residential care (Narey, cited in *Daily Telegraph*, 2009). He repeated this after becoming adoption adviser, arguing that 'the system is gripped by an unfounded optimism of the capacity of parents to change' (Narey, 2011). So within government we see the ambivalence and the tug of war between optimists, who believe in the capacity of families to change (given the right mix of support and sanctions), and pessimists, who favour early removal from neglectful families.

This polarisation is unhelpful. Both optimists and pessimists exaggerate their case. The Troubled Families initiative was trumpeted by Eric Pickles, Secretary of State for Communities and Local Government, as proof that 'these problems can be dealt with through a no nonsense and commonsense approach, bringing down costs to the taxpayer at the same time' (DCLG, 2013a). In fact, the results published alongside this speech scarcely justify these bold claims (DCLG, 2013b). They show that 2% of families enrolled in the initiative have one member who has moved from out-of-work benefits to continuous employment, and a further 3% with a family member who had volunteered for the Work Programme. Of the 152 authorities surveyed, over a third had not a single success in moving a family member to continuous employment. However, a third of families had achieved improvements in levels of crime, antisocial behaviour and school attendance. These figures were confirmed by the report issued in 2014 (DCLG, 2014). This showed that less than 3% of families had achieved employment as a result of the intervention. The proportion of authorities failing to record a single employment success had been reduced to 15%, but this hardly suggests a great turn-round. Success on the other hand with school attendance and antisocial behaviour is, however, used to claim success for the programme as a whole. Whether this will constitute a 'halo' effect as a result of the intensive support and supervision associated with it or whether families will revert to previous patterns of behaviour remains to be seen. The claim that families have been 'turned round' is bold in the absence of evidence about sustainability. There is a risk that local authorities 'will be tempted to invest their skilled professional time and resources, not on those parents and families who most need an intensive outreach service, but on those most likely to ensure that the service provider gets the results which will trigger the payment' (Thoburn, 2013).

If the evidence base for the effectiveness of 'tough love' is thin, that supporting Martin Narey's contention is even thinner. Michael Gove in a speech in 2013 made the criticism that 'social work training involves idealistic students being told that the individuals with whom they will work have been disempowered by society....This analysis risks explaining away substance misuse, domestic violence and personal responsibility, rather than doing away with them' (Gove, 2013).This was a concerted attack on the moral relativism of social work training and the tendency to attribute family difficulties to the ills of society rather than personal failings.This argument is one we return to in the concluding chapter. Here, we note that the evidence base for removing children from families in order to achieve better outcomes for children is poor. For every child who is fostered or adopted (as was Michael Gove) and goes on to university and a successful career, there are many more who cannot be easily placed, who experience multiple placement breakdowns, and whose lives are irretrievably damaged. The disproportionate representation of young people who have been in care in mental health services, in prisons and among the street homeless should give pause to those who advocate taking more young people into care.

The balance shifts regularly between rescue and rehabilitation. On the one hand is the faith in early intervention, the primacy of protecting children from neglect and abuse, and permanent placement with substitute families; on the other, the focus on rehabilitation – supporting children by supporting the birth family. Changes over the past 40 years have often reflected the latest scandal and the press and public reaction to that scandal.The current focus on increasing adoption and doing so within stricter time limits – a policy given personal backing by the current Prime Minister, David Cameron – reflects the belief in rescue.The *Daily Telegraph*, often a sound reflection of government briefing, headlined its report 'David Cameron will today demand that councils speed up their adoption processes amid concerns that vulnerable children are being condemned to years in care by red tape and political correctness' (*Daily Telegraph*, 2012). This neatly combined three favourite targets of right-wing critics – local government, bureaucratic red tape and the political correctness of social workers.

Again, those working in adoption services know that this is not an accurate reflection of the complexities of the matching process and the contribution of the court process to delays. Nevertheless, the myth has taken hold, assiduously propagated by right-leaning newspapers, that social workers driven by ideological beliefs on same-race matching or some other liberal belief are frustrating the adoption process.

It is important to disentangle the different strands of tabloid criticism of social workers. First, there are two conflicting images – the over-zealous social worker responsible for taking children from loving homes or, in a recent case, ripping a child from a loving mother's womb (although, as so often, the true facts when they emerged from the family court were very different) on the one hand; and on the other, naïve social workers blind to the neglect being perpetrated on the child for whom they are responsible. Understandably, social work struggles to defend itself when the facts in any given case can be used to fit a narrative critical of social workers.

Second, a recurrent theme is political correctness. This can be in the context of race either as a doctrinaire pursuit of racial matching at the cost of the welfare of children, or a reluctance to intervene where parents came from a different race or culture to the worker. The label of political correctness can also be used, however, if smoking, age, weight or UKIP membership are alleged to be factors in placement decisions. At times, the reluctance of local authorities to comment on individual cases in the name of confidentiality has meant that the media presents only one side of the story – that of the aggrieved individual who has been 'judged' by social workers.

A third theme is bureaucracy, with red tape and complex decision-making structures blamed for delays. While many of the delays are caused by the complexity of care proceedings, the nature of decision making in childcare is often opaque to outside critics. The individual social worker – although vilified in cases from Maria Colwell to Baby P – is rarely the lone decision maker, as such decisions are taken with a supervisor, and often (if they involve substantial resource commitments such as reception into care) at a more senior level. The structure of social services in which the director was in statute the named individual responsible for children in care militated against devolution of decision making. In the blame culture promoted by the tabloid press, it can be difficult to decide whether to attack the head of the service or the social worker. In Haringey, both came under highly personal attacks after the death of Baby P.

The critique of bureaucracy is part of the pervasive attack on public services and in particular social welfare provision. This stems from a belief that extensive welfare support, both financial and social, undermines the primary responsibility of families to care for their own. The way in which neoliberal thinking has come to dominate the response to the vulnerable is examined further in Chapter Four.

AREAS FOR DISCUSSION

Where do you think the pendulum now stands between rescue and rehabilitation?

Is the bad press that social work in childcare receives inevitable?

Does social work have a role to play in 'tough love' policies and practices?

What progress has been made in addressing the six issues identified in the Social Work Task Force interim report?

FURTHER READING

The interim report from the Social Work Task Force (*Facing up to the Task, Interim Report of the Social Work Task Force*, DCSF, 2009), is a clear-thinking analysis of the problems facing social work. It is echoed in the context of child protection by the analysis in the Munro report (Munro, E. [2011] *The Munro review of child protection: Final report – a child-centred system*, Cmnd 8062, London: TSO).

Garrett, P.M. (2009) *'Transforming' children's services? Social work, neoliberalism and the 'modern' world*, Maidenhead: McGraw Hill/Open University Press, sets the transformation agenda of New Labour in the context of neoliberalism in its pursuit of standardised processes, performance targets and large-scale data sets.

Ray Jones' book (Jones, R. [2014] *The story of Baby P*, Bristol: Policy Press) vividly describes the way in which politicians and the press combined to attack social work's failings when those of the police and the NHS were equally responsible– some would say more so – for the tragedy.

FOUR

Neoliberalism and social work practice

KEY LEARNING POINTS

» The economic foundation of neoliberalism
» Creating a mixed economy of welfare
» The significance of the Griffiths report
» Care management and personalisation
» Long-term care
» The impact of direct payments
» The growth of managerialism and employer-led initiatives

Neoliberalism is an economic philosophy based on free markets, deregulation, privatisation and the rolling back of the frontiers of the state. It is a term often used to describe the policies of structural adjustment urged by the International Monetary Fund and applied most often in Africa and Latin America. In recent years, these policies have been used in Cyprus, Spain, Portugal and Greece as conditions of a bail-out from the European Union in a financial ongoing crisis that has been affecting eurozone countries since 2009.

This economic philosophy may not seem of immediate relevance to social work, but it has had a significant impact on the development of a mixed economy of welfare and the sustained retreat of local authorities from direct provision of care. The Thatcher government was ideologically supportive of this approach. Margaret Thatcher herself was strongly influenced by Hayek (1944), whose hostility to the state was conditioned by his experience of socialism in Eastern Europe. Friedman (*Economist*, 2006) developed this thinking in economic terms, seeing any regulation by the state as the enemy of freedom. This approach in economic policy has been translated into hostility to public expenditure, which is regarded as inherently less efficient than private expenditure and more inclined to waste money on bureaucracy. This uncritical belief in the effectiveness of the market has led to the development of market mechanisms in the public sector. This was first seen in the decisions to privatise electricity, water and rail, which had previously been regarded as naturally lending themselves to national provision. It has subsequently been extended to virtually all aspects of public provision through competitive tendering and outsourcing.

Broadly this approach has held sway for the past 30 years. Even in the last years of the 1997–2010 Labour government when unparallelled investment went into public services, in particular the National Health Service, belief in the greater efficiency of the private sector remained dominant. The current state of the public finances means that neoliberalism is likely to remain dominant for a number of years to come as savings continue to be sought in the provision of services.

One aspect of neoliberalism is the desire to improve performance and productivity. In the delivery of social care, this has been expressed in a number of ways – the purchaser–provider spilt, a mixed economy of welfare, contracting out of services, the target culture, value for money, best value reviews and managerialism. These overlap, but collectively they have contributed to a major change of culture in the context in which social care is delivered.

Purchaser–provider split

In the social care context, the concept of the enabling role of local government was first articulated by Norman Fowler when Secretary of State for Health. Speaking at the Association of Directors of Social Services conference in 1984 he suggested that social services departments should switch their focus from the direct provision of care to the funding and facilitation of the delivery of care. He set out three roles for social services departments:

- a comprehensive strategic view of all available sources of care;
- a recognition that social services were only part of the local pattern;
- a recognition that social services should support and promote the fullest possible participation of the other different sources of care that exist or can be called into being (Fowler, 1984).

Fowler emphasised the importance of seeing the whole system of care. The concept of the purchaser–provider split was first developed in relation to the delivery of healthcare. It was seized on by the Thatcher government as the basis for reforming public services by separating the responsibility for planning and commissioning services from that for delivery of services. The purchaser would thus specify what was required and secure the most effective and efficient way to deliver the service from a range of potential providers.

The elegant simplicity of this concept was set out in the Griffiths report (Griffiths, 1988), which came about when the government asked a former managing director of Sainsbury's, Sir Roy Griffiths, to review the management of social care services following a review he had undertaken on the management of the NHS (Griffiths, 1983).

As befitted his background, Griffiths believed in the importance of management, with clarity about accountability, responsibility and performance. His first report on the NHS led to the introduction of general management. His prescription for social care was somewhat different. Here he saw community care as lacking a clear champion with responsibility divided between the NHS busily retreating from long-term care, local authorities acting both as providers of long term care and as funders of individuals in need of care, and the rapidly developing private care market. This had been fuelled by an open-ended subsidy, with social security funding being used to support residential care with placements made on the basis of financial need rather than any assessment of care need. The cost to the public purse rose sharply from £6 million in 1978 to £1.3 billion in 1991, with the number of private places more than doubling in the same period.

Griffiths' proposals gave responsibility for community care to local authorities rather than the NHS. He proposed a specific grant to fund the development of community-based care from savings made by capping the social security budget on residential and nursing home care. He supported the development of care management, designing packages of care to support vulnerable individuals in the community, and the promotion of the independent sector by developing purchase of service contracting.

The mixed economy of welfare

Griffiths argued that a more plural welfare system would deliver choice, flexibility, innovation and competition. This presented a dilemma for government. While it needed urgently to control the growth of social security expenditure, it was reluctant to give further powers to local authorities, in part because the majority of authorities were controlled by opposition parties. There was a long delay before a White Paper (DH, 1989) and the eventual legislation of the NHS and Community Care Act in 1990.

This introduced the concept of the local authority as the 'enabler of care' with a funding mechanism significantly different from that recommended by Griffiths. Instead of a specific grant, there was a Special Transitional Grant, of which 85% had to be spent in the independent sector. The designation of the independent sector covered both private and voluntary sector providers, but in the 1990s, the private sector became the dominant provider of residential and nursing home care. Local authorities had to assess need both on a community basis through an annual community care plan, and on an individual basis through an assessment of needs followed by a package of care to meet those assessed needs.

The effectiveness of this mechanism to provide improved community-based care has been criticised. Undoubtedly, however, it led to a rapid transfer of direct provision of residential care from local authorities to the independent sector, and increasingly to the transfer of day and domiciliary services to the independent sector. The scale of the change can be seen in the transformation in the ownership of residential and nursing home care. In 1980, local authorities provided 63% of residential care places and the private sector 17%. By 2002, those proportions had been reversed, with local authorities continuing to retreat from direct provision. By 2013, the share of local authority-provided places was down to 8% of the total (Laing and Buisson, 2013). A parallel transfer took place in nursing home care, with a reduction of 60% in the number of NHS-provided nursing home places between 1987/88 and 2009/10. By contrast the numbers of privately provided nursing home places increased fourfold (Lieveley and Crosby, 2011).

The Griffiths report on community care contained no mention of social work. The impact of these developments on social work practice has, however, been profound. The task of social workers with adults became that of assessing need and orchestrating packages of care rather than direct delivery of services. The counselling role envisaged by the Barclay report (Barclay, 1982) as part of the repertoire of skills that social workers would bring to their work was further eroded.

The demise of local authority residential care has changed provision for the better, with many new homes being built. The sharing of rooms by older people has virtually disappeared unless through choice. En-suite toilet facilities – so important for older people – are expected. Central heating is universal. Unfortunately, the undoubted improvements in physical conditions have not been matched by parallel improvements in the quality of care.

There have been significant increases in the size of care homes, particularly those offering nursing care (CQC, 2010). The proportion of self-funders – people who are unsupported by local authority or NHS funding – has increased and is estimated now to be around 45% (CQC, 2012) of all those in homes. The proportion of care home residents needing nursing care has increased. The average age of residents is rising. As a result, 'Care homes are moving away from being an alternative form of housing for frail older people towards a location of last resort for individuals with high support needs towards the end of life' (Lieveley and Crosby, 2011, p 8). For a short time in the 1980s when the social security tap was flowing freely, a move into a residential home could be a lifestyle choice. That is no longer true.

In a fascinating historical perspective, Eric Midwinter (Lievesley and Crosby, 2011, pp 9-12) notes that indoor relief in workhouses for the aged poor in late Victorian times was provided for 4% of those over 65 – the same proportion of older people now in state-supported residential care. He notes the prevalence of ill health in those in residential care in Victorian times, although current terminology has changed, with independent and dependent replacing able-bodied and infirm. The financially driven priority then as now was to make provision for those unable to care for themselves. The long shadow of the workhouse continues to influence public policy.

Tested against the original mantra of Griffiths – choice, flexibility, innovation and competition – there is no doubt that there is now more choice of homes available for potential users, although the exercise of that choice may involve moving away from their immediate network of family and friends. Care homes, too, have become more flexible in the mix of care they are able to provide, with special nursing care units augmenting the more traditional care home model. The argument for innovation is more difficult to establish. Arguably, models of care developed outside the care home market in retirement communities have demonstrated a greater capacity to try new models including telecare. Competition has certainly been evident, but probably not in the way which Griffiths envisaged.

What we have seen has been the attractiveness of the care home sector to private equity funding. A secure cash flow backed by capital assets in the shape of the property has meant that the market is now dominated by highly leveraged private equity. The vulnerability of this model is illustrated by the saga of Southern Cross, the largest provider of care home places in the UK, providing at its zenith over 37,000 places. Following a management buy-out backed by private equity in 2002, it was acquired by Blackstone Capital Partners in 2004. It then took over two other major providers, NHP and Ashbourne, and floated on the Stock Exchange. Its business model had been financed in part by the sale of leases. The financial collapse in 2008 made this model unsustainable. There was a drop in occupancy levels and the company imploded in 2011, with all its homes being taken over by the landlords. The episode exposed the vulnerability of those in care homes to arcane financial modelling mechanisms dreamed up by accountants. The quality and stability of care provided to older people had no monetary value and was not taken into account as the company collapsed.

The growth of the private sector has also been seen in the provision of domiciliary care, where over 80% of home care is now provided by the private sector. There have been concerns about quality and continuity of care provided by staff working in the sector (Panorama, 2009). The dominance of financial considerations has been blamed for the loss of personal contact between home care workers and their clients. What is striking is the gap between the rhetoric of personalised care and the reality of the scale and type of assistance available.

Care management

The accompaniment to the changes in the financial framework following the 1990 NHS and Community Care Act was the introduction of care management – a model originally developed in the US where there was a more fragmented system of providers. The intellectual heft behind care management was provided by the Personal Social Services Research Unit at the University of Kent. In a series of publications Bleddyn Davies and colleagues set out the advantages of a more systematic approach to the organisation of support packages (Davies et al, 1990; Davies, 1992). They argued that the delivery of social care could be improved by clear case responsibilities, small and targeted caseloads, trained and experienced workers with decentralised budgets, costed service packages with workers knowing the unit costs of service provision, and better record-keeping processes for assessment and monitoring (Challis et al, 1993).

What was different about this approach was the flexibility and freedom to innovate that it gave to the care managers operating with a decentralised budget. But successive reductions in local authority budgets dating back to long before the budget cuts imposed by the Coalition government after 2010 gradually squeezed out that flexibility as the thresholds for care were raised. As early as 2000, Rummery and Glendinning noted that assessments were being used as a mechanism for prioritising needs and restricting access to services for all but those deemed most at risk of harm (Rummery and Glendinning, 2000). The key function in the care management process became assessment against ever stricter and more formalised criteria and risk management.

In the initial implementation of the 1990 NHS and Community Care Act, local authorities made determined efforts to meet the needs of vulnerable people. The rhetoric had changed, however, with the government no longer expecting services to meet all needs as resource constraints tightened. The individual service user was placed centre stage as a consumer entitled to exercise choice over services – a choice facilitated by the development of a market in care. While the 1997 Labour government was less enthusiastic about markets, it 'sought to distance citizens' social entitlements from unpopular statism and articulated a new concern with the individual citizen as a reaction against the perceived rigidity of welfare state bureaucracies' (Harris and McDonald, 2000). However, a patchwork service evolved, with varying thresholds for care in different areas – a postcode lottery of provision. To address this, the government introduced Fair Access to Care Services (FACS) in 2003 (DH, 2003). This is a national framework for care, but the application of the framework is for local determination.

The FACS bandings were: critical, substantial, moderate and low. Definitions were offered. Low was where one or two personal care or domestic routines could no longer be performed, or one or two family roles could no longer be undertaken, or one or two social support systems could not be maintained. Moderate needs were where several of these routines, roles and support systems could no longer be undertaken or accessed. Substantial needs were where the majority of routines, roles and support systems could no longer be undertaken or accessed, and there was only partial choice over the immediate environment. Critical needs were an inability to carry out personal care or domestic routines, sustain a family role or vital relationships and support systems, and where there were significant health problems.

Since the introduction of FACS, it has been possible to monitor the way in which local authorities have applied these thresholds in difficult financial circumstances. The latest report from the Care Quality Commission (CQC, 2012) shows that the proportion of councils setting thresholds for publicly funded care at those with substantial needs rose from 53% in 2005/06 to 83% in 2012/13. This is likely to have increased further since then.

Setting this figure against the criteria for social care support, in practice assistance is not available until the individual's ability to manage the activities of daily living has nearly collapsed. There is no room for prevention and early intervention in this resource-driven assessment model.

A revised version of FACS in 2010 did not change the eligibility framework but contrived to include a host of current buzzwords in its title – *Prioritising need in the context of putting people first: A whole system approach to assessing eligibility for social care* (DH, 2010c). It reflected the shift in emphasis in the early years of the century towards more individually tailored services known as personalisation, coupled with a drive towards self-directed support through direct payments and personal budgets. A raft of government publications had indicated these changes (DH, 2007a, 2008c, 2009). But the volume of words produced to set out brave strategies consistently outran the reality of the changes taking place that were driven by financial restraint. The holistic attempt to meet need that had been the vision of the 1990 NHS and Community Care Act was eroded by this pressure.

The analysis by the ill-fated Commission for Social Care Inspection (CSCI) is particularly significant in examining the impact of FACS in practice. It found that assessment was often still service-led rather than needs-led and that low-level needs were sometimes receiving no assistance or even signposting to possible sources of assistance. Tellingly, the numbers receiving publicly funded home care fell by 25% between 1997 and 2006. CSCI noted the tension between a model in FACS based on standardisation and explicit decision making and a 'personalisation agenda that is about self-assessment, individual decision-making and arms-length accountability for resource decisions' (CSCI, 2008).

Personalisation

Personalisation had been the mantra since the publication of *Putting people first* (DH, 2007a), with its call for people to control their own destinies with devolved budgets and responsibility for arranging their own care. Its genesis lay in the disability movement, which, as described in more detail in Chapter Six, had a transformational impact on the way in which society as a whole, and social care in particular, viewed people with disabilities. 'Does he take sugar?' was the brilliant title of a BBC programme that perfectly captured the assumption of able-bodied people that people with physical disabilities were feeble-minded as well. The assertive demands of service users with disabilities to take control over their own destinies challenged those assumptions and changed the nature of practice. And the mantra 'nothing about us without us' first adopted by the disability movement has now been adopted by other client groups.

The key changes envisaged by personalisation were mainstream person-centred planning and self-directed support, personal budgets for all those eligible for adult social care support, a universal information advice and advocacy service for those needing services and their carers, and support for vulnerable people to enjoy equal rights as citizens. These were to be buttressed by the Joint Strategic Needs Assessment and the Community Plan. All these changes were to be coordinated and led by adult social care.

That decision, although welcomed by social care, has weakened the concept, as the introduction of these changes coincided with the severe reductions in public spending and in particular on local government spending. Adult social care was not exempt. Despite additional funding from central government to deliver this agenda of change, and later funds transferred from the NHS budget to support social care where it would help the NHS to deliver its agenda, core spending on adult care fell substantially. The interrelationship between adult social care and the NHS was a constant source of tension. Adult care was a means-tested service, while the NHS was free at the point of delivery.

In 1997, Frank Dobson, then Secretary of State for Health, referred to the 'Berlin Wall' between health and social care. Numerous initiatives have sought to bridge that divide, but financial pressures have led to accusations of cost shunting, with bitter arguments about bed blocking (when people are kept in hospital when medically deemed fit for discharge because of the shortage of suitable accommodation or support in the community) or eligibility for continuing care (when the NHS meets the cost of supporting people with acute medical or nursing needs in the community). The long-standing arguments about baths –whether they were deemed 'medical baths' or 'social baths' determining whether they were free at the point of access – exemplifies the problem. While the decision made a real difference to the bather as to whether they had to pay or not, this did not create a favourable climate for agreements about transformational agendas.

The attempt by the CSCI to reconcile the problems of FACS with the personalisation agenda led it to recommend 'progressive universalism where all citizens can expect some level of support and those with the greatest needs can access further help' (CSCI, 2008, p 7). It built on *Putting people first* (DH, 2007a) and suggested that assessment of need could usefully be separated from the allocation of resources. It proposed a different process based on the priority of intervention: immediate intervention, where without intervention a person's wellbeing would be severely threatened; early intervention, where without support problems were likely to develop within six months that would threaten independence and wellbeing; and longer-term intervention, where people's independence would be threatened within a year without targeted evidence-based interventions.

Universalism, progressive or otherwise, did not fit the new economic realities. The revised version of FACS in 2010 kept the original fourfold eligibility framework of seven years earlier. It did, however, embrace the concept of prevention, early intervention and enablement as the norm, with an enhanced focus on self-assessment and first contact as a critical element of the assessment process. In practice, however, the shift in emphasis as far as its impact on service users is concerned has been primarily cosmetic. The resources have not been there to ensure that everybody receives a preliminary assessment and the service user experience is that of an ever more narrowly targeted service.

The variability in local authority thresholds was addressed by the 2014 Care Act, which set a national minimum threshold for eligibility. This requires local authorities to consider whether needs are due to physical or mental impairment or illness, whether the effect is an inability to achieve basic care outcomes or to engage in employment education or training, and whether this has an impact on the person's wellbeing. All three criteria have to be met. The details are still subject to consultation. Although the government has given a commitment to fund the Care Act, the snag is that these new legislative responsibilities come at a time when local authority resources are being further squeezed.

We can see in this tale the influence of neoliberal thinking in four ways. First, despite the vision of the NHS and Community Care Act and the later attempt by CSCI to recast the vision in the language of personalisation, managing the money has become the dominant consideration for those delivering the service. Cost overruns are the quick route to the exit door for service managers. Second, despite the recognition and overwhelming evidence of the perverse incentives in public policy caused by social care services charging and the NHS being free, the cost implications of addressing this have scared off successive generations of politicians. Third, hostility to regulation, so disastrous in banking, has been equally disastrous in health and social care, with light-touch regulation meaning that false reassurance was given about the quality and safety of providers. Fourth, universalism is seen as too costly for the state and means testing (so hated that the Beveridge reforms were designed to eliminate it) is now viewed not only as necessary but actually desirable to ensure that resources are concentrated on those who truly need them.

Funding care for older people

The protracted debate about the funding of care for an ageing population is an example of financial constraints rather than evidence dictating policy. The growth in the population of older people has haunted policymakers for a generation, with the rise in the numbers of those aged over 80 of particular concern. This age group are heavy users of health and social care services. Over 10 million people in the UK are over 65. This will rise to 19 million by 2050, with the increase concentrated in the older group of over-80s, who will increase in number from the current 3 million to 8 million (Parliament, 2010). The crisis in how to pay for care in older age is not new, but prevarication has been the hallmark of public policy since the report of the Royal Commission on the Funding of Long Term Care (1999).

The Royal Commission called for a new partnership between the state and older people, with living and housing costs being the responsibility of the individual, while personal care costs (home care, community based nursing care and additional care costs in residential settings) should be met by the state, subject to assessment. This central recommendation was challenged by two members of the commission. In a note of dissent, Joel Joffe and David Lipsey argued that this would transfer expenditure from the private purse to the public, would discourage people from providing for their own care and would increase the level of demand.

The dissent was significant because it gave an already sceptical government room for further delay and consideration. By contrast, in Scotland, where a parallel review by the Care Development Group had recommended free personal care, the government decided to implement the recommendations in full in 2002. Unusually, therefore, we are in a position to assess the impact and cost of free personal care and see whether the Royal Commission's proposals would have been feasible in England.

Between 2002/03 and 2011/12 in Scotland the numbers in care homes actually went down by 3%. By contrast, the numbers receiving free personal care in their own homes rose by 40% in the same period, partly as a result of demographic pressure, but also because of increased demand as awareness spread of the availability of free personal care. The average hours of home care received by individuals also went up during this period, suggesting that needs were becoming more acute. Expenditure more than doubled in this period because of the increased numbers helped, higher average time spent with clients and the level of need being supported being greater than formerly (Scottish Government, 2012).

On balance, therefore, on strict cost containment grounds the case against free personal care is strong. This has to be weighed against a clear user preference for home-based care and the superior quality of life this offers. The Scottish Government is periodically reported to be reviewing its policy. The picture elsewhere is no brighter. Despite many variations on the theme of meeting care costs (private–public partnership, increasing the means test threshold, compulsory insurance), successive governments refused to make any proposals as the Treasury – already fearful of the costs of any changes – became increasingly worried.

The Dilnot Commission (Dilnot, 2011), chaired by the then director of the Institute of Fiscal Studies, was an attempt to reconcile the positions of the Treasury and the increasing cost of care falling on elderly people as the means test threshold remained unchanged. Dilnot recommended that the threshold for support should be raised from £23,250 to £100,000 and that there should be a lifetime cap on care costs at around £35,000. Once the cap had been exceeded, the state should meet the cost of care. Despite a warm reception from the press and the public, the response from the government was slow. It took over 18 months for the government to bring forward its plans of a cap of £72,000 on lifetime care costs from 2016. And even then the small print showed that the real costs to families would often be far in excess of that figure.

First, the threshold to be met before the cap comes into play was to be set at substantial, which, as we have seen, is defined as an inability to fulfil or access the majority of routines and roles of daily living. Second, the cost of a care home will be based on the local authority rate, which is often lower than that available to an individual or family because of the bulk purchasing power of local authorities. Monies paid as 'top-up fees' will therefore not count against the cap. Third, the daily living component of a care home fee will not count against the cap. Age UK called on the government to ensure complete clarity over eligibility criteria, thresholds and the cap even before the Care Support Bill was debated in Parliament (Age UK, 2013).

These impending legislative changes are set against a backdrop of continuing reductions in local government expenditure projected to continue after 2015. The focus of the new approach from government is to see the orchestration of services through the eyes of the user. That brings us back to the concept of self-directed support and the impact of direct payments on social care.

Direct payments

The tyranny of social services assessment with its circumscribed menu of options was challenged by the demand for direct payments so that service users could purchase their own care. This shift in power was facilitated by the congruence of agendas between the increased assertiveness of people with disabilities and the government's desire to introduce greater choice and competition into the care market.

The idea of direct payments came in the first instance from the disability movement and was limited in its application to people with disabilities when introduced in 1997. It was subsequently broadened out to other care groups in 2003 when direct payments were made available to anybody who sought them. The idea was that service users would have choice and control over the services they bought to meet their assessed care needs. It also meant greater flexibility, with the oft-quoted example of a football season ticket as a means of achieving greater social integration for an isolated individual. After a slow initial take-up, over half a million service users had personal budgets in March 2012, although the majority left it to local authorities to commission services on their behalf. The policy intention is that all those eligible for social care support should receive this through a personal budget in 2015 (DH, 2013).

Personal budgets were popular then with users and with politicians – a rare combination. The 2014 Care Act includes provision for personal budgets to be a mandatory part of care plans.

So what are the implications for social work and for social policy of this development of directly purchased services? First, it has taken social work out of the care equation. The evidence from direct payments is that users will buy practical services rather than those geared to improving relationships and social skills. The possible exception to this is mental health clients where the value of talking therapies is recognised but social workers are unlikely to be the profession of choice to deliver this help. The way in which social work in mental health has been marginalised is considered later in Chapter Seven.

Second, it is the triumph of neoliberalism in the sense that individuals purchasing their own care – albeit with public funding – is the exemplar of choice and control being transferred from public sector agencies to individuals. The range of choices and the development of a market in care are side benefits of this development.

Third, the popularity of direct payments and personal budgets with service users means that the long-term implications of this policy shift are virtually immune from criticism unless one wants to risk the accusation of old-style paternalism.

There are, however, legitimate questions to be raised about the pace and direction of change. The adult social care market is distinguished by a number of factors. First, the boundaries between public and private provision are blurred. In both residential and domiciliary care, most service users make a financial contribution to the provision of care through direct purchase or co-payments. Much care is provided informally without payment, thus reducing the burden on the public purse. Second, the residential care market is dominated by large-scale providers, while the domiciliary care market tends to be composed of small and locally based organisations. Third, the nature of personal care is that it is relationship-based rather than a commodity to be purchased.

There remains a tension between the political imperative to target resources in order to contain expenditure and the social imperative to improve outcomes for service users. The restriction of funding to those with substantial or critical needs means that the prevention agenda will also be more difficult to deliver. Those high-need users are least likely to benefit from preventive initiatives. Those with less acute needs are likely to have difficulty in accessing even advice services from public agencies.

The transfer of responsibility for purchasing care from professionals to service users makes it more difficult to regulate and monitor the quality and impact of what is being delivered. The responsibility of local authorities to stimulate the social care market will be constrained by their limited ability to influence user decisions and by the demise of the block contracts formerly used to influence the social care market. The key to successful delivery of this transformation may lie in advocacy and brokerage organisations, themselves controlled and run by current or former service users. Yet the funding for such organisations located in the voluntary sector is at risk in the difficult financial context where grantors may face a choice between direct service-giving organisations and infrastructure support bodies of this kind.

The polarisation of the debate between user control and professional bureaucracies is often presented in black-and-white terms. Newman and colleagues have observed that: 'The notion of self-governance through independence, control and choice (is) vulnerable to neoliberal tendencies in the policy agendas of many "modernising" welfare states especially, perhaps, in the UK' (Newman et al, 2008)..

The National Audit Office reviewed the impact of user choice and provider competition in social care (NAO, 2011). It confirmed the beneficial impact of personal budgets on the wellbeing of most service users, with less than 10% feeling that the disadvantages outweighed the benefits. It warned of the lack of commissioning and procurement skills in local authorities leading to market inefficiencies and failures in planning. It was particularly concerned at the lack of preparedness to deal with provider collapse as in the case of Southern Cross.

Personal budgets are based on giving individuals control of the funds that would have been spent on their care. They were tested in 60 pilot sites and a comprehensive evaluation was undertaken by the Personal Social Services Research Unit at the University of Kent (Forder et al, 2012). The evaluation found that there were significant improvements in the care-related quality of life and in psychological wellbeing. Budgets were most effective where users were informed of the total budget before drawing up a care plan, and where they had flexibility and choice in the use of their budget. There was some evidence that the benefits were most clear cut in relation to continuing care and mental health services.

The evidence from the major Individual Budgets Support Networks Evaluation (IBSEN) study (Glendinning et al, 2008) is more equivocal about the benefits of personal budgets, finding advantages for younger adults, those with disabilities or with mental health problems, but no gains in terms of costs for older adults. This finding was replicated in a recent study (Woolham and Benton, 2013) that suggested that older people in particular did not derive significant benefit from personal budgets. We have therefore the paradox of a policy driven by the demonstrable benefits for younger adults now being applied to all social care users and expected to deliver cost savings – truly evidence-free policy formation.

The social care market then remains an imperfect market. Choice is the mantra used to justify the transfer of power to service users, but for many people choice is a bogus concept. For those entering residential care even as self-funders, choice will often follow a period of hospitalisation or a fall that has sapped the self-care capacity of the individual whether psychologically or physically. It is rarely a lifestyle choice. The range of homes available within a geographical area facilitating the maintenance of contact with friends and family is limited, and the energy and enthusiasm of the potential resident to visit a number of homes even more so.

Market regulation is impaired by the skill deficit in local authorities and the flawed record of the Care Quality Commission. The appointment of a new head of inspection of adult social care at the commission (CQC, 2013) is an acknowledgement of past failings. Whatever the abilities of the individual, it is often a mistake to assume that one person alone can change the culture. Certainly, the appointment between May 2013 and July 2013 of a chief social worker for children's services, a chief social worker for adult social care, a chief inspector for hospitals and a chief inspector for adult social care achieved the positive headlines that were sought. The degree to which they will be able to change the landscape remains an open question.

The problems remain in the continued belief of those with the ear of government that private sector skills are invariably superior to those in the public sector – the classic ideological position of neoliberals. Despite the recent failures of private sector contractors, notoriously G4S at the Olympics and Serco in the case of allegations relating to overcharging for electronic tagging, the zeal of advocates of the private sector remains unabated. In a remarkable interview, the senior consultant at Policy Exchange said in an interview on BBC Radio 4's Today programme that 'we need to go further and faster with outsourcing … throw caution to the wind' (Today, 2013). Any failures of procurement are attributed to the lack of skill in the public sector. The solution for zealots of the private sector lies in the recruitment of private sector skills to undertake this task. As an example, the consultancy firm McKinsey was famously employed by the government in working out the NHS reforms that have increased the role of the private sector in the NHS.

Titmuss, in his classic text (Titmuss, 1970), used the donation of blood as proof of the virtues of altruism expressed through the NHS compared with the US model of a private market in blood. It is therefore bitterly ironic that the storage and supply of plasma has now been outsourced to Bain and Co, the US-based hedge fund.

The issue for social policy is whether the trend to individualisation and privatised solutions is now irreversible. The extension of the concepts underpinning personal budgets in social care to the NHS in the form of personal health budgets is the latest example of the continuing shift. A jointly agreed care plan sets out the person's health and social care needs, the health outcomes sought, the budget available and how the person wishes to spend that.

The combined impact of these changes has been to bring about a dramatic change in the role of social work. The 1990 NHS and Community Care Act placed social workers in the role of care managers at the heart of delivering high-quality services, responsive to the needs of the user. With the development of personalisation, the social work role became less significant, shifting to that of adviser and advocate and sometimes a service broker. With the extension of personal budgets and the shift of control to service users, social work has become further marginalised.

Care itself has been monetarised. The Treasury is anxious to avoid a repeat of the cascade of monies into residential care through social security funding in the 1980s, but its failure to protect adult social care in the face of demographic pressures has transferred the pressure to the NHS budget. While the public sector still has an assurance role in ensuring probity in the use of public monies, the purchase of care has effectively been privatised.

The new managerialism

These changes have to be seen in the context of the growth of managerialism and what is known as the 'new public management'. This phrase describes a number of aspects of management that built on the 3Es – economy, efficiency and effectiveness – espoused by the Audit Commission in the 1980s.

Economy is the responsibility of all managers in the public sector – delivering services in a way to achieve the best value for money. Unfortunately, economy has tended to be interpreted as reducing costs without regard to the other two Es – efficiency and effectiveness. There has been too little attention to ensuring that services achieve the desired outcome and maximise the impact of the inputs of staff time and resources.

More recently there has been an emphasis on outcome management, whereby the goals of policy are set, leaving it to providers to decide how best to achieve those outcomes within the cost envelope available. While this has had some success, it is too early to be confident that mechanisms are in place to avoid providers 'gaming the system' by manipulating data supplied to commissioners, as evidenced by Serco and G4S, or by cherry picking those clients most likely to succeed.

Although the focus on outcomes was first developed under the Conservative government led by John Major, the modernisation agenda of New Labour adopted many of the same techniques. While it stressed the importance of joined-up government and the importance of multi-agency working and partnerships, the Labour government 1997–2010 accepted many of the neoliberal arguments. It believed in light-touch regulation. It accepted the superiority of the private sector. It sought reforms of the public sector introducing elements of competition.

Marquand notes the hostility of the neoliberals to professionals who are seen as self-interested and who 'can be motivated only by sticks and carrots. If possible privatisation must expose them to the stick and carrots of market competition. If not, they must be kept on their toes by repeated audits, assessments and appraisals' (Marquand, 2004, p 3).

As a consequence, Labour was reluctant to use established public services as the vehicle for change, preferring the creation of new multi-agency initiatives and partnerships. An increasing role was seen for the private sector and for voluntary organisations and charities. Drug action teams, Sure Start, family intervention projects, Connexions and youth offender teams were established. New funding mechanisms – the Children's Fund, Health Action Zones – came and went. Only a minority of the initiatives survived for more than four or five years.

Social workers had a role in these multi-agency partnerships, but the influence of social work was diluted. Day care for pre-school children had been located in social services, but Sure Start was centrally funded and managed by boards with strong local representation. But despite the promise of 10 years' funding Sure Start was transferred to the new local authority children's services departments and as such is now suffering from the prolonged squeeze on local government expenditure.

The Children's Fund was established in 2000, aimed at tackling social exclusion among children aged five to 13, with local partnerships as the governance vehicle. The initiative lasted five years, but the final evaluation reported the difficulties in partnership working, agency commitment and securing parental participation, which made the fund less successful than had been hoped.

Health Action Zones were established on a pilot basis in 1999 for seven years to tackle health inequalities. Like so many of the initiatives of New Labour, they came to an end long before their projected lifespan and were subsumed into primary care trusts. They failed to make any direct impact on health inequalities. In evidence to the Health Select Committee, the researcher and academic Ken Judge noted that the projects 'were conceived and implemented too hastily, were too poorly resourced and were provided with insufficient support and clear direction to make a significant contribution to reducing health inequalities in the time that they were given' (House of Commons Health Committee, 2009, para 117).

The most successful initiative so far has been family intervention projects, which have mutated into the Troubled Families initiative, under which there is a sustained short-term effort to turn round the lives of families with a multitude of problems bringing them into conflict with police, schools and authority.

Many of these initiatives were natural territory for social workers with their training and experience in working with troubled families, their expertise in relationship building and their understanding of deprived communities. Instead, we had new groups of personal advisers, support workers and development workers, all with a sanction in their back pocket if they encountered non-compliance. Rogowski notes that 'work that was once the preserve of highly trained professionals is now being carried out by less qualified staff' (Rogowski, 2010).

The rise of employer-led initiatives

We have seen, too, a steady increase in the role of employers in shaping the nature of training and the way in which social work is practised. The final progress report of the Social Work Reform Board was enthusiastic about 'the opportunities for driving further the implementation of social work reforms through an integrated and coordinated sector led approach' (DfE, 2012a, p 8). The Children's Improvement Board brought together the Local Government Association, the Association of Directors of Children's Services and SOLACE, the Association of Local Authority Chief Executives, to drive improvement in children's services, working particularly with councils experiencing difficulty. The aim was to use peer challenge and support as a vehicle for improvement and to reduce the numbers of councils subject to central government intervention. The range of work covered was impressive (LGA, 2014).

In April 2013, the Department for Education (DfE) withdrew its funding from the Children's Improvement Board. While the partners have reaffirmed their commitment to sector-led work, the loss of funding has inevitably had an impact on the range of work undertaken. It also calls into question the value which DfE placed on the joint work.

In adult services, the major drivers for change were the government's *A vision for adult social care* (DH, 2010b) and Think Local Act Personal (2010). These set out a way forward for adult social care and were followed by a White Paper (DH, 2012) and subsequent legislation. It mirrored the Children's Improvement Board model of sector-led delivery by the establishment of Towards Excellence in Adult Social Care (TEASC), a similar model but also including input from the Social Care Institute for Excellence (SCIE) and Think Local Act Personal. The reform board took a rosy view of these changes, suggesting that 'this will place social workers firmly at the heart of adult social care. It will recognise the important role of social workers in promoting people's independence, providing personalised services and in upholding their human rights' (DfE, 2012, p 9).

The TEASC progress report (LGA, 2013) contains much valuable information produced in a timely fashion. It shows a fall in the numbers receiving local authority help, with care and support reflecting the budgetary pressures. There was, however, an increase in those receiving self-directed support and in those receiving direct payments. Most tellingly, the report records that 'there has been a rapid reduction in most forms of traditional community based services, such as meals, equipment, day care, professional support, and short term residential care' (p 43). For all the fine rhetoric in the White Paper about prevention, the report also shows that preventative support delivered through low-level home care has been reduced more severely than intensive support. The number of older people receiving professional support from a social worker or occupational therapist fell from 156,000 in 2010/11 to 66,000 in 2012/13. In the progress report there is no mention of social work.

These trends were confirmed in a study showing a 15% real-terms reduction in spending on adult social care between 2009/10 and 2012/13 and a 13% reduction in spending on residential care. Completely contrary to the professed policy goal, the biggest reductions were found in community-based services, with a 23% reduction in domiciliary and day services and a 36% reduction in meals services (Ismail et al, 2014).

The role that could be played by social workers in the new model of care is not clear. While social workers will welcome the emphasis placed on prevention and early intervention, this will be delivered by advice and information, meeting low-level needs within communities by more housing options and better support for carers, reablement services and effective crisis response before intensive care and support services become involved. Giving people the right to plan their own care through a personal budget builds on the success of direct payments, but few service users have seen the purchase of a social work service as a priority.

Government and the media

The role of the media in shaping the public discourse is an important factor in the interaction between social policy and politics. The advent of the 24-hour news cycle has exacerbated the already existing tendency to seek the 'headline-grabbing announcement'. And every report in the media of problems in health or social care demands a political solution to be promulgated by government. The Blair government, with its obsession with creating a story to control the news cycle, produced the instability described earlier, in which new initiatives were rarely given the time to establish themselves before being succeeded by other new ideas.

In Chapter Three, we examined the disastrous consequences of the cyclical shift between rehabilitation and rescue in childcare policies and the influence of the media in shaping social policy.

The issues raised are about the role of government in society. Winning elections has become the driving force of governments. Margaret Thatcher and Tony Blair – despite their numerous and vociferous critics within and outside their respective parties – won respect for their skill in winning elections and creating stable majority government. While the move to fixed-term parliaments introduced by the 2010 coalition was designed to prevent government manipulation of the economic cycle for political advantage, it has not lessened the influence of electoral calculation in framing governmental social policies. The rhetoric of debates about those receiving social security benefits is the result of the hardening of public attitudes towards those on benefits (JRF, 2014). It reflects too the attitudes of the Poor Law, attributing dependency on benefits to individual failings rather than to social injustice.

The relationship between the state, the individual and the market at a time of austerity is a fundamental political debate. Is the financial crisis attributable to self-deluding bankers forgetting some basic principles of lending, or it is it an existential crisis of capitalism? Whichever explanation is accepted, what is intriguing is the separation in social attitudes. While bankers are vilified for their contribution to the economic collapse, so too are those at the bottom of the socioeconomic system for their lack of enterprise. They have to be incentivised into work by cutting benefits through the 'bedroom tax' or the cap on housing benefits, although the evidence suggests that it is the working poor who are the primary victims of such policies.

Austerity and the pressures on household budgets have not produced the social solidarity of the mass unemployment of the 1930s or the resilience shown by the British people during the privations of the Second World War. Social work has been blamed for supporting minorities. The blame for our problems is ascribed to foreigners, whether as individuals – Roma beggars, Romanian or Bulgarian criminals, Muslims, asylum seekers, or those 'milking the system' – or as collective bodies such as the impersonal European Union. (Interestingly, in 1875 the Charity Organisation Society produced a paper on what to do about Italian children begging on the streets of London.)

The post-war Labour government demonstrated reforming zeal in an age of rationing and scarcity, but that kind of radicalism is absent from current political discourse. Social work has a value base of promoting social justice and the worth of each individual. It has a role in building communities. Yet it has still to find a voice challenging the prevailing attitudes.

Why has social work become silently complicit in the changing social culture? First, social work itself is under threat, with reductions in public expenditure, the marginalisation of the profession, lack of popular support because of its identification with childcare failures, and lack of a defined professional identity. Second, the profession lacks clear leadership. In part, this is because of the division between the College of Social Work and the British Association of Social Workers. In part, it is because of the widening gap between academia and the social work workforce, with the preoccupations of academics rarely speaking to the condition of the front line. The demolition job by Sue White and colleagues on the integrated children's system is a rare exception (White et al, 2010). Third, challenging government policy is not career-enhancing when governments hold considerable leverage through research grants, commissions and patronage. When the basic social policies are common to the major parties, this challenge becomes even more difficult.

In analysing the mechanisms used to extend market disciplines, Carey argues that:

> Market hegemony has succeeded in establishing now largely accepted rituals such as resource and contract-led practice, as well as a sustained emphasis placed upon accountability, efficiency, performance, audit

and the application of scientific laws and new technologies to vastly regulated and standardised practices. (Carey, 2008)

Working within resource constraints has become accepted practice.

Lymbery (2001) wrote: 'Power has flowed from practitioners to managers.... It is managers who are the dominant voices in social work.' The Association of Directors of Social Services established a close relationship with the Department of Health and was approached for professional views. By contrast, the British Association of Social Workers had less frequent contact with officials and much less influence. Tackling the dominant role of managerialism and how best to deal with the neoliberal consensus on public policy is the theme of the concluding chapter.

AREAS FOR DISCUSSION

Did the mixed economy of welfare develop in the way envisaged by the Griffiths report?

Has the emphasis on market principles in social welfare delivered benefits to service users? How does the practice of care management match up to the expectations invested in it 25 years ago?

What are the strengths and weaknesses of personal budgets from the user perspective?

What do you see as the next steps in the application of neoliberalism in social welfare? Is this inevitable?

FURTHER READING

There are many texts analysing the development of neoliberalism and how it has changed social work. Among them, Rogowski, S. (2010) *Social work: The rise and fall of a profession*, Bristol: Policy Press; Ferguson, I. and Woodward, R. (2010) *Radical social work in practice: Making a difference*, Bristol: Policy Press; Ferguson, I. (2008) *Reclaiming social work*, Bristol: Policy Press; and Lavalette, M. (2011) *Radical social work today*, Bristol: Policy Press, are significant.

Harris, J. (2003) *The social work business*, London: Routledge, is a brilliant analysis tracing the application of business principles to social work.

Garrett is a prolific writer and has a challenging take on the consequences for social work practice of the neoliberal agenda; see Garrett, P.M. (2009) *'Transforming' children's services? Social work, neoliberalism and the 'modern' world*, Maidenhead: Mcgraw Hill / Open University Press.

Webb, S. (2006) *Social work in a risk society*, Basingstoke: Palgrave Macmillan, is a thoughtful analysis that looks at neoliberalism in the context of society's preoccupation with risk and how it is reflected in day-to-day practice. Some of these themes are developed more contentiously in Webb's joint work with Mel Gray: Gray, M. and Webb, S. (2013) *The new politics of social work*, Basingstoke: Palgrave Macmillan.

FIVE

Education or training for social work

KEY LEARNING POINTS

» The rise of vocationally based training from the Certificate in Social Service and the Diploma in Social Work to the social work degree
» The struggle adequately to define social work
» The Social Work Task Force and Social Work Reform Board analysis and agenda
» The development of specialist and fast-track training
» The tension between social work education and social work training
» Foucault, postmodernism and class as academic preoccupations
» Two reviews of social work education: the Narey and Croisdale-Appleby reviews

It is a paradox that more social workers are being trained and trained to a higher standard than was true 40 years ago while the territory exclusively occupied by social workers has contracted. This chapter explores this paradox and how it has developed.

Council for Education and Training in Social Work

With the Seebohm report's (1968) call for one central body responsible for promoting the training of staff in the personal social services, the days of the three training councils – the Central Training Council for Child Care, the Council for Training in Social Work and the Advisory Council for Probation and Aftercare – were numbered. A unified Council for Education and Training in Social Work (CCETSW) was created in 1970 to develop a basic qualification with less emphasis on a particular setting.

The advent of CCETSW coincided with an unprecedented and never to be repeated period of expansion in personal social services. The remit of the CCETSW extended also to residential and day-care settings where the deficit of trained staff was even more acute. The pell-mell expansion of training places also posed issues of quality. The ready access to promotional opportunities in fieldwork settings meant that academic positions rarely attracted the highest calibre of applicant, leading to some training courses being of indifferent quality.

There was much discussion about the nature of training required for residential work, regarded then and now as the poor relation of fieldwork. After a CCETSW working party report boldly asserted *Residential Work is Part of Social Work* (CCETSW, 1974), the debate focused on whether the skill set needed in residential settings was identical to that required in fieldwork or whether the training should be geared to competence in particular roles. CCETSW was understandably reluctant to open again the vexed issue of specialisation – this time by setting and not by client group – and instead opted for a new qualification – the Certificate in Social Service (CSS).

The distinctive features of CSS were its modular form and its focus on fitness for the role. In practice, therefore, CSS became a qualification fitted to the particular role occupied rather than a fully portable qualification. The temper of the times was hostile to elitism. The British Association of Social Workers (BASW) had moved to open its membership to unqualified staff in 1978 after a series of divisive debates. CSS holders objected to their qualification being regarded as inferior in status to the Certificate of Qualification in Social Work. It took a decade to achieve but the two were effectively merged in 1988 with the creation of a single Diploma in Social Work first awarded in 1991. In the process, the employer-led basis of CSS became the norm for social work qualification, with competencies drawn from the framework of National Vocational Qualifications taking their place in social work curricula.

The Diploma in Social Work

The debate leading to the creation of the Diploma in Social Work reflected the questioning mood of the time, with CCETSW in the firing line of the government because of the social activism and alleged political correctness manifest by those coming off courses. Attempts to match black children in care with black and minority ethnic foster carers or adopters were a particular source of attack from right-wing newspapers that featured the numbers of white prospective adopters denied a child on grounds of ethnicity. Like so many contested areas of social work practice, this debate rumbled on for over 30 years, reaching a resolution in the 2014 Children and Families Act. This has removed the requirement that adoption agencies and local authorities should give due consideration to a child's religious persuasion, racial origin and cultural and linguistic background. It was argued that these were factors to be taken into account, but the dangers of delay in seeking a perfect match were greater than the risks from transracial adoption.

Social work then was under fire from the Right for its failings in child protection and for the assumed over-emphasis on political correctness and social activism. At the same time, it was criticised from the Left for its individualisation of the problem rather than seeing structural solutions as key to addressing social ills. Steve Rogowski (2010) argues that welfare bureaucracies were seen as anti-democratic and unaccountable.

The balance within the governing body of CCETSW shifted, with increased representation from employers and managers. And with it the demand grew for training that was fit for purpose and required students to demonstrate competencies rather than 'education, research, knowledge and understanding' (Rogowski, 2010). CCETSW Paper 30 was roundly attacked for its references to endemic racism, but Lena Dominelli criticised it from a different perspective for:

'• a competency driven, technicist approach to social work education which has bleached out the political nature of social work intervention and emphasized decontextualised practical skills;
• the marginalisation of social work educators, practitioners and consumers;
• an employer and government led training agenda in social work;
• the absence of substantial independent (of government objectives) funding in social work education;
• forms of intervention which disempower users whilst clothing their activities in the rhetoric of citizenship and empowerment' (Dominelli, 1996).

The Diploma in Social Work (DipSW) was criticised from the outset. First, it had not met the aspirations of social work educators for a degree-level entry to social work. Second, by incorporating aspects of the former CSS qualification, it was seen by some to be 'dumbing down' social work. Third, it was seen as reframing social work education to produce staff suited for work in public sector bureaucracies at a time when the employment pattern for social work was beginning to be more fragmented. Fourth, employers continued to complain that some products of training courses were still ill suited to employment.

What it did, however, was to offer a range of entry routes at non-graduate, graduate and postgraduate level over four, three and two years respectively. Some conversion courses were offered, enabling holders of the CSS to upgrade their qualification. Courses were offered at a range of institutions, from further education colleges to leading research universities.

With the advent of New Labour and the modernisation agenda that came with it, a new approach was required. Reviews were launched of CCETSW itself, of the DipSW, of post-qualifying education and training, of practice placements, and of the delivery arrangements for DipSW. A consulting firm – JM Consulting – was employed at the outset of New Labour's long love affair with external consultants. The government had already announced the establishment of a new regulatory framework with a General Social Care Council in England and parallel care councils in Scotland, Wales and Northern Ireland to replace CCETSW.

Recognising the criticisms of social work education, the consultants asserted:

> It would be false to expect that changes in the content of the DipSW alone could achieve the significant improvements in public confidence in social work that we all seek. This will require action on a broader group of issues which include the selection of students; the content of the qualification; the relevance and integration of the practice education; the way the DipSw is managed and delivered; and the way in which employers induct and support their newly qualified workers. (JM Consulting, 1999, para 2.12)

It would be another decade before the Social Work Task Force addressed these broader issues. The report of JM Consulting went to some familiar territory – Is social work a profession? What sort of social workers do we need? – before making its recommendations. It concluded that 'social workers in future need to work to a framework of individual accountability, standards and ethics, continuing education and development and research and evidence based practice and in this sense need to become recognised as "professional"' (JM Consulting, 1999, para 3.4a). In addition to a set of competences, social workers needed 'the critical thinking, analytical and inter personal attributes normally associated with professionalism' (JM Consulting, 1999, para 3.9).

The review called for an extension of the programme, implying – although not explicitly stating – that this should be a degree-level qualification. It called on employers to recognise the importance of their responsibility for post-qualification support and development.

The modernisation agenda of the Labour government was addressed to the deficits in training throughout the personal social services. Its White Paper (DH, 1998) had led to the creation of the Training Organisation for the Personal Social Services (TOPPS), which itself produced a training strategy (TOPPS, 2000). This contained strategic objectives including national occupational standards as the foundation for social care work planning, job definition, skills assessment and audit, development of training provision and performance appraisal. It set priorities for the five-year period 2000–05 for registration and inspection staff, heads of homes for both adult and children, day-centre managers, domiciliary care managers and staff, and NVQ level 3 for mental health and child care staff. Social work itself was not seen as a separate priority. The ambition to secure a fully trained workforce was laudable, but the reality was far different.

The mapping exercise undertaken as part of the strategy showed alarming gaps in the numbers of trained staff – three quarters of residential care staff had no qualification, 85% of day-centre staff had no qualification, and in domiciliary care over half the managers had no qualification and virtually no frontline staff had a qualification.

Although social workers were not a priority, the document had some useful data about trends in social work recruitment and retention. While there was a 24% increase in the numbers of social workers in the decade, there was a worrying decline of 55% in the number of applications to social work courses. The strategy noted a concern about the quality of DipSW in terms of gaps in curricula, a lack of outcome consistency between programmes, and variations in the experience and background of course tutors.

The confusion within the field about roles requiring a qualified social worker, the lack of good-quality practice placements and the lack of employer commitment to staff development were all worrying factors, but the strategy reasserted the importance of employer-led initiatives. The critical thinking and analytical ability to use evidence required in a profession were subjugated to the requirements of employers – and then predominantly to the requirements of public sector employers despite the rising numbers of social workers in the private and voluntary sectors.

The social work degree

The government's White Paper (DH, 2000a) set out a strategy for improving the quality of social work training. This led to the degree programme being introduced, with the first intake of students graduating in 2003. The qualification was available through a number of different entry routes as well as conventional undergraduate degree programmes. But the picture was confused by the division of responsibilities between TOPPS, which defined occupational standards, the General Social Care Council, which validated the curriculum and approved courses, and universities and colleges, which delivered the programmes.

The degree programme did indeed reverse the slump in applications for courses and the numbers of social workers continued to grow. Between 2003 and 2009, the numbers of social work students graduating increased by over 60%. But despite the degree, the same issues remained:

> Some employer representatives are concerned that the introduction of the social work degree is focussed on academic achievement at the expense of work experience, with graduates finding it difficult to pass practice-based assessments. (Centre for Workforce Intelligence, 2012).

Two big questions remained unanswered: What did social workers do that required their mix of knowledge, skills and competencies? What were the boundaries of their occupational role?

Looking across the field once occupied exclusively by social workers, it is possible to identify many tasks now carried out by those without a social work qualification. In adult care, there are personal advisers, advocates, brokers and personal assistants. In childcare work, staff in children's centres and family intervention project workers come from a multiplicity of backgrounds. The area reserved for social work seems to be narrowing. Probation has abandoned a social work qualification. The formerly restricted role of approved social worker has now been opened up to other disciplines with the advent of the approved mental health professional.

What is the social work task?

The debate about the appropriate structure for social work training has been characterised by a number of attempts to differentiate those tasks that require a qualified social worker. In 1976, the Birch report (DHSS, 1976) suggested circumstances involving loss of liberty or a change of home for the client, and those situations demanding complex assessment or treatment/planning. In 1977, BASW (BASW, 1977) did not offer a categorisation of tasks, but suggested that decisions should be made on the basis of client vulnerability – physical psychological or social – the degree of case complexity, and the significance of the decision for the client. In 1982, the Barclay report (Barclay, 1982) identified situations where life and liberty are at risk; a major change of living situation may be involved;

counselling may be needed when relationship problems are escalating to life crisis proportions; the client, family or group seems unable to make use of available resources; and a network of resources needs to be established and monitored.

Attempts to define social work have continued, with the International Definition of Social Work being most widely used (IFSW, 2014). This is more broadly based than looking at social work tasks:

> Social work is a practice-based profession and an academic discipline that promotes social change and development, social cohesion, and the empowerment and liberation of people. Principles of social justice, human rights, collective responsibility and respect for diversities are central to social work. Underpinned by theories of social work, social sciences, humanities and indigenous knowledges, social work engages people and structures to address life challenges and enhance wellbeing.

This certainly bears the hallmarks of being written by a committee. Ministers periodically seek a concise statement of what social workers do, but this has eluded many of the regulatory bodies. The College of Social Work was widely criticised in its first attempt to define those tasks that only social workers could perform but that included many tasks currently undertaken by other healthcare professionals. Its latest guidance revisits the territory but is much less prescriptive (College of Social Work, 2014). It differentiates between those situations where a social worker must be used, usually one requiring the exercise of functions defined in statute, and those where a social worker should be used. It also maps these against the Professional Capabilities Framework. The document does not achieve either clarity or conciseness. Arguably the most useful statement to date comes in the interim report of the Social Work Task Force, which sets out concisely a public description of social work outlining situations where social workers might be needed, how social workers operate and the specialist training they require and why (DCSF, 2009a).

Undaunted by the difficulties previously experienced, the Narey review of social work training (Narey, 2014) returned to this territory. In addition to analysing the complexity of curriculum requirements and alleging disproportionate attention to anti-oppressive practice, Narey argued that 'there needs to be a concise, single document drafted, drawing on the advice of the College of Social Work, academics and, *particularly*, employers, which offers in a single publication, a GMC style summary of what a newly qualified children's social worker needs to understand' (Narey, 2014, p 13; emphasis added). This thankless task is allocated to the chief social worker for England. The GMC document to which Narey refers is *Tomorrow's doctors* (GMC, 2009), a statement by the General Medical Council of what newly qualified doctors need to understand. As a foundation for that work, Narey suggests that the chief social worker should first draft a definition of social work.

Malcolm Payne (2013) argues that the quest for definition is illusory, as social work practice is shaped by the political, social, legislative and cultural context in which social work operates. He notes that different theories of social work serve to define the content of practice. Psychodynamic practice deals with emotional and psychological problems; cognitive-behavioural practice aims to modify ways of thinking or behaving; task-centred practice helps individuals to identify problem areas and agree an approach to tackle them; systems practice looks at the relation between the person and the environment, helping adaptation where needed; humanistic practice helps to develop people's understanding of their social identity in relation to others; and critical practice incorporates concepts of empowerment, anti-oppressive practice and feminism to explore how social relationships and institutions constitute barriers to individuals and how they can be overcome. These modes of practice are very different. They are all, however, legitimately regarded as social work, addressing the interaction between the individual and the social.

The lack of a research culture

One of the most disappointing aspects of social work at degree level is the relative absence of a research base. At its best, research can help to assess the effectiveness of social work intervention, examine the costs and benefits of social work, compare social work with other forms of intervention and thus inform the development of practice.

Social work courses may afford less opportunity for research than other university programmes, as tutors are required to maintain contact with students on practice placements while other colleagues are able to concentrate on research projects without the distraction of students. Social work research also raises ethical issues if households that might benefit from assistance are denied it in order to create the research gold standard of a randomised control group. 'Soft' research looking at changes in attitudes and behaviours does not have the same status as research undertaken in large-scale clinical trials. Most importantly, research activity has never been integrated into social work as a core component of practice. In this respect, social work is very different to medicine and nursing, where research is highly valued.

Social work research formed a significant part of a review of social work education carried out by David Croisdale-Appleby that concluded that social work needed to develop its social science base so that 'its own rigorous research must underpin its teachings and beliefs' (Croisdale-Appleby, 2014, p 16). The review included the recommendation that 'all qualifying education should equip newly qualified social workers with the capability to engage in research throughout their career, inculcating an understanding that the ability to carry out research is an essential component in their future professional capability in practice' (Croisdale-Appleby, 2014, p 87).

Those research findings with the most impact on social work practice have been concentrated in the field of childcare work. *Children who wait* (Rowe and Lambert, 1973), *Child protection: Messages from research* (Bullock et al, 1995) and *Caring for children who live away from home: Messages from research* (DH, 1998) have been particularly influential. In adult care, a series of publications by the Personal Social Services Research Unit at the University of Kent in the 1980s shaped the development of care management, but there have been few subsequent publications with a similar impact.

Social Work Task Force

The Social Work Task Force in 2009 was given the unenviable task of attempting to bring coherence to education and training and the future pattern of careers in social work. It did so with a report (Social Work Task Force, 2009b) setting out a new framework for career development based on a professional capabilities framework, mapping competencies and skills expected over the lifespan of a social work career. The task force recommended a reformed system of initial education and training with clear and consistent criteria for entry to social work courses; courses where the content, teaching, placement opportunities and assessment are of consistently high standard; and a new assessed and supported first year in employment (ASYE). These changes to training would then be supported by a framework for career development, including a Master's in social work practice.

The government responded positively and swiftly to these recommendations with the establishment of the Social Work Reform Board chaired by Moira Gibb, who had chaired the task force. The reform board operated for just under three years, overseeing significant changes to secure the implementation of the task force recommendations.

The Professional Capabilities Framework has nine domains – professionalism, values and ethics, diversity, rights justice and economic wellbeing, knowledge, critical reflection and analysis, intervention and skills, context and organisation, and professional leadership – and each domain is backed up by a number of statements defining competence in that area. There are frameworks for seven stages of a career from initial qualification through the first ASYE to social worker, senior practitioner, advanced practitioner, practice educator and social work manager.

Unfortunately, the Health and Care Professions Council (HCPC) shortly afterwards adopted standards of proficiency for social workers in England (HCPC, 2012a), which it mapped against the Professional Capabilities Framework. Two different documents covering the same territory was a recipe for confusion. If the two reviews of social work education by Narey and Croisdale-Appleby agreed about little else, on this they were united. Croisdale-Appleby is clearly confused that 'the profession is regulated and endorsed by two very different sets of criteria, which is a continuing major problem which needs to be addressed' (Croisdale- Appleby, 2014, p 18) and recommends that the two processes should be brought together. Narey, characteristically, is more blunt. He states that the document 'Standards of Proficiency does not remotely provide adequate guidance to universities about the skills and professional knowledge required of graduate social workers' (Narey, 2014, p 7). He is also critical of the Professional Capabilities Framework, and although he regards this as the better document, he is scathing about the HCPC publishing 'a twenty one page document that maps their Standards of Proficiency to the Professional Capabilities Framework. Simultaneously the College of Social Work has produced its own twenty four page document mapping the PCF to the Standards of Proficiency. This is frankly embarrassing' (Narey, 2014, p 8). It is hard to disagree. It is as embarrassing as the Department for Education commissioning a separate review of social work education shortly after the Department of Health had done so.

If the Professional Capabilities Framework has had some criticism, the ASYE has been widely welcomed. It was the first change to be introduced in autumn 2012. Early evidence was ambiguous, with some suggestion that employers were not showing the necessary commitment to release staff and provide protected caseloads (Naqvi, 2013). Certainly the introduction of a new model could hardly have come at a more difficult time with a sustained squeeze on local authority budgets. It had teething problems, as the speed of implementation and the late issue of guidance meant that both employers and staff were uncertain about how to meet the requirements of ASYE. Reasonable expectations from practitioners that there would be a national standard of support guidance and assessment similar throughout the country did not fit with an employer-led model that left employers to devise their own methods of delivering support. There were also concerns about the effect of an increasingly diversified employment market. There remains a difficulty for social workers working in agencies or in the private and voluntary sector where small employers lack the infrastructure to meet the requirements of ASYE. But getting a new scheme established is a major achievement. It will become a permanent part of the landscape, building on degree programmes and encouraging a culture of continuing professional development.

Admission requirements for social work degrees were tightened from 2012, with a minimum threshold of academic attainments set at the level of the average in 2009, holistic assessment including both academic and interpersonal qualities set against the Professional Capabilities Framework, and a requisite level of proficiency in English and IT.

Addressing curricula was a more difficult task and changes were implemented in 2013. A series of curriculum guides were developed, seeking to achieve some consistency in course content. The areas covered included social work law, assessment and risk, disability, social work intervention methods, inter-professional and inter-agency collaboration, diversity and oppression, physical health, dementia and end-of-life care, personalisation, relationships, relationship stress and/or breakdown, migration and refugees, communication skills, human growth and development, mental health, substance use, children's behaviour and parenting problems, neglect, violence and abuse of children and adults, research and research-mindedness. This formidable litany should achieve some greater consistency across programmes. What it cannot do is address the balance between the various components of a programme or the quality of the teaching. The changes were not reflected in the Croisdale-Appleby and Narey reviews and it remains to be seen if they succeed in driving improvement.

The critique set out in the Narey (2014) review of training for children's social work is scathing about the variability in the quality of degree programmes from admissions criteria to course content. It notes that less than a third of social work students on degree courses had one or more A-levels and that the proportion of entrants to social work degrees with less than the recommended number of university admissions points (240) was double the proportion of those undertaking nursing or teaching degrees.

Narey argued that social work teaching gave disproportionate attention to anti-oppressive practice, empowerment and partnership working, with the result that social workers tended to over-identify with parents, seeing them as victims of an unequal society. As a consequence, social workers were reluctant to use authority in their work with resistant clients. The lack of availability of practice placements in local authority settings further compounded the problem, as many students had no experience of using statutory powers.

Sector-led initiatives

The data available about ASYEs raises question marks about the consistency of the commitment to sector-led approaches to development. While the progress made on the recommendations of the Social Work Reform Board about a national standard for employers on supervision, professional development and career progression is extremely welcome, there has to be a concern that implementation will be similarly patchy.

These reforms are taking place at a time of great changes in social work. Not only are there deep cuts in local authority budgets, with consequences for staffing levels and workload, but there are also major changes being made to the infrastructure that has supported social work and social care.

The references to social workers in the White Paper (DH, 2012) on the future of care services were limited to the appointment of a chief social worker, now in post, using evidence from the social work practice pilots where social workers are liberated – or so it is claimed – from case management to concentrate on community development and linking older people at risk of isolation with community groups and networks, and endorsement of the programme of the Social Work Reform Board. The area that is specific to social work was not clearly identified. The lead role in identifying and linking isolated older people was given to the voluntary and community sector elsewhere in the White Paper. Educating social workers to play their part in the new structure is not going to be easy – not least because there is no curriculum guide on community development and courses in recent years have moved away from seeing community work as a central part of social work.

The social work practice pilots are important, as they tested a model that is attractive to social workers. They were small, social worker-led, independent of local authorities, person-centred and outcome-focused. They were established in 2010 following the Social Work Task Force report to test whether a social enterprise model led by social workers could deliver better outcomes. The benefits to the staff working in this model are clearly set out in the progress report (Stanley et al, 2014).

Future directions?

Two other initiatives launched by the Department for Education may contain indicators of the future direction of social work education. The first, Step Up to Social Work, is a 14-month programme aimed at graduates with at least a 2:1 degree and based on an apprenticeship model with students who are employed in children's services and are paid a salary but who combine workplace learning with academic study. Around 200 graduates have been recruited each year to this programme, now in its third year. In a sign of changing times, the programme is run by a major recruitment and human resources consultancy.

The second programme, Frontline, is based on the successful Teach First initiative and provides an intensive, 12-month, work-based programme for top-quality graduates. It includes summer schools and weekend academic elements as well as distance learning, leading to qualification as a social worker within one year and a Master's degree within two years.

Both schemes have been the subject of controversy and accused of dumbing down standards. The evaluation of Step Up to Social Work (DfE, 2013; 2014b), however, was positive, both in terms of the improved calibre of those undertaking the programme and in the constructive dialogue between course providers and the agencies. Criticism has been most intense in relation to Frontline, partly because of the early immersion into practice after a few weeks' study and partly because of the marketing for the programme, which contained exaggerated promises of accelerated promotion. Croisdale-Appleby notes tartly that 'I am unclear where the pedagogical research is to be found which would validate the different direction of travel in England to shorter courses to that of other countries' (Croisdale-Appleby, 2014, p 30) and goes on to recommend a proper evaluation of fast-track initiatives.

Despite this lack of evidence, the Department of Health is launching a fast-track programme for graduate social workers to work in mental health – Think Ahead – again borrowing heavily from the Teach First approach. Due to start in 2015, it will offer a two-year programme including one year of on-the-job training.

Despite fears that the two reviews of social work education (Croisdale-Appleby, 2014; Narey, 2014) would lead to a complete separation of social work training for adult social care work and for children's services, there is a measure of agreement on course content. The style and content of the reviews is very different. Croisdale-Appleby is explicit that all newly qualified social workers should be able 'to work successfully, after an initial period of supported and supervised practice, in any context and with any user group' (p 67). Narey, meanwhile, argues for degrees for those intending to work in children's social work, with 'the first year common to all social work students but the second and third years focussing exclusively on children and related issues' (p 39).

It is the related issues referred to by Narey that undermine his case for specialisation. The reality is that children live in families that include substitute and reconstituted families. Social workers need to be able to work with domestic violence, substance misuse, mental health problems and dysfunctional families regardless of their primary specialisation. Narey's concern with child protection and his over-optimistic assumptions about the benefits of removing children from troubled situations have led him to ignore the context in which many children have to grow up.

What do we want from social work education?

It is time to address the big questions about social work education and training in the light of the ever-narrowing territory that is unique to social work. Have social work programmes prepared students adequately to do a professional job? The answer from both employers and the Social Work Task Force appears to be a resounding negative. Rogowski and others would argue that this is the result of a reductionist approach, judging social workers by their ability to fulfil prescribed tasks in a prescribed way, with individuality and creativity squeezed out by the demands of employers. But it is also true that social work educators have failed to communicate that element of creativity in practice that makes social work at its best so fulfilling. The virtues of self-directed support for service users are rightly trumpeted. Managerial control over social work has grown to the point where social workers are unable to exercise self-direction over their working lives.

The Narey critique raises the difficult issue of course content and whether the preoccupations of social work tutors have distorted the education of social workers in a way that contributes to the present malaise. To many tabloid commentators, social work itself is riddled with political correctness and Marxist claptrap. While that is far from the reality, as most of the curriculum is devoted to issues pertinent to social work practice, it is undoubtedly true that many social work educators approach their work reflecting the value base of social work that demands a commitment to social justice. This involves being politically aware and that awareness often translates into a political perspective influenced by a Marxist analysis of the class structure.

Unfortunately, as was true of the radical social work movement in the 1970s, debate tends to be polarised and sometimes conducted in acrimonious and personal terms. It is not helped by the inaccessible language used to discuss theories of class struggle. A Marxist perspective of social work history would be predicated on the conflict between the owners of the means of production – the bourgeoisie – and those forced to sell their labour – the working class. Social work can be viewed variously as a means of assuaging the worst excesses of capitalism by offering support to the most vulnerable and thus decreasing the radical fervour of the proletariat; as propping up capitalism by reinforcing social norms around work and family relationships; and as a form of benign social control. But the language of the class struggle and the prescription of alliances with trade unions as the organised expression of the working class have seemed increasingly irrelevant. Some writers (Ferguson and Woodward, 2009; Rogowski, 2010) have sought to replace the trade union alliance by calling for alliances with service users. Of course, it is important to work in partnership with users, but many user groups regard social workers as in part responsible for their oppression and do not see them as natural allies. While a Marxist perspective has contributed greatly to the analysis of society, it is – like social work itself – better at diagnosis than it is at providing remedies and solutions.

Yet if the political expression of Marxism seen in the Soviet Union and the satellite states of Eastern Europe has collapsed, its analysis in terms of the dominance of capital has been vindicated by the banking collapse and global financial crisis resulting from speculation and over-borrowing against flimsy security. The price of the crisis is being paid by the poorest in society in terms of reduced social security protection, less investment in public services and pay rises lagging behind inflation levels. Public discourse has hitherto been dominated by how to secure growth in the economy rather than the impact on the poor of worsening inequalities. The surprising best-seller by Thomas Piketty (2014) may be indicative of a growing awareness that the widening gap between rich and poor has social costs. The inequalities in society are a legitimate and important topic of study for social work students, who need to understand both the cause and the impact of an increasingly polarised nation.

Foucault and postmodernism

The other characteristic trope of academic discussion about social work's role in society is the use of analysis drawing on Foucault, modernism and postmodernism. Michel Foucault, a French writer and philosopher, contended that the relationship between power and knowledge was central to an understanding of society. Power was used to control and define knowledge. In this way, supposedly, scientific knowledge was used as a means of social control. The anti-psychiatry movement seized on this idea to support the view that madness was a social construct.

There is an overlap between this approach and a Marxist analysis of social work in the shared argument that social work has been used to draw the sting from the impact of unbridled capitalism on the most vulnerable. The link is often made between Foucault and postmodernism, a term used to describe a suspicion of any global large-scale narrative seeing such narratives as a series of social constructs defined by a specific time and place rather than a movement. It is called postmodernism because it rejects the scientific objectivity and rationalism that modernists saw as the dominant characteristic of the 20th century.

To use a crude example to illustrate this point, Al-Qaida was characterised by the media, particularly in the US, as a global conspiracy determined to secure world domination for militant Islam. Postmodernism, however, is sceptical of narratives and is more interested in diversity as it expresses itself in society. Postmodernists therefore would see a loose grouping of Islamic movements whose activities and motivations are determined by time and place, so its actions in Mali are different from those in Yemen, which differ again from those in Afghanistan.

The other elements in this litany of philosophical approaches are structuralism and post-structuralism. Structuralism was a predominantly French intellectual movement that drew on linguistics, psychology and anthropology to develop an understanding of the underlying meaning in texts. Post-structuralism seeks to deconstruct texts to see them in their historical and cultural context and apply that understanding both to the author and to the contemporary context. The reader rather than the author becomes the primary focus in terms of how the reader interprets the text.

As numerous books have been written on each of the four movements, many of great length and impenetrable in their use of language, the sketchy account given here is open to challenge and certainly requires further reading. The issue for social work education is whether our understanding of social work's place in society has been clarified and enhanced by the preoccupation with these movements in much social work writing. Rogowski's excellent book (2010) discusses this, arguing that it provides a context for practice that is very different from a mechanistic approach to prescribed tasks.

The problem with course content of this nature is that it takes time at the expense of equipping students for their future role. This can be seen in the sustained criticism of the quality of those completing social work courses from employers, from the Social Work Task Force and from governments of different political persuasions. Despite the impact on the numbers of qualified social workers achieved by the move to a social work degree, there has not been a comparable advance in quality. Is the task of social work educators to locate social work's place in a postmodernist world or to work effectively in safeguarding children?

The argument against a strictly functional view of social work education is most clearly stated by Rogowski, who views social work as a profession with a particular set of skills and knowledge that is more than an employment role. It is portable between client groups because it has a common core of values of self-determination and individual worth and a developed understanding of people and their relationships. It locates its work in the environment in which clients live because of its awareness of the impact of debt, poor housing, and unhealthy and crime-ridden neighbourhoods on wellbeing and development. That broader knowledge is at risk if a reductionist approach means that social work programmes are judged only by the ability of their graduates to work in a local authority social work setting.

This tension is captured in Wilson and Campbell's research on social work educators:

I think there are tensions there because on the one hand we want them to be for agency practice and on the other ... we want them to resist....I would like to see them leaving us a little radical – more questioning and critical of the system. (Respondent in Wilson and Campbell, 2013, p 91)

The study found educators concerned that practice learning had become overly prescriptive and outcome-led rather than process-led.

The first element of this criticism about prescription is widely shared. However, outcomes are important. What matters in social work is whether social workers can bring improvements in the social functioning and quality of life of the people with whom they are working. That requires an ability to understand and to analyse the factors in the household and environment that are having a negative impact and to decide with the clients where and how to effect change. It also requires a readiness on the part of social workers to be judged on whether those agreed outcomes are being achieved.

The danger is that Narey's criticism of the political context of social work may mean that those who undertake the Frontline programme to act as safeguarders of children within a statutory framework will be expected to ignore the social conditions that produce hopelessness and despair. Social work cannot be a value-free activity. Social work education has then to equip practitioners with a skill set that enables them to operate in the interpersonal domain but also to influence the social environment. Empowerment of service users, enabling them to take control of their own lives and by so doing enhancing their self-esteem, is an essential part of social work. Working with clients as partners is the most effective way of securing change. Narey's concern with rescuing children has led him to view empowerment and partnership as negative factors alongside anti-oppressive practice and to contend that these elements are given disproportionate attention in social work education. If they were excluded from the curriculum, central elements of social work practice would be lost.

The broader vision of the Croisdale-Appleby review (Croisdale-Appleby, 2014), which considers the three roles of social workers as practitioners, as professionals and as social scientists, is more appealing. First, Croisdale-Appleby sees social workers as more than the reductionist vision set out by Narey. Second, he sees social workers as professionals, influenced and guided by the accumulation of skills and knowledge about social work. Third, he sees the potential for research and evidence-based policies, drawing on and collating the experiences of social workers. Equipping social workers for that latter task is a challenge for educators.

Social work education will be kept under constant review, but distilling the reviews of Croisdale-Appleby and Narey offers a way forward. Selection processes for degree programmes need to be more rigorous, with minimum academic requirements. Greater rigour is also needed in assessing course content and quality. The hotchpotch of overlapping regulatory mechanisms needs to be clarified, with unified guidance on course content and a single course approval mechanism. Practice placements should continue to be a central part of programmes, but need to include statutory settings. The programmes should remain generic, with the post-qualifying year having the primary role in developing specialist knowledge for the occupational setting. Future decisions about course length and content should be based on research evidence about effectiveness and not on assumptions unsupported by evidence. Above all, a proper system of continuous professional development should be developed with a rigorous process of revalidation after a number of years (Croisdale-Appleby suggests five years).

The future pattern of training will continue to be contested territory. Social work has not always spoken with a united voice. It will need to do so to combat the challenges of improving standards without compromising on its core values.

AREAS FOR DISCUSSION

Should a social work degree equip people for frontline practice from day one?

Is the knowledge base of social work transferable between different client groups or would service users be served better by specialists?

What are the advantages and disadvantages of the proposed fast-track programmes?

Are poverty and inequality part of the core of social work education, or is too much time spent on anti-oppressive practice?

FURTHER READING

The two reviews of social work education should be read, one because it is a careful, thoughtful analysis of social work education and what it should aim to achieve (Croisdale-Appleby, 2014), and the other as an illustration of how little evidence is required to win the ear of ministers if you tell them what they wish to hear (Narey, 2014).

The cursory treatment of Foucault's work in this chapter can best be redressed by the detailed and relevant discussion in Chambon et al (1999) *Reading Foucault for social workers*, New York, NY: Columbia University Press.

SIX

The evolution of radical social work

KEY LEARNING POINTS

» The seminal work of Roy Bailey and Mike Brake
» The influence of feminism, anti-racism, and the independent living movement on anti-oppressive practice
» The growth of service user movements
» The influence of class on radical movements
» The rediscovery of relationships

Case Con was a radical magazine first produced in 1970 and published until 1977. Its clever title was a 'deliberate attack on the term "case conference", the con of all those earnest professionals sitting around discussing an endless stream of cases' (Weinstein, 2011). It published a manifesto as its critique of aspirations for the professionalisation of social work. It argued that by claiming a particular knowledge and skill, the profession separated itself from the population at large. It led social workers to see themselves as part of a specialist group on a par with doctors and lawyers. It encouraged business-like career structures. Most fundamentally, *Case Con* criticised the pseudo-science of casework with its language of controlled emotional involvement as implying that clients needed to be changed to meet the demands of society. But community work, group work and welfare rights work were not exempt from this critique, as they, too, were seen as instruments of control for the ruling class (*Case Con*, 1975).

The remedy as viewed by *Case Con* was to oppose capitalism and its administrative tool – the state – by working through trade unions, by direct action with other militant tenant groups and squatters and by organising in defence of the working class. This prescription for action bears the hallmark of the time in its use of the class struggle and in its heroic assumptions about the trade union movement as the organised expression of the working class.

The arguments of *Case Con* were refined by Roy Bailey and Mike Brake in a hugely influential book (1975). This was a collection of essays showing some of the strengths and weaknesses of the *Case Con* manifesto. Peter Leonard argued that radical social work required a new praxis with critical reflection on reality and how it is constructed. Drawing on Paulo Friere's pedagogy of the oppressed that had dominated the development of social work in Latin America, Leonard set out a paradigm for radical practice to develop both individual and collective conscientisation. He concluded that 'the operationalising of conscientisation for radical social work in Western Europe is a major task for the future' (Leonard, 1975, p 55). It remains so 45 years on.

Bailey and Brake published a second collection of essays five years later, seeking to develop the practice implications of radical social work (Bailey and Brake, 1980). Social workers were seen as working with individuals in a way that maintained the self-respect of the client, but also as having a responsibility to develop the consciousness of the client about their social reality and to locate their problems and issues in a wider social and political context. At a time when we are confronted with attacks on social security benefits and changes that further widen social inequalities, this message has considerable appeal. Bailey wrote of the impact of cuts in welfare spending and the need 'to translate our theories of society into a practice that at once helps and assists the victims of our system, and simultaneously, contributes to the creation of conditions which will transform our society into a socialist democracy' (Bailey and Brake, 1980, p 13). Today's social workers confront similar issues but can no longer assume that salvation lies in developing links with the trade union movement as the organised expression of the working class.

There is a striking continuity in the arguments deployed by those who identify themselves as radical social workers. The critique of social work by Bailey and Brake (1975, 1980) still has resonance 40 years on. Some of their original passion about racism and discrimination has now become mainstream. But while still heavily influenced by Marxism, radicalism today has found a different voice.

Bailey and Brake argued that the structural determinants of inequality and discrimination meant that a radical practice required a commitment to collective action through the social work team and involving service users. This needed to include work through trade unions and through community politics. They argued that welfare rights work and community work were legitimate areas for radicals. This was not a universally held view among radical social workers. Others in their earlier book had warned of the dangers that such advocacy would shore up the welfare state by dealing with the most acute grievances (Cannon, 1975; Mayo, 1975) that were most susceptible to direct action. There is a recurrent tension between those committed activists seeking to mobilise the deprived and disadvantaged in political action and those more modest reformists who see virtue in achieving changes that improve the position of the deprived. Conscious of the criticism that radical social workers ran the risk of patronising clients by seeking to politicise their situation, Bailey and Brake accepted that workers should start 'with their definition of the situation and their values, and then trying to extend these into a wider understanding of self and of society' (Bailey and Brake, 1980, p 24).

Just as *Radical social work* had struck a chord with the beleaguered social workers in what were disparagingly called 'Seebohm factories', Bailey and Brake's later book (1980) was pioneering in discussing feminism, sexuality and racism in the context of social work. These contributions were to challenge the view of oppression in society as rooted exclusively in a class-based analysis as suggested by the *Case Con* manifesto.

Feminist social work

Elizabeth Wilson (1980) located feminism in theories of ideology and of women's oppression with the nuclear family as a model sustaining the dependency and inferiority of women. Social work was viewed as expressing 'a concern central to our society: the maintenance of family life in the face of disintegrating or atomising influences that may naturally tend to undermine, loosen or at least change it' (Wilson, 1980, p 32). She went on to note the differing views of social workers about domestic violence. Some saw this as another form of neurotic relationship requiring treatment; some rejected the middle-class reformist nature of refuge provision; and a smaller group located the women's aid movement in a broader analysis of patriarchal culture.

There are many variants of feminism, sometimes characterised as first wave, second wave and third wave, and sometimes as liberal, socialist and radical.

The first wave of feminism refers to the campaign for voting rights and fundamental equalities in the 19th and early 20th centuries. The second wave often identified with the women's liberation movement brought to the fore issues of gender violence, reproductive rights and continuing gender discrimination. Third-wave feminism influenced by post-modernism leads to a more nuanced debate about difference incorporating issues of race, class and culture. It explores how society has shaped concepts of gender identity and sexuality. It has made use of modern media and developed specific campaigns against everyday sexism as part of a wider concern for gender, racial, economic and social justice.

Parallel to the analysis of feminism as first, second and third wave was the characterisation by political ideology, but this does not map directly to the three waves.

Liberal feminism was concerned with improving the position of women in society through recognition of unequal relationships in the family, improving access to childcare, and direct intervention with women victims of domestic violence. It locates women's disadvantage as remediable by securing equal rights and equal treatment in the workplace, and views equality in gender relationships as a matter for education. It is strongly associated with legislative advances for women including equal pay.

Socialist feminism was more far-reaching in its analysis and prescription for practice. It saw gender oppression as predating the emergence of capitalism, but sought to pursue a class-based analysis. Patriarchy was seen as modelling the class system, with women as the exploited proletariat and men the bourgeoisie. In terms of practice, non-statutory services were seen as the best location for a female-centred practice as they were less likely to be agents of state control.

Radical feminism developed the concept of patriarchy expressed in the family, ideology and political structures by which male-dominated institutions shaped culture and expectations. It viewed gender as the central social division with race and class as subordinate. Women-only groups were important in valuing women as women and in challenging the patriarchal culture. This meant that often men were viewed with suspicion both as workers and as service users (Featherstone, 2001). This form of feminist absolutism resembled the preoccupation with class of earlier radical social work theorists.

The distinctions between these strands of feminism can be overstated, but in turn they were all challenged as understating the significance of race and class and being rooted in a white middle-class and heterosexual perspective. The perspectives of feminism have transformed our understanding of society and family relationships. Gender relationships have been altered by the changing place of women and the drive to equality. While the traditional roles of male and female remain powerful influences, not least in the media's treatment of women who fail to meet those expectations, there are changes towards greater equality in parenting and greater awareness of emotional communication (Giddens, 1992).

Is a feminist social work practice possible?

The degree to which social work practice is influenced by a traditional view of family structures can be seen in family courts where mothers are still assumed to be the primary care giver and any failings in that role are used against them. Poor parenting is seen as a failure of the mother. In contrast, a semi-detached or wholly detached paternal role is socially accepted. Social workers need to question the assumptions underpinning family structures in both their training and their practice. The caring role expected of women does not stop when children move to adulthood but is likely to be transferred to that of care for elderly parents as the state retreats from responsibility for that role.

Annie Hudson noted that the majority of senior managers in local authorities were male and argued that 'feminists and others on the left have a responsibility to enter the debate to ensure that principles such as participation are an integral component of definitions of "effective" management' (Hudson, 1999). This is a valuable counterbalance to the too ready assumption that entrepreneurialism and risk taking, generally viewed as desirable managerial characteristics, are associated with males.

Those proponents of a feminist practice are influenced by concepts of patriarchy as a dominant force in society. This has been challenged by Harry Ferguson (2001), who sees the transformation of gender relations, in which feminism has been an active positive and creative influence, as moving the debate into a different dimension. He depicts a move away from traditional sources of authority to self-actualisation. He regards the use of self-help groups and books together with social media support groups as ways in which people can regain a sense of mastery over their own lives and thus transform the dominance of patriarchy and authority.

This is an important challenge to critical social work theorists who have been suspicious of individual narratives as detracting from a broader societal analysis. The challenge was played out in articles in the *British Journal of Social Work*, in which Garrett and Ferguson debated the issue (Ferguson, 2003; Garrett, 2003,

2004). The degree to which social changes justify this challenge is a theme throughout this chapter.

Racism

The discourse of feminism in the 1970s and '80s was criticised for its failure to incorporate the different experiences of black women. Treating people with equal needs equally was a common mantra in social work. It was, however, based on the assumption that needs are individual demanding an individual response. It was less sensitive to the impact of the social and cultural environment on the way in which those needs presented. Too often services were colour-blind, refusing to recognise that some communities required a different approach.

A study by Juliet Cheetham noted 'well-intentioned assertions that the achievement of equality rests on a refusal to perceive racial, sex or ethnic differences' (Cheetham, 1982, p 17) – the colour-blind approach. But the Scarman report (Scarman, 1982), following the Brixton riots in 1981, led to a much greater awareness of the need to combat racist attitudes, conscious and unconscious. Anti-racist training was used extensively in social services departments and research studies drew attention to the disproportionate numbers of minority ethnic groups in care, and in the criminal justice system.

As understanding developed of the impact of racism on social work practice, Dominelli (1988) argued that it was expressed in social work by extending social control through the perpetuation of existing inequalities, by accepting the apolitical nature of social work, and by stereotyped assumptions about cultural patterns. For instance, it is often assumed that Asian families will look after their own elderly and vulnerable family members. This can mean that they do not access – and sometimes do not get offered – the support services they may require.

While the Scarman report rejected the concept of institutional racism in the Metropolitan Police Service in response to the riots, social work thinking became aware of the degree to which racist stereotypes were built into the structure of social work. The over-representation of black people in secure mental health services has many causes but racially based assumptions about drug misuse and violence, and lack of awareness of how emotions are expressed in some cultural contexts, are major contributory factors in the disproportionate reliance on compulsory admissions (Morgan et al, 2006).

The Central Council for Education and Training in Social Work (CCETSW) in its paper *Rules and requirements for the Diploma in Social Work* (CCETSW, 1989) proposed that social work training should tackle racism by recognising that the major institutions of society were institutionally racist. This concept was ahead of its time. It was nine years later that the Macpherson report was able to define institutional racism as:

> The collective failure of an organisation to provide an appropriate and professional service to people because of their colour, culture

or ethnic origin. It can be seen or detected in processes, attitudes or behaviour which amount to discrimination through unwitting prejudice, ignorance, thoughtlessness and racist stereotyping which disadvantage minority ethnic people. (Macpherson, 1998, para 6.34)

But CCETSW at the time came under fierce attack from the press and from politicians because to talk of endemic racism in society was regarded as a politically motivated critique of government. CCETSW, under heavy political pressure, was obliged to withdraw the section of the paper referring to endemic racism, yet now the concept of institutional racism is widely recognised (although not universally accepted).

Yet while substantial progress has been made, racism is capable of infinite mutation. It finds new expression. Hostility to immigrants, asylum seekers, Roma beggars, health tourists and Muslims are current manifestations of racist attitudes evident in the right-wing press. A limited number of examples are used to stigmatise the entire group.

Just as feminism was challenged for ignoring considerations of class and race, so too anti-racist training was criticised for focusing on that particular form of discrimination without also recognising the pernicious effects of discrimination on grounds of sexuality, disability, age and religious belief. Neil Thompson brought these concepts together in 1992 in a ground-breaking work that has been a social work best-seller, now in its fifth edition, selling over 70,000 copies (Thompson, 2012).

Thompson argued that each instance of discrimination, whatever the basis, led to oppression because of the exercise of power by the person doing the discrimination. It had an impact on the identity and self-image of the person subject to discrimination in terms of marginalisation. This is not 'a simplistic one-dimensional model of oppression as the evil or unenlightened behaviour and attitudes of certain social groups' (Thompson, 1992, p 19), but a complex interweaving of multiple factors.

Thompson introduces the concept of PCS: P, the personal and psychological, the basis traditionally of much social work individual practice; C, the cultural level of shared assumptions about what is normal; and S, the structural implications of practice. This joining up of the three domains is a helpful framework to integrate thinking about practice. Thompson warns against the danger of splitting off anti-discriminatory practice as something separate from everyday social work.

Anti-oppressive practice has been integrated into social work training. It has, however, been criticised for its focus on 'changing the attitudes, behaviour and language of individual workers, as opposed to changing the conditions in which clients live (with the emphasis on language in particular making it an easy target for the accusation of political correctness)' (Ferguson and Woodward, 2009, p 29). Language is important in framing how we view certain groups. The vituperation that can be seen in the right-wing press against alleged examples of political correctness is indicative of the power of language to reinforce existing power relations.

Disability movement

In terms of impact on practice, the disability movement has had the most direct impact. From the early pioneering writings of Oliver (Oliver, 1983, 1991), there has come the recognition that disability is a social construct. The issue is how people with impairments can be enabled to participate fully in the life of the country. An exclusively individualistic perspective that has characterised much social work practice risks ignoring the wider structural issues that reinforce disability. The challenge laid down by the rise of the disabled people's movement was how to reframe a model in which things were done for disabled people to one in which they were done with disabled people. The powerful slogan 'Nothing about us without us', subsequently adopted by other user groups, captured the demand of the independent living movement.

The movement rejected the negative focus on the deficits of disability and argued for a social model of disability that looked at barriers to full participation and sought to dismantle them. The success of the approach was seen first in legislation with the 1995 Disability Discrimination Act, later to be incorporated in the 2010 Equality Act, which also covered gender and sexual orientation. Ironically, the definition of disability used in the Act was a medical model, but the approach requiring employers to make reasonable adjustments to premises, policies and practices was very much a social model geared to removing barriers to participation. The definition of discrimination now covers both direct and indirect discrimination.

The legislative advance has been matched by a transformation in the context of practice in both health and social care with an increasing emphasis on service users and carers. The 1990 NHS and Community Care Act was explicit in its belief that a market should be created in social care. It sought to introduce market mechanisms and stressed the importance of consumer choice over the services to be provided. The patient as consumer was to be involved in service planning. Further guidance followed in the *Patients Charter* (1991), which stressed the importance of patient-centred care. This was echoed in the NHS Plan (nine years later under a different government) (DH, 2000) but also still talking about a patient-centred service.

The concept was developed in the NHS Plan and its preceding White Paper, *Patient and public involvement in the new NHS* (DH, 1999a). It envisaged patients being fully involved not only in decisions about their care but also in service planning. The same language had been used ten years earlier to little avail, so this time detailed guidance was provided about the mechanisms needed to deliver genuine involvement – patients' forums in every NHS trust, patients' surveys to inform planning and decisions, and a commission for patient and public involvement established at national level. These mechanisms lasted five years before being abolished to be replaced by local involvement networks (LINKs). These proved no more effective than their predecessor bodies and by 2008 new guidance was issued (DH, 2008a). This set out a range of activities that could constitute involvement.

More significantly, the White Paper *Equity and excellence: Liberating the NHS* (DH, 2010a) and the government's mental health strategy (DH, 2011) adopted the principle of 'nothing about me without me' originally coined by the disability movement. This promised a NHS with patients at the centre with greater choice and control, and with personalised services. It also indicated that LINKs were to be replaced at local level by Healthwatch, backed by a national body, Healthwatch England. These changes took effect from 2013.

We see here a yawning gap between the rhetoric adopted by national government and the reality on the ground. The constant changes in the delivery vehicles for patient and public involvement would suggest that these are seen as having failed to secure public engagement. The failure is rather that of those in positions of authority in the NHS and social care to move beyond a form of involvement that can be characterised as 'This is what we are proposing and why. Any comments?'. It is a long way from co-production.

Empowering service users has always been an important concept in social work practice. Originally, it was expressed in the language of client self-determination. For many years, that was delivered in a paternalistic way, with 'guided' self-determination encouraging the client towards what was felt to be the right decision. The disability movement has moved on by claiming for itself the right to determine the shape and content of the services needed.

Before looking at the mechanism by which this is being achieved, it is worth reflecting on the various ways in which involvement benefits both the service user and those responsible for commissioning and delivering services.

For service users, the benefits are both short term and long term. In the short term, it delivers enhanced self-respect for users whose views are taken seriously rather than being passive recipients of what others have deemed right. It can improve the quality of life for service users through incremental improvements – changing the positioning of phones or televisions, for example. It can enhance the quality of care, especially if service users are involved in training practitioners. In the long term, effective involvement should lead to better relationships between service users and staff, and to improved outcomes. Here we are on trickier ground, as user-defined outcomes may differ from practitioner-defined outcomes. The latter may be driven by the imperative of securing exit from a caseload or a discharge from a hospital bed, which may not be the priority of the user.

For commissioners of services, the benefits are clear. Effective involvement will lead to services that are more relevant to the needs of service users. The involvement of service users has, however, to be more than a single event – for example, consulting users on a proposed change in service. It needs fully to embrace the concept of co-production, with service users involved in planning the shape of services, delivery and implementation of services, and, importantly, in monitoring services. The recent changes in hospital inspections announced by the Care Quality Commission have embedded the concept of patient and carer involvement in the inspection process.

For those delivering services and for frontline staff, the benefits are similar in terms of improved relationships between service users and staff, more relevant and timely service provision and immediate feedback on service quality. But this does require a whole-hearted commitment to co-production and there are practical obstacles in the way. First, it requires a significant change in the culture of many organisations and teams engaged in service delivery. Second, good involvement is not something that can be wished into being. It requires a significant additional time commitment from staff and can be viewed as slowing things down when staff are hard pressed to achieve their primary tasks within the allocated time. Third, the consequences of empowering service users may require radical changes to the way in which services are delivered that do not benefit staff. Strong and committed leadership is essential to overcome these obstacles.

Service users have now achieved through the mechanisms of direct payments and personal budgets the opportunity to determine the pattern of their care. But there is a long way to go before service users and carers are at the heart of practice. Branfield and Beresford (2006) noted that service user knowledge is not taken seriously by professionals and services, that issues of access in the broadest sense (resources, support) are not given due weight by providers, and that user organisations are often fearful of the impact on funding if they are critical of current services. Beresford has been a consistent advocate of good practice in service user involvement and has produced a guide for service users (Beresford, 2013) particularly aimed at reaching those users often categorised as hard-to-reach groups.

While personal budgets and self-directed support enjoy cross-party support, the evidence base for better quality care at lower or the same cost (the transformational vision of personalisation) is thin (West, 2013). Personalisation, personal budgets and self-directed support are often conflated, but are separate concepts. Personalisation is the overarching concept, describing a model of care that provides supports and choice to service users, giving them control over their lives. Self-directed support is the process by which service users acquire control over their lives and may include a variety of financial support mechanisms to enable them to do so. Personal budgets enable service users to purchase the services and supports that are relevant to them using a formula – the resource allocation system – to calculate how much public services would have spent on their support.

This latter element has been the most contentious, as it has served to weaken the original vision of personalisation. A highly critical analysis of the gap between notional allocations under the resource allocation system and the actual funds made available shows that the number of assessments and reviews has fallen sharply, as have the numbers receiving professional support. Most worryingly, the correlation of self-directed support and users' feelings of being in control is negative. Those authorities with the least numbers on self-directed support have more users feeling in control than do those with the highest numbers on self-directed support (Slasberg et al, 2013). The authors argue that the cash limits on local authority resources have led to an increased gap between notional allocations and the real level of resources available. The process has become a bureaucratic exercise rather than the exercise in empowerment originally envisaged.

Radical social work today

Would Bailey and Brake recognise radicalism in today's social work, with its emphasis on anti-oppressive practice and its concern for human rights in the politics of difference – gender, race, disability, sexuality and age? Certainly, their work explored the political nature of social work and the difficulty in separating practice from the political context. But their concern with class in the sense of the potential of the organised working class to bring about transformation in social structures seems dated, given the accelerating decline of the trade union movement both in terms of membership and influence. The distribution of power and how that is exercised may be more fruitful territory for radical social work today. The high level of unemployment, the impact of austerity and the sharp increase in the gap between rich and poor create the classic conditions for the Left to argue for a traditional response, but there seems little appetite for this from the union movement.

There is a danger for the politics of difference to be seen as creating a hierarchy of oppressions, some of which are more heinous than others. To do so runs the risk of pitting one marginalised group against another. To use an example from current political rhetoric, the government claims that if it does not cut welfare payments to those out of work, it will have to cut pensions for older people, when in reality, Trident, Iraq and the bank bail-outs have cost the public purse far more than the welfare spending. As always, it is how you frame the question that matters.

McLaughlin is critical of the way in which social work practice has become focused on individual practice within a regulated and prescribed context, be it care management for adults or the five outcomes of Every Child Matters and the integrated care system. He argues against this 'micropolitical regulatory approach, substituting as it does a focus on interpersonal rather than social or structural politics' (McLaughlin, 2008, p 140). He is critical of those who would recast the 1970s nostrum of forging alliances with the trade unions and working-class movements with proposals to forge alliances with self-help groups. He doubts that this would be in the interests of already successful user groups or that they would derive much benefit from engagement with social workers as a group.

So is class still as relevant today as in the assertion by Bailey and Brake that understanding the position of the oppressed in the social and economic structures of the time was essential for radical social workers? The decline of trade unions, the rise in home ownership, the decline in manufacturing industry and the lack of radical fervour would indicate that radicals today need to find a new model, as the traditional working class no longer exists as a recognisable community. But the success of the UK Independence Party in northern Labour strongholds has focused attention on the sense of disenfranchisement of members of the residual white working class who do not identify with their current political representation.

Yet social class remains a powerful predictor of life chances. Inequalities of wealth are greater than at any time since the Second World War. Migration has become a touchstone for right-wing politicians aware of the problems of the disenfranchised white population unable to find work and competing with more motivated and often better educated workers from eastern Europe. It is questioned whether free movement of labour within the EU is a tenable policy when there are over two million unemployed people in the UK. And migration has changed the dynamic of the working class, for while many from black and minority ethnic groups are in the lowest decile of household incomes, they identify themselves by ethnicity rather than class.

The neoliberal explanation for differentials in income continues to be rooted in the failings of individuals, whether couched in terms of the cycle of deprivation by Sir Keith Joseph, the underclass by Charles Murray or the broken society by David Cameron. Social work has always been uneasy with the notion of individuals being exclusively responsible for their failings. Social workers are more likely to identify rather with Geoffrey Rankin, a gifted family service unit manager and my tutor on a social administration placement, who wrote of those regarded as social failures in the following terms:

> We believe however that they are what they are for two reasons: a) they were born with a well below average potential of strengths and skills into an environment that has aggravated these inborn weaknesses b) a vertically structured competitive society has to have a bottom and they are the natural bottom rung of the ladder. (Rankin, 1971)

Social work has never bought into the discourse of neoliberalism but has struggled to articulate an alternative thesis. The most influential critics of neoliberalism have come together in the Social Work Action Network (SWAN). The network developed following a social work manifesto, written in 2004 (SWAN, 2004). This described social work as 'shaped by managerialism, by the fragmentation of services, by financial restrictions and lack of resources, by increased bureaucracy and workloads, by the domination of case management approaches with their associated performance indicators and by the increased use of the private sector' (p 1). It called for 'a modern engaged social work based around such core anti-capitalist values as democracy, solidarity, accountability, participation, justice, equality, liberty and diversity' (p 2). One can question the facile assumption that these values are anti-capitalist. Most liberal societies would also claim these as their core values. The weakness of the manifesto was that its rhetoric was not accompanied by a clear prescription for what engaged social work would look like. The remedy is seen to lie in engaging with and learning from some of the strong user movements. As observed earlier, it takes two to tango. Strong user movements with an identity of their own by virtue of their independence are unlikely to see a similar need for alliances.

The critique set out in the manifesto has resonated with many social workers. SWAN has held some very successful annual conferences, attracting numbers far beyond the reach of British Association of Social Workers or the College of Social Work.

The intellectual case for an engaged, actively radical social work has been further developed by two of SWAN's leading protagonists – Iain Ferguson (2008) and Michael Lavalette (2011). Ferguson does not view the radical social work of the 1970s as a coherent movement, but rather as one of loose and sometimes overlapping strands with three central positions – acknowledgement of the structural roots of poverty and developing strategies to address these, recognition of social casework as a 'con' pathologising problems as individual, and a rejection of the trappings of professionalism as elitist. He is highly critical of the adoption by New Labour of moral authoritarianism and its robust dismissal of any attempt to draw out social explanations. Ferguson contends that social workers need to be more vocal in analysing how social policies impact on the life of their clients.

There is a tension between those radicals who see class as the major factor in social inequalities and those who adopt the broader agenda of anti-oppressive practice. Hilary Spearing argues that social work 'is actually very weak on the oppression of working class people. This is because the profession has been taken over by the middle class and has chosen to support those groups who do not threaten its interests eg black gay and disabled people' (Spearing, 2013). Leaving aside the false premise that social work was ever a working-class profession, this view elevates class as the only appropriate target for social workers concerned with inequalities. In doing so, it marginalises those whose primary identification is with gender, ethnicity, sexual orientation or disability and represents a regression to an over-simplified view of the working class.

Social work has struggled to move on from the radical critique of the 1970s because of the preoccupation of some social work academics with a class analysis derived from Marx. What should concern social workers is inequality and those structural factors that worsen inequality and limit the life chances of those at the bottom of the social structure. A more nuanced view of disadvantage and how it is reinforced would recognise the impact of other social factors. The media, including social media, can reinforce disadvantage. Newspapers and social media readily adopted the word 'chavs', illustrating the ease with which stereotypes can be created. Not only was the word itself used to describe uneducated, loutish, poorly dressed white people, which in Jones' (2011) words serve to demonise the white working class, but the suggested derivation 'council house and violent' (Manley, 2010) also gained currency. The study of power in society and how it is distributed owes much to the writings of Foucault. The challenge for social work practice is how those lessons can be translated into effective practice.

Ferguson and Woodward (2009) offer several examples of how this may be achieved. They suggest the application of community development approaches, working with community-based groups to support change; building alliances with social movements such as the survivors groups in mental health or upholding human rights in relation to asylum seekers and refugees; and forming links with global social movements. They identify four strands in a radical social work practice (Ferguson and Woodward, 2009, p 153): retaining a commitment to good practice; encouraging guerrilla warfare and small-scale resistance; working alongside service users and carers; and fostering collective activities and political campaigning.

The first strand – retaining good practice – is more than common sense, despite the efforts of politicians to reduce it to the level of 'streetwise grannies' (Bottomley, 1991) or 'a very practical job' (Smith, 2002). It has an intellectual component involving the integration of heart and head. Relationship-based practice became unfashionable for a while, as it was seen as a return to the emphasis on psychosocial work that had been the model of the 1960s. Without a relationship with clients, no strategy for change is likely to succeed.

Good practice is not solely about building relationships. It is about using those relationships to bring about change in clients' lives. That may come through collective action in the community that changes the circumstances in which clients live. It may be quasi-contractual, in working systematically towards agreed outcomes. It may be about interventions agreed with the client that relieve some of the stresses in the social environment. Social work, like human behaviour itself, is multi-faceted, and the good worker will use techniques and skills that are tailored to the circumstances of the client.

The second strand – small-scale resistance – is cited as continuing to present managers with well-documented evidence of unmet need or examples where earlier intervention would have been effective in diverting later difficulties.

The third strand – working with service users and carers – is important, both in refreshing the insights of the worker into the real needs of service users rather than their assumed needs as well as in affording users and carers the chance to influence the structure of services and social work courses. If there is to be a whole-hearted commitment to engaging service users, there must be an acknowledgement of the subsequent costs to users and carers in terms of their time and money – for example, paying for substitute carers in order to free up time to make the necessary preparations. Their involvement should not be regarded as a free resource for professionals to exploit.

Ferguson and Woodward's fourth strand is collective activities and political campaigning. One feels that this is where the emphasis really lies – in a practice committed to challenging neoliberalism and fighting for social justice. Lavalette shares this perspective, arguing that:

> The key element is the orientation of the practitioner as they undertake good quality work: whom they involve in work processes and how they communicate and keep service users informed; how they speak 'truth to power'; how they fight for service users' rights and needs and how they locate (and explain) the problems service users and

workers face in the context of local and national power structures. (Lavalette, 2011, p 6)

In their recent text, Gray and Webb articulate the case for a 'new social work Left' that is 'inherently antagonistic against its adversaries: neoliberalism and parliamentary capitalism, while projecting an emancipatory activism of new social movements without ignoring the longstanding problems of economic inequality and social injustice' (Gray and Webb, 2013, p 6). It is not surprising that Narey found ample material here for his critique of the politicisation of social work.

The progressive militant agenda for social work is drawn on thinkers 'from Marx to Simmel, Gramsci to Bourdieu, Adorno to Habermas, Fraser to Honneth and Kristeva to Butler' (Gray and Webb, 2013, p 5). Georg Simmel was a German philosopher and sociologist writing in the early 20th century. Antonio Gramsci was an Italian political theorist. Pierre Bourdieu was a French philosopher and sociologist who developed concepts of social and cultural capital. Theodore Adorno was a German philosopher writing predominantly after the Second World War. Jurgen Habermas also was a German philosopher, interested in critical analysis of contemporary society and who wrote about the student protest movement. Nancy Fraser is an American political philosopher who has written extensively about critical theory and feminism. Axel Honneth is a German moral philosopher.

The observant reader will note that these writers, with the exception of Ian Butler, have two things in common – they are all philosophers and none of them is a social worker. It seems a strange foundation for a 'new social work Left'. The reference to parliamentary capitalism as the enemy leads one to suspect that parliamentary democracy is subordinate to emancipatory activism for the authors.

The fight against neoliberalism, while a worthy cause, is not one for social work alone. There is a risk that the zeal of those who seek to align themselves with social movements in order to secure the overthrow of capitalism may lead to the interests of clients taking second place. Social workers need to have a strong ethical framework to provide guidance about what degree of involvement of clients is appropriate. In reviewing the history of radical and critical social work, Pease argues that 'discourses of empowerment, strengths and social justice serve to legitimise normative mainstream approaches, while providing a radical veneer to conservative practice' (Pease, 2013, p 23).

Empowerment of service users, building on their strengths in relationship-based work and fighting for social justice is a big enough agenda for this writer. One can be radical without signing up wholesale to the overthrow of capitalism or engaging in the academic debate about redistribution/recognition. With the exception of Ferguson and Woodward, and Lavalette, few writers from the critical school offer material relevant to practice. There is a gap between the academic preoccupation with social theory and the politics of class on the one hand, and the daily reality of frontline practice on the other. That gap has militated against effective improvements in the quality of social work. Practitioners have not been provided with the tools successfully to secure the integration of personal and political in their work.

It is sometimes asserted that the legacy of radical social work is to be seen in the degree to which anti-oppressive practice and insights from feminist and antiracist perspectives allied to work with service users has been incorporated into the mainstream (McDonald, 2007). If this is so, it remains surprising that social work has been quiescent in the destruction of services and supports for service users. The critical social work movement remains divided on the importance of personal relationships between worker and client, with some seeing this as a distraction from structural analysis. Others, like Ferguson, argue that engaging clients in social action will only be ethical and effective if there is a pre-existing relationship. This does not have to lead to the psychosocial casework so criticised in the late 1970s, but it is the foundation for a shared analysis of the situation.

AREAS FOR DISCUSSION

Why was the Bailey and Brake book so influential?

Do you think that anti-oppressive practice successfully encompasses the issues of race, gender and disability?

Are alliances with service user movements likely to produce a similar impact to the links with trades unions advocated in Bailey and Brake?

Is the nature of radical social work practice determined by the context of social work? Is it possible in a public sector agency?

FURTHER READING

The leading lights of SWAN have written extensively on their vision of radical social work. Ferguson, I. (2008) *Reclaiming social work*, Bristol: Policy Press; Ferguson, I. and Woodward, R. (2009) *Radical social work in practice: Making a difference*, Bristol: Policy Press; and Lavalette, M. (2011) *Radical social work today*, Bristol: Policy Press, provide a good background.

The Marxist view at the time of Bailey and Brake is best set out in Corrigan, P. and Leonard, P. (1978) *Social work practice under capitalism: A Marxist approach*, Basingstoke: Macmillan.

A more recent analysis, reflecting the crisis of global capitalism, is Gray, M. and Webb, S. (2013) *The new politics of social work*, Basingstoke: Palgrave Macmillan. This fascinating collection of essays sets out a new agenda for political engagement that explicitly argues that capitalism is the central problem to be addressed rather than 'the plurality of anti-racist, feminist and post-modern resistances'.

SEVEN

From the mainstream to the margins: two case studies

This chapter is divided into two sections, which examine in detail the role of social work in probation and mental health respectively.

Thinking about social work's role in adult care, I am struck by the similarities between two examples where social work has been relegated from a position of influence to the periphery. In probation, it is a deliberate act of public policy to reaffirm the government's toughness on crime, an approach enjoying bipartisan support. In mental health, it is more paradoxical. Policy statements continue to stress the social factors in mental health problems and the importance of tackling these early including primary prevention. Social work, however, is no longer seen as a key player in the delivery of care despite its capacity to address both the individual and social context.

Probation: no longer a social work service

KEY LEARNING POINTS
- » Probation: the impact of the IMPACT study
- » The shift from rehabilitation as a core value to punishment in the community
- » A national service or local services
- » Probation as junior partner in National Offender Management Service
- » Outsourcing and payment by results

Chapter One looked at the early days of probation. The roots of the service lay in the temperance movement and the Christian faith. They came together in the Church of England Temperance Society and the initial requirement that missionaries had to be communicant members of the Church of England. Redemption was the goal of much practice and this was to be achieved through a combination of practical assistance and befriending.

The court missionaries were replaced over time by a professional service that developed its training based on social work. In 1930, the Home Office introduced a national training scheme for probation officers. Vanstone's study of articles in the *Probation Journal* in the 1930s concludes that they show 'not only the influence of psychology and social awareness but also the resilience of moral judgement, Christian mores and class perspectives' (Vanstone, 2004, p 87).

Insights from the development of psychology were an important influence on the development of probation because they added psychological problems to moral defects as an explanation of delinquent behaviour.

The service, which had always been strongly male, began to change after the Second World War as concepts of rehabilitation gained ground. The Ingleby Committee's radical recommendation to raise the age of criminal responsibility from eight to 14 was watered down, and the age was fixed at 10 in the 1963 Children and Young Persons Act. But the central role of the probation service was reaffirmed by the report of the Departmental Committee on the Probation Service in 1962 (Morison, 1962). This confirmed the probation role as one of treatment, rehabilitation and reformation. It endorsed the creation and utilisation of a relationship between the offender and a trained social worker as the basis for probation practice. This unequivocal statement led to social work becoming the entry route to the service as it shed its reliance on former military and police officers with a strong sense of discipline.

I trained for the service in 1964/65 at Rainer House, the Home Office training centre for probation, located in Chelsea. Its location meant that it was able to call on talented academics and practitioners from psychiatry, psychology, sociology, addictions and social work. The course was unfashionable in its use of block fieldwork placements with a three-month residential programme embracing theory in contrast to the integration of theory and practice offered by concurrent placements. There is no conclusive proof about the superiority of one form of training over the other, while my own fond memories of the residential element may be coloured by the fact that I met my wife on the course.

The core content was based on the concept of probation as a form of therapeutic intervention, using the relationship with the offender as the vehicle to change behaviour. It was important to help offenders gain insight into the reasons for their offending and to build on their strengths to secure change. The relationship, however, was set in the context of authority, with the potential sanction, albeit rarely used, of a return to court on breach of probation.

That period represented the highwater mark of probation's embrace of social work. Biestek (1961) and Monger (1964) provided a clear framework for taking the social history of a client, establishing a relationship, and using one's own personality in the relationship as the instrument to bring about change. The Home Office course provided a social work qualification alongside the increasing number of generic courses developing at this time.

As a callow 22-year-old, I found myself responsible for a caseload of around 50 probationers made up of young offenders, adult petty offenders and some 'matrimonials' – the name given to those referred from the police and courts following domestic disputes and court hearings. The staple method of keeping in contact was reporting so each week I would set aside two afternoons to see probationers, usually at 15-minute intervals. After chatting inconsequentially about the local football team or Saturday night's activities, I would seek, usually with conspicuous lack of success, to explore their feelings about the offence or problems within the family in order to help them gain some insight into the reasons for their offending. The exchange would be dutifully recorded and then we would arrange to meet again the following week or in two weeks, depending on the length of the probation order already elapsed.

The possibility of a breach was there, but in practice a further offence often preceded any possible action over failure to sustain contact with the probation officer. Probably the most useful aspect of the work was in compiling the social history reports. These provided magistrates and courts with a picture of the probationer's family background and offending history, and an opinion on the likelihood of repeat offending. This information then helped the court to reach a view on sentencing.

The training on which I drew for this work was that of social work but not all my colleagues saw their role in that way, with a mixed bag of ex-Army officers believing in the virtues of discipline and evangelical Christians believing in the virtues of forgiveness and the possibility of redemption. One colleague would end his reporting session with the injunction 'let us pray together'.

The Seebohm Committee was obliged by its terms of reference to exclude probation from its examination – a decision it clearly regretted, possibly looking at the model in Scotland where probation had recently been integrated with local authority social work departments. The decision by the National Association of Probation Officers (NAPO) in 1970 to stand outside the newly established British Association of Social Workers (BASW), discussed in Chapter Two, was to mark a turning point for probation in its identification with social work.

The responsibility for prison aftercare, previously discharged by voluntary aftercare societies, was transferred to probation in 1967, and the 1972 Criminal Justice Act introduced a raft of non-custodial disposals to supplement the probation order – community service, suspended sentence supervision order, bail hostels and day training centres. The community service order, successfully piloted in six areas, was particularly significant. Initially seen only as an alternative to imprisonment, it swiftly became popular with magistrates and demand for the orders exceeded the supply available.

The 1970s saw an accumulation of research findings calling into question the effectiveness of probation. The IMPACT experiment (Folkard et al, 1976) seemed like a dream come true to many probation officers. It studied the impact of low caseloads on outcomes and afforded an opportunity to do really intensive supervision using casework skills. Unhappily, no evidence of improved outcomes was discerned, leading to the conclusion in an official Home Office publication for sentencers that 'probationers on the whole do no better than if they were sent to prison, and that rehabilitative programmes – whether involving psychiatric treatment, counselling, casework or intensive contact and special attention, in custodial and non-custodial settings – have no predictably beneficial effects' (Brody, 1976, p 37).

Throughout the 1970s probation officers enjoyed more autonomy than their colleagues in social services departments. They made their own recommendations to the courts, whereas – at least notionally – actions by the social services departments were implemented on behalf of the named officer – the director of social services. The welfare model of probation based on the needs of the individual offender was, however, increasingly challenged by society's concern for a justice model as a result of increases in juvenile delinquency. Rising crime, and in particular juvenile crime, was attributed to 'soft' sentencing. The change of government in 1979 was to accentuate the shift to more of a control role for the probation service.

Crime was a significant issue in the 1979 general election campaign, but there were few legislative commitments in the Conservative manifesto. Securing value for money in the criminal justice system through pursuit of the three Es – economy, efficiency and effectiveness – was seen as the priority. With the benefit of hindsight, the Thatcher years can be seen as a continuation of the policy stance that the Home Office had held previously, that the criminal justice system itself had limited impact on crime. Priority was therefore given to 'designing out crime' by improved security and better management of housing estates, and the creation of opportunities for young people.

The rhetoric of politicians did have an impact in sentencing policy where there was a 30% increase in custodial sentences between 1979 and 1985 and a consequent growth in the prison population to 45,000 in 1985 (a figure that seems very modest compared with nearly double that figure at present). The rise in the prison population and the widening gap between capacity in the system and the need for places presented a policy dilemma for the government. The 1982 Criminal Justice Act drew a distinction between more serious offenders for whom longer sentences were introduced and those who posed no threat to the public for whom alternatives to imprisonment were actively sought.

Punishment in the community

In 1984, the government published a national statement of objectives and priorities for probation (Home Office, 1984). This represented the first attempt by government to define the role of the service and set explicit priorities. It saw as a first priority ensuring 'that wherever possible placed offenders can be dealt with by non-custodial measures and that standards of supervision are set and maintained at the level required for the purpose'(Home Office 1984,Vi a). Significantly, those standards were still defined as being delivered 'through the exercise of social work skills and use of available facilities' (Home Office, 1984, B (V)). It began the shift in emphasis within the service towards working with more serious offenders but with probation supervision redefined as 'punishment in the community' (Home Office, 1988).

The publication of two major papers in 1990 – one White Paper, one Green Paper – further developed the role of the service as a key element in the delivery of community sentences. The White Paper, *Crime, justice and protecting the public* (Home Office, 1990a), was designed to reassure magistrates and judges that probation was not a soft option. Probation could be linked with other penalties and was to be viewed as a punishment, not the alternative to punishment that had been the origin of the service. The language was stronger in the Green Paper, *Supervision and punishment in the community: A framework for action* (Home Office, 1990b), which floated the possibility of a national probation service, contracting out the provision of some services and placing greater emphasis on accountability and performance.

The 1991 Criminal Justice Act placed probation squarely in the arena of the management and administration of punishments in the community, with the order no longer seen as an alternative to punishment but as a punishment in its own right. This was counterbalanced by a requirement that custodial sentences had to be justified by the seriousness of the offence and the possibility of longer sentences, where, following violent or sexual offences, these were needed to protect the public from harm. The Act also introduced national standards for court reports and community sentences, adding to those already introduced for community service. The delicate balancing act between the rhetoric of punishment and the broadly progressive aim to limit imprisonment to serious offenders began to fall apart after the 1992 general election and the 1993 Criminal Justice Act marked a sharp policy reversal.

Michael Howard as new Home Secretary told the Conservative Party conference in 1993 that 'prison works'. He announced at the same time the building of six new prisons, secure training centres for persistent young offenders, a review of community sentences – with a view to making them more punitive – and increases in the maximum length of sentence for some juvenile offenders. He was supported by the pledge of the Shadow Home Secretary Tony Blair to 'be tough on crime and tough on the causes of crime' and by a right-wing press concerned at the impact of liberal do-gooders on penal policy.

The murder of three-year-old Jamie Bulger in 1993 by two young boys was material for headlines for weeks and retains traction as a tabloid story 20 years on. The judge in the trial described the killing as an act of 'unparalleled evil and barbarity', but the sentence he gave the killers – a minimum term of eight years – provoked outrage in the tabloid press. The Lord Chief Justice increased the minimum term to 10 years, and Michael Howard, responding to a petition organised by the *Sun* newspaper, subsequently increased it to 15 years. The episode was seen as indicative of moral decline, leading to calls for traditional approaches to punishment rather than understanding in dealing with juvenile crime. Social workers as an occupational group were seen as apologists for the bad behaviour of young people and thus out of step with the mood of the times.

In a thoughtful analysis of the influence of the media on politicians, Silverman (2011) sees the mid-nineties as a time when a resurgent Labour Party was seeking to lead the agenda on crime and the Conservative Party was determined to demonstrate its firm touch. This was the basis for the emergence of a tacit consensus that penal policy could no longer be left to the Howard League for Penal Reform.

The dramatic shift from a policy geared to keeping offenders out of prison to one that asserted the effectiveness of prison had immediate consequences. The prison population went up by 50% between 1992 and 1997. A more questioning approach to the work of the probation service led to a number of key performance indicators to measure the effectiveness and efficiency of the service, including predicted and actual reconviction rates, average days to produce reports, and the satisfaction levels of courts with the service provided.

At the same time as this inexorable rise in the prison population, the Home Office decided to reshape probation training and break the links with social work. Instead of a nationally recognised academic qualification, it decided to move to on-the-job training and practical experience, using distance learning as the route to a National Vocational Qualification. It was thought this would attract mature students. A Green Paper (Home Office, 1995) and a White Paper (Home Office, 1996) argued for the importance of prison and the need to strengthen the punitive element of community sentences.

The advent of the Labour government in 1997 led to some change of emphasis, but the concern to be seen as tough on crime remained. The Labour government accepted the argument for retaining a link with higher education in training for the service, but the Diploma in Probation Studies was essentially unchanged in its core emphasis on criminal justice.

A prisons–probation review launched in 1997 did not lead to a merger of the two services as some had anticipated. Instead, the probation service was nationalised, with the appointment of a national director, and the establishment of a unified service with local operational areas coterminous with police authority boundaries run by a probation board. The service was 100% funded by central government and all members of staff became civil servants. So in 15 years, the service had moved from a statement of national objectives and priorities to a national service.

The National Probation Service came into being on 1 April 2001. Before it had been in existence for 12 months, a review of correctional services was initiated. This concluded that despite the increased use of prison, there was no evidence that increasing the severity of sentences had any effect on reoffending (Carter, 2003). Sentences were poorly targeted, with inappropriate use of prison for first offenders. Carter proposed a new National Offender Management Service (NOMS), bringing together prisons and probation under a national director and with 10 regional offender managers. Custody would be reserved for serious dangerous and persistent offenders with an enhanced range of community punishments. The new Sentencing Guidelines Council would review sentencing annually, with a focus on what works in terms of reducing reoffending.

Much of Carter's report was well received, although there were anxieties among probation workers that its influence would be limited and its resources minimal compared with those of the prison service. This anxiety was confirmed when nine of the 10 regional management posts were secured by former prison service staff. Less welcome, although not of immediate impact, were Carter's proposals for 'contestability', with the provision of both custodial and non-custodial sentences being opened up to a range of providers, which was intended to lead to greater efficiency, value for money and innovation. The Carter proposals were warmly received by the government and NOMS came into existence just over three years after the birth of the National Probation Service in June 2004.

NOMS aimed to achieve 'end to end' management of offenders from admission to custody through to discharge support as a key element in the reduction of reconviction. Probation officers were central to the delivery of this process as 'offender managers'. In practice, the vision was rarely achieved. The limitations of the prison estate meant that offenders were often placed many miles from home with an inevitable detrimental impact on the frequency of contact with family and friends. NOMS was also subject to numerous reorganisations, in part as the result of its hasty introduction.

In some ways, NOMS has been good for probation. Its workload in terms of offenders under supervision and reports prepared for the courts has substantially increased. The number of offenders supervised rose by 39% between 2000 and 2011 as a result of new orders and the increased numbers of offenders subject to pre- and post-release supervision. The number of court reports prepared, however, peaked in 2004, since when there has been an increase in reports prepared on the day of sentence. To long-serving professionals, this is reminiscent of the days when a probation officer had a 10-minute interview with the offender in his cell in order to glean some background information to proffer to at the court hearing.

The increase in workload outstripped the increase in resources over this same period. The House of Commons Justice Committee (2010) calculated that in real terms resources dropped by 14.8% between 2002 and 2008. Much has been lost along the way in terms of the traditional values that once underpinned the service. Describing the changes since the *Statement of national objectives and priorities for the probation service* (Home Office, 1984), Whitehead and Statham argue 'the people-based nature of the organisation is being transformed into a more rigid, authoritarian, and centrally controlled bureaucracy. There is ... less room for care and compassion as the culture is transformed' (Whitehead and Statham, 2006, p 282).

This comment has to be seen in the context of the shift in emphasis in the work of probation and its embrace (possibly reluctant) of the enforcement of community sanctions. In the key performance indicators for the service set by its first and last national director, enforcement was given most prominence (National Probation Service, 2001). The ideology of enforcement and compliance within a national framework of standards and performance indicators fundamentally shifted the role of probation and its culture from its historic roots in social work and its ethos of 'advise, assist and befriend'.

The restructuring of NOMS resulted in a downgrading of probation and even under the Labour government the culture was clearly hostile to the 'softness' associated with probation. The scope for discretion was reduced, with the adoption of risk assessment scales and categorisation prescribing the level of response required.

Worse, however, was to come, in terms of the abandonment of the last elements of social work within probation. The degree of political control over probation had been illustrated by the *Sonnex* case, where two French citizens were killed by an individual under probation supervision. The Chief Officer for London Probation was effectively forced to resign as a result of this case and subsequently launched a withering assault on both NOMS and the justice secretary, Jack Straw.

> Nothing had prepared me for the duplicity of the agency (NOMS) nor more shockingly the posturing of the then Justice Secretary in the national media. Why the Justice Secretary should state that I had been suspended when I had not remains a mystery to me. His assertion that I would have been sacked (prejudging any hearing) is deeply ironic coming from the head of the Ministry of Justice … is [this] just another symptom of the political life in our country which has descended to such tawdry depths. (Scott, 2010)

Wendy Fitzgibbon (2011) notes the parallel with Ed Balls' purported dismissal of the director of children's services in Haringey, another example of ministerial interference with due process apparently driven by the demands of appearing tough to the popular press.

The concern to demonstrate toughness continued with the incoming Coalition government, which launched a Green Paper (Ministry of Justice, 2010) floating the idea of rehabilitation programmes delivered by independent providers on a payment-by-results basis. Following consultation, the government proposed that three quarters of discharged prisoners would be dealt with on this 'contracted out' basis, with independent providers paid according to their success in cutting reoffending. Despite vigorous protests from probation interests, including strike action by NAPO, the proposals are going ahead.

Criticism can be expected from the probation service, which will be left only with the most serious offenders. In the meantime, the plans have already been attacked by the Social Market Foundation for providing perverse incentives and by Matthew Taylor for being modelled on the unsuccessful Work Programme. Taylor notes that 'charities lacking the contract planning and negotiation capacity of the private sector generally failed to get on the original framework of preferred providers' (Taylor, 2013). Even when they did, they found that the structure of the contracts, the low referral rate, the exacting compliance regime and the low margins made it a costly and unattractive option for third-sector providers.

Despite the issues raised by the exclusion of two of the leading contenders – Serco and G4S – for any such contracts (because of allegations of overcharging taxpayers for electronic tagging), the government continues to press ahead with its plans for outsourcing. It is doing so with what the House of Commons Committee of Public Accounts (2014) described as 'a highly ambitious time table … with evident risks arising from the scale and pace of the reforms' (p 3). Most striking is the lack of evidence that outsourcing and payment by results will be successful. It is more indicative of the success of neoliberalism than evidence-based policy.

The effect will be to limit the probation function to the supervision of long-term and more serious offenders. It has been a long journey from the social work base of the probation service, but it has been accomplished in a remarkably short time. There are important lessons to be drawn by other social work services from this sorry tale.

AREAS FOR DISCUSSION

What factors have driven the emphasis on punishment and the growth of prisons?

What part do you think politicians have played in leading this process or has the press been more influential?

Would the retention of social work training as the basis for probation work have made any difference to the outsourcing programme?

FURTHER READING

Inevitably for those who have spent years in probation there is an undertone of anger at the changes under way detectable in the books below.

Whitehead, P. and Statham, R. (2006) *The history of probation: Politics, power and cultural change 1876–2005*, Crayford: Shaw and Sons, provides a good historical context to the changes.

Fitzgibbon, W. (2011) *Probation and social work on trial: Violent offenders and child abusers* Basingstoke: Palgrave Macmillan, uses specific cases to illustrate the distorted treatment in the press and the consequent impact on politicians.

In Scott, D. (2010) 'Who's protecting who?', *Probation Journal*, vol 57, no 3, pp 291-5, the searing anger of the author over his dismissal in the wake of the *Sonnex* case, discussed earlier, comes across strongly.

Mental health social work: a study in displacement

KEY LEARNING POINTS
» The emergence of the mental welfare officer
» The approved social worker role
» The Clunis case and its impact
» The changing social worker role in community mental health teams

The duly authorised officer

We have seen elsewhere how the long shadow of the Poor Law influenced the development of social work. This is no less true in the context of mental health. The 1890 Lunacy Act gave the power to the duly authorised relieving officer to apply on behalf of a patient for admission to hospital. This was both an issue of capacity on the part of the patient as well as an important administrative procedure to ensure that the public purse would pick up the costs of the hospitalisation.

The duly authorised officer (DAO) role was not seen as a social work role and was staffed by former nurses and other staff, predominantly male, who saw it as a quasi-enforcement role. The legislation required the development of links with community resources, so DAOs, later to be redesignated as mental welfare officers, 'became more expert at resource finding, developing good relations with her local authority departments such as housing and with voluntary organisations' (Pierson, 2011, p 189).

By contrast, the development of psychiatric social work took a different path. Its practitioners were highly qualified and skilled in psychotherapeutic interventions. They worked predominantly in the context of child guidance and those few specialist hospitals with a strong therapeutic orientation. Psychiatric social workers were regarded as the elite of the social work profession.

The reform of mental health law was driven by the recognition that large overcrowded mental hospitals were not a suitable setting for therapy or asylum. Pharmacological advances had rendered surgical treatments like lobotomy and leucotomy, and physical treatments like electro-convulsive therapy, outmoded. The aim of the 1959 Mental Health Act was to start the process of community care by giving local authorities responsibility for social work for patients not receiving hospital treatment and those who had left hospital. They were expected to develop a range of residential alternatives, including half-way houses, group homes, hostels and day-care services.

The development of services was, however, extremely patchy. Sixteen years later, the White Paper, *Better services for the mentally ill*, noted that 'by and large the non-hospital resources are still minimal, though where facilities have been developed they have in general proved successful ... hospital staff ... have become increasingly unwilling to act as social care custodians for those who would not need to remain in hospital were supporting facilities available in the community' (DHSS, 1975, p 11).

There had been some positive changes, with social workers actively involved in developing services, but the pace of contraction in hospital places exceeded the rate of expansion of community places. A number of long-stay patients were transferred to life in bed and breakfast accommodation in seaside resorts – a move that brought the concept of community care into disrepute.

The case for reform of the 1959 legislation was led by the mental health charity Mind, which, supported by BASW, argued for the protection of the civil liberties of patients and a strengthening of patients' rights. Mind argued for wider availability of counselling and talking treatments (a call still echoed over 30 years later), and greater safeguards for patients against dangerous treatments and lengthy detention in hospitals without external review.

The 1983 Mental Health Act introduced the concept of the approved social worker, who would have specialist training and be responsible for application on behalf of patients for admission to hospital. Before making an application, the approved social worker had to consider whether there was a less restrictive option. Social workers were expected both to act as advocates for the patient and also to balance that with the protection of the public from unnecessary risk (Prior, 1992).

As so often, advances in practice requiring the development of specialist training happened at a time when public spending was being constrained. No additional funds were made available for the training of approved social workers (ASWs). There were two protracted disputes – one between the National Association of Local Government Officers trade union and BASW about whether this new role demanded separate negotiations about salaries and conditions of service, and one between the local government associations and central government about the cost and duration of the specialist training. The eventual compromise of a minimum 60-day training leading to ASW status and the transitional approval of previous mental welfare officers allowed the Act to operate.

There were problems with the operation of the ASW role. The role itself was a relatively small part of social work in mental health. The majority of the workforce did not have access to this specialist training. The emphasis on the least restrictive alternative meant that social workers found themselves vulnerable in the event of high-profile cases like that of Christopher Clunis, a schizophrenic who killed a passenger at a tube station after a long period of contact with hospitals and social services. The inquiry report (Ritchie et al, 1994) found that hospitals and social services failed to contact his family or GP, repeatedly treated his hospital admissions as separate incidents, failed to check his false claims that he abused drugs and discharged him from hospital prematurely because of a shortage of beds or to save money. The case was seen as indicative of what was widely perceived as a failed policy of community care. As the implementers of the policy, social workers found themselves under scrutiny in the same way as their colleagues in child protection. In mental health, the emphasis on multidisciplinary working meant that the responsibility for weaknesses was often shared with other agencies.

The main vehicle for delivering community-based care was community mental health teams (CMHTs), including a psychiatrist, psychologist, occupational therapists, mental health nurses and social workers. Over time, CMHTs became focused on those with the most complex health and care needs. The role involved working flexible hours, including at weekends, to allow patients full access to the team; providing patients with practical help with everyday living such as shopping and transport; day care; and delivering a range of therapies, including group therapy and counselling. No profession had a monopoly of wisdom, although the control over hospital bed places exercised by the psychiatrist meant that they had a particular status in the team.

A national study of CMHTs in the year of the Clunis report found over 500 such teams. Their number expanded rapidly with the publication of guidance from the Department of Health (DH, 1996). Onyett noted a growing tension for team members between their professional allegiance and loyalty to the team. It was, however, identification with the team and role clarity in the team that correlated most strongly with job satisfaction in a field notorious for burnout and stress (Onyett, 1997).

Teams work with an allocated key worker, usually chosen to reflect the needs of the client, to provide coordinated care. Thus a client unable to cope with some of the basic requirements of daily living, such as shopping, budgeting or transport, may be allocated a support worker, while one with problems managing their medication may be allocated a mental health nurse. Care coordination is the preferred term in mental health for the care management widely used in adult social care, reflecting the multidisciplinary skills within the team and the reality that different needs require different assistance. Care coordination is based on the care programme approach (CPA). This has been in place since 1990 as the means of delivering care to those with severe and enduring mental health problems. Service users are involved in drawing up and agreeing a care plan to meet their needs. This will cover all of their treatment, care and support needs, including medication, social relationships, housing and employment.

The CPA had two levels – standard and enhanced – reflecting the degree of complexity of the needs of clients. A review of CPA in 2008 led to the removal of the lower level. Those with less complex and more straightforward needs remain entitled to an assessment of their needs and a care plan subject to regular review. The more complex cases will continue on a CPA based on an assessment of the level of mental disorder, the risk presented by the client to self and others, history of instability, co-morbidity and engagement with relevant agencies. The review, however, presented a bleak picture of how ineffective user involvement had been, with many care plans unsigned and even unseen by the client (DH, 2008b).

The advent of New Labour in 1997 had produced a spate of modernisation White Papers and national service frameworks setting out policy and practice guidance. The 2000 White Paper, *Reforming the Mental Health Act* (DH, 2000), followed a Green Paper (DH, 1999b) and the report of an expert committee (DH, 1999c). While the proposals in each were broadly similar – a broad definition of mental disorder, clarity about compulsory powers and compulsory treatment in the community, and new powers to deal with those with personality disorders – Grounds refers to the change in tone over the three documents: '[the proposals] became harder in tone, less balanced, liberal and principled' (Grounds, 2001). In particular the balance between the extension of compulsory treatment in the community and entitlement with a duty on local authorities to provide appropriate services was replaced by a general reliance on existing duties and the National Service Framework.

The proposals were extremely controversial and were opposed by many professional groups, especially in relation to community treatment orders. They seemed to be based on the failings such as the Clunis case and the mistaken belief that there were large numbers of dangerous offenders unsupervised in the community. Campaigners argued that compulsion per se would achieve little that could not be achieved by a well-resourced range of community-based services.

In 2006, the government dropped the proposals and instead brought forward the 2007 Mental Health Act, which retained elements of the original 1983 legislation. The community treatment order was retained and the approved social worker role was to be replaced by that of an approved mental health professional (AMHP).

The proposals continued to be contested in the House of Commons and House of Lords and a number of concessions were made. Interestingly, the AMHP role itself was not a source of controversy because it reflected the increasingly multidisciplinary way in which care was delivered. What was contentious was the inadequacy of the training proposed and the loss of independence in the ASW role. As officers of the local authority, trained and validated by the local authority, ASWs were independent of the mental health trust. Under the new arrangements, all the professionals involved in assessing an individual for detention could be employed in the same multidisciplinary team, with a consequent loss of real and perceived independence. There was already concern that the pressure on crisis teams to reduce admissions as a result of the lack of mental health beds was leading to decisions to retain people in home settings that were potentially risky.

The specific social care role of the ASW, familiar with the range of community services and support systems and thus well placed to assess the least restrictive option for the patient, was lost without a fight. Does this matter as long as social work plays a full part in the multidisciplinary team?

It does for two reasons. First, the ASW role was backed by high-quality training of those already familiar with the social care system. Its specific identification of the independent decision-making powers vested in the role was a tribute to the high calibre of many social workers in mental health. In a multidisciplinary team, it is essential that the contributions of each professional are valued. The demise of the ASW made it seem that this role was not fully appreciated. Second, the loss of the role was exacerbated by the 2008 financial crisis and the consequent austerity programme implemented by the government. The split between the substantial budget reductions sought from local authorities and the standstill budget for the NHS meant that local authorities' ability to maintain the level of social work staffing supporting mental health teams came under pressure. Partnership agreements were broken or rewritten, with local authority staff being withdrawn altogether in some cases.

What has been the impact of the 2007 Mental Health Act in practice? To help answer this question, we can examine two areas – community treatment orders and compulsory powers – which are particularly relevant for the social work role.

In 2008, the *British Journal of Psychiatry* ran a fascinating debate article on the pros and cons of community treatment orders (CTOs) (Lawton-Smith et al, 2008). CTOs were designed to deal with the problem of patients not taking their medication after being discharged from hospital, with the sanction of compulsory rehospitalisation in the event of non-compliance. In his contribution, Lawton-Smith noted how 'stranger danger occupies the media and public imagination and in England the murder ... by Christopher Clunis looms larger over the debate despite occurring fifteen years ago'. He argued that although the measure was targeted at the 'revolving door' patients with a history of repeat admissions, the legislation was couched more broadly and would extend the numbers subject to compulsion.

By contrast, Burns and Dawson in the same article argue that the walls of hospitals are porous, with the majority of treatment taking place in the community. They suggested that Australasian and North American experience indicated that compulsion is an effective means of securing greater compliance with treatment plans often without the necessity to use the sanction of rehospitalisation.

Five years on from the introduction of CTOs, the evidence is accumulating of the impact of the change. A randomised controlled trial studied the use of CTOs. It found no evidence that the level of readmissions was different in those subject to CTOs from those discharged without supervision. It concluded that 'in well coordinated mental health services the imposition of compulsory supervision does not reduce the rate of readmission of psychotic patients. We found no support in terms of a reduction in overall hospital admission to justify the significant curtailment of patients' liberty' (Burns et al, 2013).

Around 4,000 CTOs are made each year but the lead researcher on the 2013 study, Professor Tom Burns – a protagonist in the earlier debate – is now questioning whether their continued use can be justified. Just as in Chapter Eight it is noted that the findings of the research studies of integrated care have failed to produce evidence of what intuitively seems good practice, so too the absence of evidence to support the efficacy of compulsion is counterintuitive but sufficiently compelling to prompt a review of the policy.

The use of detentions overall has grown by 6% between 2006/07 and 2010/11, but the largest increase has been in the number of people compulsorily detained by the police, which has doubled in the same period. This may reflect the scarcity of acute hospital beds or the problems in accessing crisis services particularly where the individual was not previously known to services.

Reflecting back on the controversy surrounding the Mental Health Act, it seems as if the issue of risk, which was so salient in the parliamentary discussions of the legislation, has become the dominant factor in assessment replacing the welfare of the individual patient. Glover-Thomas has suggested that there has been a shift in the mode of assessment, with an increase in defensive risk-averse practice both from psychiatrists and from approved mental health professionals (Glover-Thomas, 2012).

New Ways of Working

At the same time as the controversy about the Mental Health Act, the Department of Health launched a parallel initiative, New Ways of Working. This was designed to reflect the flexibility in working required in effective multidisciplinary teams while continuing to recognise distinctive professional roles. Each profession contributed to the final report (DH, 2007b). The section on social work identifies four themes emerging from the widespread consultation exercise that preceded the report: social work identity, social work research, career pathways and leadership.

Traditionally, the social work role in mental health had been to empower service users and carers through a range of interventions using a social model and understanding of mental distress. The consultation, however, found that 'although they may be part of a particular mental health team, they often feel that they are professionally isolated, that their contribution is not valued, that they are not receiving effective professional supervision, and that they are under enormous pressure' (DH, 2007b, para 7.10.5).

The lack of opportunity for social work research in contrast to the extensive research programmes available to other occupational groups was a source of disquiet, further reinforcing the sense of marginalisation within mental health social work. Pay differentials were a source of discontent, as most mental health social workers were seconded from their local authority employment and thus remained on local authority scales. Nursing colleagues, as a result of the banding introduced in 2004 under the Agenda for Change initiative which regraded many nurses, often enjoyed higher levels of remuneration. Opportunities for advancement to more senior levels were also far more limited for social workers. The absence of professional leadership was a major problem. Local authorities, having seconded their staff, often did not retain a clear responsibility for their employees' professional support. The worsening financial climate for local authorities in the wake of the 2008 global financial collapse has been a further destabilising factor.

Work in community settings

Compulsion is at one end of the spectrum of mental health. Most people with mental health issues are living at home with friends and family supported by community services. These services differ from those provided by community mental health teams, in that support is provided by assertive outreach teams, crisis intervention teams, early intervention in psychosis teams, support time and recovery workers, and counsellors delivering psychological therapies (predominantly cognitive behavioural therapy but also other talking therapies).

Assertive outreach was designed to reach severely mentally ill patients who did not engage with mental health services. Using a team approach, workers would seek out their clients at home, in a park, in a café or in a social security office and would maintain regular contact. The results of this approach were positive in terms of reduced hospital admissions, although some studies suggested that they were no more effective than CMHTs (Burns et al, 1999; Killapsy et al, 2006). Social workers were members of the team along with nurses, psychiatrists, support workers and sometimes former service users.

Crisis intervention teams, again usually comprising community psychiatric nurses, social workers and psychiatrists, were established to intervene at a time of crisis where severe mental health problems were evident. The model developed was to deliver home-based support to prevent hospital admissions and to help the patient stabilise. The results from these teams have been positive, with a recent Cochrane review (Murphy et al, 2012) finding evidence that intervention from such teams reduced the level of admissions, produced greater stability at three-month follow-up and were preferred by patients and families.

Social work still has a role in mental health, but stitching together a network of support for the patient is the task of the care coordinator who may come from a different discipline. But for many with mental health problems, the clinical care is not their foremost priority. Their prime concern is managing the daily reality of surviving in a world of bills to be paid, jobs to be held onto or sought, friendships to be sustained and families to be cared for. The development of peer support has been a significant shift in the past decade. Services have used experts by experience (users of services or those who have experienced mental health issues) to advise on policies. Some trusts have shown the changing attitudes to the employment of people with a history of mental health issues by taking into their workforce people with mental health difficulties as a means of supporting the process of recovery.

Recovery means different things to different occupational groups, but in the mental health world it is a concept that is dependent on the circumstances of the individual involved. That does not necessarily mean full clinical recovery free of symptoms. It does involve leading a meaningful and satisfying life and learning to live with the constraints of mental illness. It is based on the strengths possessed by individuals and reinforcement of those strengths. Peer support from those which have lived through severe mental illness can be a powerful factor. Many mental health trusts are now formalising recovery in their training and support programmes, sometimes as recovery colleges. But social work, while historically at the forefront of championing the interests of service users and working with them to promote a holistic model of care, has not been at the forefront of this shift and is still struggling to define its role.

The search for social work identity has been compounded by the development of the Improving Access to Psychological Therapies programme. This programme was adopted in 2008 to offer psychological treatments for anxiety and depression based on clear evidence of the effectiveness of these talking therapies. In the first three years of the programme over one million people entered treatment programmes. A recovery rate of 45% was achieved and over 4,000 practitioners were trained.

Initially, the programme concentrated on cognitive behavioural therapy, but has now been extended to include interpersonal psychotherapy, counselling for depression, couples therapy and brief dynamic interpersonal psychotherapy. The programme is delivered by a mix of experienced and newly trained staff, with the experienced staff taking the more complex cases and offering supervision to trainees and recent graduates. Again we see a major initiative well funded and supported by government that has broadened the range of choice open to service users but one in which social workers – the traditional apostles of talking therapies – have played at best a marginal role.

The social work role in mental health work

The question one always has to ask in public policy is whether it is conspiracy or cock-up? Has the diminution of social work's influence in mental health been a deliberate act, possibly as retribution for the association of social work with hostility to conventional psychiatry? There is no evidence to support this view. More realistically, it is the consequence of the location of social work in local government rather than within the NHS, which is where the majority of mental health services are located. While social work and social care have made a contribution through group homes and day-care provision, and through supported housing, they are cut off from the mainstream of policy development. The diversification of services within flexible teams and the recognition of psychological therapies may be consistent with what social work would wish to see in mental health, but the profession has not been at the forefront of change. There has been a lack of leadership in the development of social care in mental health. The thresholds for referral to social work in adult care are set so high that only a small minority of those with mental health conditions are eligible for help.

This combination of factors has a powerful message for social work, given the current discussion about integrated care. The physical, financial and political separation of social care services, unless addressed, will lead to social work being relegated to the margins of public policy. Yet the government's strategy *No health without mental health* (DH, 2011) is a statement of high-level commitment to wellbeing that recognises the impact of social factors on mental health more clearly than any previous document. The argument for a social model has been won, yet 20 years ago such a statement would have been explicit about social work's contribution to building social capital for those with mental health problems. Despite references to personalisation, self-directed support and the outcomes framework for adult social care, there is no reference to social work in the publication.

The proposed fast-track programme Think Ahead is designed to address recruitment issues in mental health social work, but is clear in its analysis of the present malaise. It argues that the move to integrated teams has been problematic in some areas where social workers have been undervalued and left isolated by their medical colleagues, that social workers feel 'deprofessionalised' by acting as care coordinators following procedural assessments, and that recruitment is impaired by the lack of practice placements in mental health settings (Clifton and Thirley, 2014).

The College of Social Work recently set out its view on the role of social work in mental health. In the foreword, the Minister of State for Care and Support, Norman Lamb, argued that 'in modern mental health social work ... there will be a move to earlier intervention, building resilience, reducing and delaying dependency, and ensuring people have all the information and enabling support they need for better self care' (Allen, 2014).

The publication itself identifies five key roles for social workers:

'• enabling citizens to access the statutory social care and social work services and advice to which they are entitled, discharging the legal duties and promoting the personalised social care ethos of the local authority;
• promoting recovery and social inclusion with individuals and families;
• intervening and showing professional leadership and skill in situations characterised by high levels of social family and interpersonal complexity, risk and ambiguity;
• working co-productively and innovatively with local communities to support community capacity, personal and family resilience, earlier intervention and active citizenship;
• leading the approved mental health professional workforce' (Allen, 2014, pp 19–22)

These roles accurately capture the role of social work in an ideal world, but they do not capture the current reality of social work practice in mental health. The 'services and advice to which they are entitled' become more restricted year by year as spending cuts reduce the range of options available. While recovery has been adopted as a mantra by most mental health trusts, it is not an area in which social work is ascribed the lead role. The exclusive skills for situations of complexity are not viewed as those of social work alone. Co-production and community capacity building are tasks for the whole organisation and not exclusively the domain of social work.

The judgment of the Supreme Court in 2014 in *R v Cheshire West* provided a more extensive definition of deprivation of liberty than had been applied previously. The court ruled that those in care arrangements made by the state who lacked capacity, who were subject to continuous supervision and control and who were unable to leave were to be regarded as being deprived of their liberty and thus subject to the safeguards within the legislation. The impact of this judgment is considerable, with the Association of Directors of Adult Services claiming that the number affected will be in excess of 18,000 as the ruling extends to supported living and shared living placements. While this will give a clear role for mental health social workers, it is, like the AMHP role, one defined by statute. Despite the use of partnership funding, social work as a discipline has lost its place at the top level in mental health policy. Social work remains influential through the move that some social workers have made into commissioning and general management roles within the NHS. Its emphasis on the rights and strengths of users is now widely acknowledged as best practice. The task now is to carve out a distinctive role for social work that protects its separate identity while contributing to the development of policy and practice. The value base of social work means that recovery approaches and peer support models fit well with the ethos of social work. However, if social work asserts the contribution it can make in these areas, the territory will doubtless be contested by other professions.

AREAS FOR DISCUSSION

How has the separation of the NHS from local authority social work influenced mental health development?

Has social work identity been affected by approved mental health professionals?

Why have social perspectives flourished while social work has declined in impact?

Has the social work role in assertive outreach and crisis teams been sufficiently developed?

Why has the AMHP not been attractive to other occupational groups?

Do you find the College of Social Work's publication (Allen, 2014) on the role of the social worker in mental health persuasive?

FURTHER READING

The best introduction to a broader view of social work is Tew, J. (2011) *Social approaches to mental distress*, Basingstoke: Palgrave Macmillan.

Mental health: New ways of working for everyone (DH, 2007b) sets out the argument for breaking down traditional professional boundaries.

Allen, R. (2014) *The role of the social worker in adult mental health services*, London: College of Social Work, sets out a clear view of the social work role, although some of the areas she cites are likely to be claimed also by other professions.

Conclusion

In different ways, these two case studies demonstrate the vulnerability of social work. In probation, the residual service is left with high-risk offenders, with less serious offenders dealt with by contractors on a payment-by-results basis. It is why moves to outsource the provision of some children's services were met with such fierce resistance and regarded as potentially deskilling the social work functions in relation to children's care.

In mental health, the area in which social work formerly played a lead role in developing community-based support services and counselling has been taken over by other occupational groups. Mental health nursing has moved out of its hospital base to community settings. New groups of staff, like support time and recovery workers, are providing help to patients in the community. Social work is left with its statutory roles in relation to the approved mental health professional task and to the Deprivation of Liberty Safeguards (introduced by the 2005 Mental Capacity Act) to ensure that people in care homes, hospitals and supported living are looked after in a way that does not inappropriately restrict their freedom.

As the drive for cost savings continues, these examples offer a clear warning of the danger to social work.

EIGHT

The impossible dream: integration of health and social care

KEY LEARNING POINTS

> » Different funding, different cultures, different control
> » The Northern Ireland model
> » Better Care Fund
> » Integration and its many meanings
> » Evidence of effectiveness
> » Coordinating care

Breaking down the barriers between health and social care is not a new idea. It was not the invention of Frank Dobson, who referred to the Berlin Wall between the two when he became Secretary of State for Health in 1997. Collaboration between the two agencies has been a statutory duty since the 1974 reorganisation of the National Health Service and a succession of joint planning mechanisms, joint consultations, joint committees and joint finance have tried to lubricate the wheels of the health and social care system. There remain, however, profound differences of history, culture and principle separating the two. The title of this chapter reflects the almost universally held view that integration would be a good thing but the impossibility thus far of addressing the deep-seated differences.

Money is arguably the most important obstacle to integration. The totemic belief in health care free at the point of access – the phrase used by Aneurin Bevan when introducing the NHS Act in 1948 – contrasts with social care where charges are levied for services, especially those required by older people in need of care after leaving hospital, one of the pinch points in the system. The roots of this distinction can be found in the Poor Law where the provision of free social care including residential care was thought likely to encourage pauperism and create a disincentive to thrift and self-reliance. The 1948 National Assistance Act transferred to local authorities the residual Poor Law functions including residential care.

After the introduction of local authority social services in the early 1970s, reliance was placed on collaboration between health service agencies and social services. The priority groups for joint planning were older people, the mentally ill and mentally handicapped (using the customary terminology at that time) – areas where the policy thrust was to reduce the numbers of long-stay beds in hospitals and build up services in the community.

Follow the money

To encourage coordination, central government prescribed indicative growth rates and indicated its priorities for action. It required local authorities to submit three-year plans and introduced joint finance – a funding stream to be used on social services where jointly agreed projects would serve the purpose of the NHS. Initially, joint finance was used where there was a direct correlation between spending on community-based facilities, such as homes and hostels for those with physical or mental disabilities and those with mental health problems, and a desired reduction in the numbers of hospital places. In theory, this was an easy win, as hospital-based care was far more expensive than care in the community. Releasing the funds, however, often proved difficult. Buildings had fixed costs in maintenance that still had to be met. Not all the staff savings could be realised, as those remaining in hospital had the most complex needs requiring a high staff ratio.

As a further refinement to joint finance, the 1999 Health Act introduced mechanisms to allow health bodies and local authorities to delegate functions to each other, known as Health Act flexibilities. These were used to create lead bodies, for example in services to those with mental health problems, which might be led by the NHS, and to those with learning disabilities, which might be led by local authority social services. Patterns varied across the country, with a range of staffing arrangements including secondments, new employment structures like care trusts, and – albeit less often – transfers of staff from local authority to NHS and vice versa.

The Health Act flexibilities could also be used to pool funds, with a common fund being allocated to specific services or functions. They could be used to support lead commissioning, with one partner taking responsibility for achieving an agreed set of joint objectives using a single budget. And they could be used to create integrated provision, with a single management structure and with resources and staff effectively transferred to that structure.

The greatest use of pooled funds to date has been in relation to people with learning disabilities and those with mental health problems, and in the provision of community equipment. But it is the care of older people that is the most severe pressure point in the system and one with the greatest potential for tension in the relationship between health and social care. When people are assessed as medically fit for discharge from hospital, there are sometimes problems in achieving this immediately. Although, in theory, discharge planning should begin on the day of admission, there are blockages in the system. A shortage of occupational therapists may mean that nobody has been able to assess what aids and adaptations are needed to enable the individual to live at home. The package of home care support may not have been agreed. A stair lift or wider doors may need to be fitted to enable someone confined to a wheelchair to live at home.

The cost of 'blocked beds' to the NHS is substantial. In 2003, it was estimated by the Public Accounts Committee to be £170 million a year and in 2012 the NHS Confederation estimated it as £200 million. Given the 66% growth in NHS spending during that period, it is evident that the numbers of elderly people in hospital for non-medical reasons have decreased significantly, and as a share of NHS spending they represent less than 0.2%. Nevertheless, this situation produces a disproportionate amount of tension. The deputy director of the NHS Confederation has been quoted as saying 'the Health service cannot go on picking up the costs of a broken social care system' (*The Times*, 2012).

Money is one source of tension, but there are others relating to culture and control. These have been thrown into relief by the recent transfer of public health to local government at a time when local government expenditure is being cut at an unprecedented pace.

Culture

The organisational cultures of social care and the NHS are different, but so, too, are the approaches of the staff employed in social work and their colleagues in healthcare. Both organisational contexts have their virtues, but an understanding of difference is essential if effective integration is to be achieved.

Medicine is focused on remedying the problems of sick patients. It proceeds from diagnosis to prescription. Historically, there has been an imbalance of power between doctor and patient and even more so between hospital consultant and patient. But much has changed since Bywaters wrote that 'social work finds itself at odds with medicine in its central belief in a respect for a client's self-knowledge and right to choice, and in its growing recognition of the value of mutual support and exchange. Medical expectations of patient passivity fit uneasily with social work objectives of a self-directed and empowered clientele' (Bywaters, 1986). While those social work values remain, modern medicine now takes a more holistic view of the patient's needs and recognises the importance of giving patients full information and the opportunity to discuss and question. The General Medical Council guidance is explicit:

> You must work in partnership with patients sharing with them the information they will need to make decisions about their care ... treat each patient as an individual.... You must listen to patients, take account of their views and respond honestly to their questions. (GMC, 2013, paras 31, 49)

Patient-held records would have been anathema to doctors for a decade after client access to records became the norm in social work practice, yet here, too, there has been change. The greatest cultural difference now lies in social work's explicit commitment to social justice and its engagement with housing and income issues as they affect clients.

In relation to nursing, this difference of emphasis can be seen in a comparison of the codes of ethics governing the professions. The British Association of Social Workers (BASW) code (BASW, 2012) talks of groups and communities as well as individuals, whereas the Nursing and Midwifery Council (NMC) code (NMC, 2008) is very much focused on the individual. Thus, the BASW code says that social workers should 'work to promote the best interests of individuals and groups in society … and focus on the strengths of individuals groups and communities and thus promote their empowerment'. The NMC code makes no reference to groups and communities except to mention a responsibility 'to work with others to protect and promote the health and wellbeing of those in your care, their families and carers, and the wider community'.

Similarly, the BASW code is much more assertive in relation to social justice, saying that 'social workers have a responsibility to promote social justice in relation to society generally, and in relation to the people with whom they work' and includes reference to challenging discrimination, recognising diversity, distributing resources fairly, challenging unjust policies and procedures and working in solidarity with others to challenge policies that contribute to social exclusion, stigmatisation and subjugation. The NMC code refers to a professional commitment to equality and diversity.

Even allowing for the different styles in which the codes are presented, the difference between the two is striking. One demands an active role of its practitioners in tackling oppression and discrimination throughout society (arguably cast so widely that it is unachievable), while the other views the nurse's relationship with authority as unproblematic and even when patients are put at risk by the working environment limits the responsibility to reporting the problems immediately and in writing to 'someone in authority'.

The GMC guidance is specific in the responsibilities of doctors 'where patients are at risk because of inadequate premises, equipment or other resources, policies and systems you should put the matter right if that is possible. You must raise your concerns in line with our guidance and your workplace policy. You should also make a note of the steps you have taken' (GMC, 2013, para 25b).

The clear distinction between the individual orientation of the health codes and the collective orientation of the social work code is reflected in the way in which the two services are organised. Decision making in local authorities is hierarchical, with the director in theory taking responsibility for all decisions, whereas the tradition in medicine is that GPs and consultants are responsible for their own decisions, and in nursing frontline practitioners have more autonomy in decision making. This is because of the different statutory base of local authority social work, with the chief officer being the accountable individual. Decisions taken by social workers may also involve substantial resource commitments. For example, a decision to take a child into care often has to be referred to more senior levels for agreement because of the financial commitment involved, possibly stretching over many years. This often causes frustration to health colleagues who see only bureaucracy and procrastination when they seek urgent action from their local authority colleagues.

Control

The boundaries between health and social care have shifted over the past 40 years. They are shifting again with the establishment of the Health and Social Care Transformation Fund, which in short succession became the Integration Transformation Fund and then the Better Care Fund. They will continue to change. But all boundary changes are contentious and create winners and losers.

In 1974, responsibility for the medical social worker role shifted from the NHS to local authorities, and over time many workers were moved out of hospitals to undertake health-related social work in community settings. That was resisted by hospitals, which felt a loss of a valued resource from their control. The same legislation – the 1973 NHS Reorganisation Act – took public health medicine out of local authorities and placed it in the NHS. This in turn was regretted by local authorities, which valued the health input to their decisions. This particular boundary shift was reversed in 2013, with equal anxiety expressed by the NHS about the move.

These changes at the margin were significant, but the real issue was one of political control. The direct intervention of politicians in health has always been resisted, although local authorities have had some representation on the ever-changing management structures for health. As the 1979 Royal Commission on the National Health Service noted tartly:

> The evidence we had received tended to divide according to the interest of the organisation concerned; local authorities often argued for local government control of the NHS, and health authorities advocated the absorption by the NHS of the social work services. (Royal Commission on the National Health Service, 1979, para 22.59)

The Commission stopped short of such a radical solution, but noted that joint administration of the two services had its attractions if linked to regional government. Regional government did not become a reality, but the arguments for linking the two services have not gone away and have gained greater currency in the straitened financial circumstances facing both health and social care.

The Northern Ireland experience

In Northern Ireland, the advent of direct rule in 1972 led to a major restructuring of health and social services, drawing the two together under one administrative setting – the Department of Health and Social Services – with services administered at local level by four health and social services boards. The structure was an uneasy mix of a model specific to Northern Ireland with its population of 1.8 million, yet heavily influenced by the changes in England and Wales with the advent of general management, foundation trusts and payment by results. The current position is that health and social care services are delivered through five geographically based health trusts responsible for both acute and community services. These were established in 2006/07, with the inclusion of acute hospitals in the integrated structures. The commissioning responsibility is carried by one body, the Health and Social Care Board for Northern Ireland.

The benefits of the joint management structure proved difficult to realise. Bamford (1990) noted five areas of tension between social services staff and health staff in the integrated structure:

- Client participation in recording reviews and planning sat uneasily with a culture where decisions were taken for patients.
- There was little health care input to social services run residential and day-care facilities.
- There were different attitudes within social services to the display of logos and the virtues of bulk buying.
- Risk taking was seen as an essential element of normalisation by social services working with people with disabilities and with mental health problems but this was alien to health colleagues.
- There were different organisational models for district nursing and health visiting from those used in social care.

A recent review of health and social care in Northern Ireland (Compton, 2011) charts a new direction, drawing heavily on best practice elsewhere. It envisaged a focus on prevention and early intervention, integrated care and the promotion of personalised care to enable support to be provided in the community closer to people's homes where possible. Historically, Ireland, north and south, has relied heavily on hospitals and institutional care to a greater degree than elsewhere in the United Kingdom (the numbers living in nursing homes are three-and-a-half times greater per head of population than in England and Wales). The review signalled the need to reduce the number of acute hospitals and the number of residential care places and to develop integrated care in the community. It commented that 'professionals providing health and social care services will be required to work together in a much more integrated way to plan and deliver care' (Compton, 2011, p 94). Birrell and Heenan note that 'there was little analysis or evaluation of the failings of existing integration but ... implied criticism' (Birrell and Heenan, 2012).

It is worth examining exactly how this is to be achieved. First, the review proposes 17 integrated care partnerships responsible for planning and delivering integrated services that will draw together GPs, community health and social care providers, hospital specialists and representation from the independent and voluntary sector. Second, more specialist care including outpatient appointments will be available in the community. Third, more use will be made of technology, including self-monitoring by people with long-term conditions. Fourth, substantial reductions in inpatient beds will be achieved by allocating home treatment teams to those with mental health problems and providing virtual wards with specialist care at home rather than in hospital.

Taken together, the proposals represent a break with the past legacy of fragmented services backed by a large institutional sector. But one must question whether they will achieve what 35 years of nominally integrated services have failed to achieve. The focus appears to be on bridging the divide between primary and secondary care. The risks for social care identified by Birrell and Heenan include the difficulty in getting resources out of acute care short of closing down buildings, the lack of IT compatibility between health and social care systems, and the likelihood of medical dominance in the new structures with the attendant risk of insufficient attention to developing the user voice in care. They have, however, one major advantage over proposals for integrated care in England and Wales in the single line of accountability to one Health and Social Care Board and one funding stream, so the budgetary imbalances that have crippled social care in England do not apply.

Partners or uneasy bedfellows

Pinker, in his minority dissenting note to the Barclay report, observed that 'when our policy makers reach an intellectual impasse they cover their embarrassment with the figleaf of community' (Barclay, 1982, p 242). Some words, like community, do cast a rosy hue over what follows. Partnership, coordination and integration have similar characteristics. We are all in favour of working together if the alternative is fragmentation and silo working. But why then do partnerships so often founder?

Part of the explanation lies in the overuse of the word in a myriad of different contexts. Glasby and Dickinson (2008) suggest that a sense of added value, reciprocity and a formal and ongoing relationship are some of the criteria that differentiate partnerships from cooperation (although the latter can be valuable in itself).

The enthusiasm for partnerships, some formal and some informal, was a characteristic of New Labour, which from 1997 launched a variety of initiatives outside the formal statutory services. Yet this very fragmentation, accentuated by market-based approaches to public services, quickened the need for partnerships across traditional boundaries. The growth of consumerism placed more emphasis on the rights of service users and the requirement of services to be responsive to consumer needs. This led to consequent targets focused on the front end of access to social care and waiting times for hospital care, both for elective surgery and in accident and emergency. Linked to these was a growing scepticism about the traditional professions and in particular the degree of power exercised by the professions on the way in which care was delivered.

Financial pressures

The separation between local authority social care and healthcare has been accentuated by the very different financial pressures facing the two services. NHS spending went up 66% between 2003 and 2012. In the same period, social services expenditure rose from £15.1 billion to £17.2 billion, an increase of 14% (Health and Social Care Information Centre, 2013), and even that figure is distorted by the transfer of just under £1 billion of Valuing People funds from the NHS to social services in 2010/11.

We have then a situation in which one service, having expanded rapidly, is now facing major efficiency savings just in order to meet demographic pressures within a standstill budget. Social care, having been severely constrained for the past decade, is faced with a requirement to find up to 10% further cuts per year. It is an unpropitious climate in which to talk about integrated care because the financial pressures have thrown up inevitable tensions. Belatedly, the government is recognising that there is a huge overlap between the NHS and adult social care in supporting older people. Sixteen years after Frank Dobson referred to the Berlin Wall between the two, the Treasury recognised the urgency of the problem by announcing in its Spending Review 2013 a transfer of £1.1 billion from the NHS to social care in 2014/15 (increased from £859 million in 2013/14) and creating for 2015/16 a pooled budget of £3.8 billion to establish the Better Care Fund.

As often with central government, this is not all new money. It includes existing carers' break funding, reablement funding for clinical commissioning groups, and capital grant funding including disabled facilities grants. The new money is effectively £1.9 billion – a significant figure in the personal social services context. There are conditions attached – jointly agreed plans, seven-day working in health and social care to address weekend discharges and unplanned admissions, a lead professional for integrated packages of care and protection of social care services. There is a clear risk of cost shunting, with the fund being used to put money back into social care services to plug the gaps left by cuts in funding to meet budget targets set by the Department for Communities and Local Government (DCLG). There is no evidence of joined-up thinking here between the Department of Health and DCLG. The call for integration as the answer has yet to be heard in central government.

The fund is likely to be used where spending on social care will deliver improved outcomes for the NHS in terms of shorter bed stays for older people or enhanced community support preventing hospital admissions. These are worthy objectives, but they are hardly new. There is a long history of attempts by government to promote joint working between the NHS and local authorities, from joint finance introduced in 1982 through joint guidance on priorities for health and personal social services, joint planning mechanisms, health improvement programmes, pooled budgets, joint investment plans, joint strategic needs assessments and, most recently, health and wellbeing boards, with the transfer of the public health function to local authorities (where it resided until 1974). All have shared the objective of getting the two services to work closely together, to share resources and to develop joint plans.

Why has this endeavour failed despite the acknowledgement on all sides that this is essential – even more so at a time of scarce resources? First and fundamental is the different funding structures. Local authorities have annual budget cycles, while the NHS works to a longer budgetary cycle. Second is the political control of local government, which is anathema to the ostensibly politics-free zone of the NHS. Third, the acute sector – hospitals offering a full range of services including accident and emergency services – has historically been the dominant element of the NHS both in terms of expenditure and of public attention. Finally, in the language of priorities, cutting waiting lists and waiting times, and improving surgical outcomes, has always been a higher priority than keeping people out of hospital. The proposed integration fund will still be less than 3% of NHS funding in total.

So there is ground for some scepticism over whether the new initiative will be more successful. It has been buttressed by the publication of a joint commitment from key players – NHS England, the Local Government Association, the leading professional bodies, the regulators and National Voices (a health and care charity coalition) (DH, 2013). This pledges that integration will be the standard model of care by 2018, with pathfinder pilots being in place by 2015 so that lessons can be shared. For those with long memories, it has the flavour of a statement by a former health minister John Hutton, who said that he expected nearly all social care to be delivered by care trusts by 2005 (Hutton, cited in *Community Care*, 2000).

Will the new commitment address the problems of the past? In terms of funding, the ground has shifted from the previous position when NHS funding provided long-term security compared with local government's annual budget cycle. The Spending Review now provides three-year allocations, albeit diminishing year by year, for local government, while NHS allocations are on an annual basis, and, as foundation trust regulator Monitor has observed with studied understatement, an uncertain financial outlook can make it difficult for commissioners to plan and make strategic decisions (Monitor, 2013). Payment by results introduced another element of uncertainty into the finances of provider trusts.

The controls exercised by central government over local government by limiting their ability to raise revenue through increasing the council tax has greatly reduced the potential scope for politics at local level to change priorities as dramatically as in the past. The growing experience of joint working, with councillors involved with primary care trusts and clinical commissioning groups, has also served to diminish the hostility with which the medical profession has historically viewed political involvement.

More significant is the explicit shift in priorities within the NHS. There is a new emphasis on the development of primary and community care, with incentives built into the GP contract that are designed to encourage integrated working.

What do we mean by integrated care?

Integrated care means different things to those working in health than to those in social care, and different things between primary and secondary care. The King's Fund identified 175 different definitions in the literature (Goodwin et al, 2012). Integration was defined in *Integrated care and support: Our shared commitment* by

National Voices from the perspective of the individual as 'being able to plan my care with people who work together to understand me and my carer(s), allow me control and bring together services to achieve the outcomes important to me' (DH, 2013, p 7). This document mirrors much of the material in the Northern Ireland review (Compton, 2011) in its emphasis on ending the institutional divide between physical and mental health, primary and secondary care, and health and social care, and creating person-centred coordinated care and support.

Building care around the individual makes eminent sense, but there are systemic obstacles to achieving this. A review of integrated care (Goodwin et al, 2012) identifies these as follows:

- differences in staff contracts, employment arrangements and payment contribute to problems in achieving multidisciplinary teamwork;
- social care being means tested at the point of access remains a problem for integrated care;
- the NHS culture is risk-averse about local service developments, especially where they threaten the territory of local hospital care.

In addition, a lack of time and resource committed to demonstration sites and the absence of shared electronic patient records continue to impede development. There are also persistent weaknesses in commissioning, with an approach to care services that concentrates on individual providers rather than building partnerships.

Payment by results incentivises acute hospitals to maximise activity and reduce length of stay, which is a win-win situation for the hospitals but a closet transfer of costs to social care and community-based provision by virtue of earlier discharge. The promotion of choice and competition by commissioning from any 'willing provider' further reinforces the focus on individual providers rather than the partnership model best calculated to achieve integrated care.

It is important to distinguish between integrated care and service integration. Hitherto much of the argument between health and social care has been about control because it was focused on management arrangements. Integrated care is focused on the individual patient and building care around that person. Integration at service level does not necessarily require explicit management changes with their accompanying tensions. It does require clear connections and coordination of the service systems serving the individual.

Shaw and colleagues (2011) identify five types of integration:

- systemic, where policies rules and regulatory frameworks are aligned;
- normative, where shared values and cultures are nurtured across professional boundaries;
- organisational, where structures and governance are coordinated, as, for instance, in Northern Ireland's integrated care partnerships;
- administrative, where back-office functions, such as finance and IT, are aligned; and

- clinical, where patient care is integrated in a single process with information and services coordinated.

These are not a hierarchy and indeed different aspects of each type may be present in individual models of integration. They offer a way of thinking conceptually about integration beyond the assertion that it must be a good thing to collaborate in the interests of the patient.

Research on integrated care

The most comprehensive review of research findings on integrated care is set out by the Social Care Institute for Excellence (SCIE) in a research briefing (SCIE, 2011). The results were disappointing. While a number of studies reported positive impact on quality of life and capacity for independent living, it was difficult to find a consistent pattern because of differences in the models of joint working, the arrangements for employment and the scheme design. There was greater consistency in the identification of factors that helped to promote integrated working.
    These included:

- a shared understanding of aims and objectives and involvement of staff in the development of policies and procedures;
- good communication both of the objectives of the project and within the multidisciplinary team;
- clarity about respective roles and responsibilities at every level from strategic management to frontline practitioners.

Some of the factors were obvious but not always achieved, for example, adequate resources to provide back-up in the event of sickness or leave and shared information systems. Co-location of staff and strong professional and management support were important positive factors. Regular inter-professional team meetings were important in addressing the cultural differences that can obstruct progress.
    The factors that hindered joint working were the other side of the coin where no shared aims and objectives were agreed and where there was confusion and lack of clarity about respective roles and responsibilities as well as the procedures to be followed. Organisational problems resulted from different attitudes to risk management (a point previously noted in relation to risk-averse healthcare staff) and even health and safety issues. Confidentiality was sometimes used to justify withholding of information from other professionals. Constant reorganisation and a lack of coterminosity were other negative factors because reorganisation is not a once-and-for-all event but something foreshadowed for years ahead, creating uncertainty and defensiveness, and stifling innovation and creativity.
    The ambiguous nature of the evidence from research was confirmed by the evaluation of 16 integrated care pilot projects (RAND Europe/Ernst and Young

LLP, 2012). The staff involved in the projects were enthusiastic, reporting more interesting jobs and improvements in teamwork and communication. Service users, however, were less enthusiastic, with a marked drop in the percentage who felt involved in decisions about their care.

The study identified six key design features:

- personal – a holistic focus that helps service users and carers to become more independent and manage their own care;
- clinical – multiple referrals channelled to a single entry point with a named care coordinator to provide continuity;
- community – building trust and engagement with the local community to support the care-giving process;
- functional – effective and regular communication between members of the multidisciplinary team;
- organisational – effective targeting of services;
- system – integrated health and social care commissioning to build stability and long-term support.

Social work would be a crucial player in the first three areas: delivering a personal and holistic focus, assuming the role of care coordinator and building community engagement and support.

Two major difficulties identified in the study were, first, the disengagement of GPs, although public policy envisages the central role for them in coordinating the care of people with chronic long-term conditions. The researchers suggest that this may be attributable to their role as independent practitioners, their lack of time, and their distinctive payment model, which puts them outside the wider health and social care system. The second area of difficulty was the lack of integration of these primary care-based studies with secondary care.

Deconstructing integrated care

It is time to deconstruct integrated care and see if we can identify both the reasons for its popularity and whether the current initiative through the Better Care Fund is likely to enjoy more success than its predecessors. The first task is to be clear about what we are seeking to integrate. The fund itself by virtue of its transfer of funds from the NHS to local authorities through transfers from clinical commissioning groups is clearly targeted at the health and social care divide. The likelihood is that the bulk of resources will be spent on older people in an attempt to reduce unplanned admissions and sustain people in their own homes for as long as possible. The definition proffered by National Voices, with its emphasis on allowing the user control and achieving the outcomes important to them, may not always be consistent with the overall policy objectives for the NHS. For example, the priority of maintaining people in their own home may cause disproportionate pressure on carers and relatives.

Second, we should acknowledge that gaps in the care offered arise throughout the care system and not only in the boundary territory between health and social care. In a telling case history, Brand (2012) illustrates the problems facing a 91-year-old widow with a wide range of physical, sensory, mental health and personality problems. There were weaknesses in communication between primary and community services and the hospital, where medical staff relied on their own diagnosis without knowledge of the home situation. There was confusion about the meaning of private care, with hospital staff unaware of the reality that for those with assets above the threshold private residential care was often the only option. There was a division between medical and psychiatric services that obscured the real needs of the patient. And there was little effective communication between ward staff and relatives.

Third, the increasing numbers of older people and those with chronic illnesses poses a problem for healthcare systems in many countries. Shorter hospital stays and a clear user preference for home-based care where possible mean that the links between prevention, home care, social care and palliative care are important.

Fourth, as the Brand example shows, the issue of co-morbidities poses particular problems for services in achieving the seamless care long sought by policymakers and demands adjustments in approach from all professionals.

Finally, putting the service user at the centre of plans and procedures requires a challenging culture shift for many, especially where the expressed preferences of the user are in conflict with medical advice or established procedures.

These factors mean that the quest for integration will continue and will continue to take many forms with no single model of integration likely to deliver the Holy Grail. The example of care trusts is a salutary warning against pursuit of a structural model to achieve integration. The NHS Plan in 2000 proposed the establishment of care trusts to commission and deliver primary and community healthcare as well as social care. This model of integration was trumpeted as the future by the then health minister, John Hutton, who anticipated that 90% of social care would be delivered by care trusts by 2005. In practice, only around 12 care trusts were established, and of these, a number focused exclusively on mental health and social care. Although one trust, Torbay, is often cited as an example of successful integration, the others foundered for a variety of reasons. No formal evaluation of the model was ever carried out so lessons have not been learned.

Work in progress

One detailed study carried out in north-west London is being evaluated in considerable detail. It offers the most comprehensive attempt to secure service integration in the UK by merging services from two acute hospitals, two mental health services, three community health service providers, five local authorities and over 100 GPs to secure coordinated multidisciplinary care for those over 75 and/or with diabetes. The explicit objective was to reduce the level of hospital admissions and to improve quality of life. The savings projected were in excess of £10 million.

The evaluation looked at service cost and utilisation, care processes and intermediate health outcomes, and the quality of patient care. The findings are devastating for those who see integration as the key to unlocking efficiencies, achieving savings and improving the quality of care. Despite the attempt of the researchers to put the best possible gloss on the findings, even taking refuge in the time-honoured plea that the evaluation 'has demonstrated the need for thorough evaluation and research over a long period of time in order to detect impact' (Curry et al, 2012), the message is gloomy on every count.

First, the intervention group did not show any reduction in emergency admissions, accident and emergency attendances, or total inpatient costs. Second, there were few changes in health outcomes, with the exception of an increase in dementia case finding. Third, over half of the patients responding to the survey found no improvement in the quality of patient care, although the study was very popular with patients.

The project initiated a series of multidisciplinary meetings, risk stratification and care planning and reviews to embed a true multidisciplinary approach to care. While the meetings succeeded in drawing together a range of professionals, the researchers found that they tended to be dominated by GPs and consultants.

Despite these findings, it is intriguing to note the presentation of the project elsewhere. On the principle set out by Joseph Heller in *Good as gold* (Heller, 1979), 'nothing succeeds like failure', a larger project is now under way in outer north-west London. The NHS website Right Care (2013) reported that the pilot was found to improve communication and the planning of services. The *British Medical Journal* report on the pilot was headlined 'Integrated care: a story of hard won success' (*British Medical Journal*, 2012). Imperial College London (2013) tells us that 'good progress made in integrated pilot'. Herein lies the problem. We want to believe that collaboration and effective joint working will deliver results. That wish blinds us to the reality that the accumulating evidence from the integrated care pilots and from the north-west London study is that this will not reduce unplanned admissions or accident and emergency admissions. As this is counterintuitive, we need to look elsewhere in the healthcare system for the reasons.

Healthcare has developed as a series of professions. It has a history of increasing specialisation. The general surgeon covering virtually all surgical procedures is now relegated to memory, with professional specialisation driven by the advance of knowledge and of medical technology. Only in the powerful trade unions – the British Medical Association and the Royal College of Nursing – is the major overarching discipline given pride of place. But specialisation inevitably brings with it the possession of exclusive knowledge and skill and a claim to be uniquely qualified to deal with certain kinds of problems. Those claims set up tensions with other professional groups and more so when they do not share the discipline, or as in the case of social workers, approach from a very different perspective.

Multidisciplinary working sounds good but raises the question of whether all the professionals in the team are equal or some are more equal than others. The evaluation in north-west London noted the dominance of GPs and consultants in the multidisciplinary meeting. To a degree this reflects their knowledge derived from long years of training, but it shuts out different perspectives, for example about the social environment to which a social worker or occupational therapist would be able to make a better informed contribution.

The pressures on the NHS mean that success is judged on outputs – reductions in admissions or accident and emergency attendances – rather than outcomes in the longer term. While sceptical about the distorted claims for the north-west London pilot, it may be that in five years' time (if the substantial investment in the project is not aborted) it will show improvements in the quality of care as perceived by patients and better coordination of the services and support needed by older people. But this may have little or no impact on admissions and attendances. Unfortunately, projects that do not cover their costs in terms of savings generated are unlikely to be favoured if quality improvements are the only ones to be delivered.

The New Zealand experience

The importance of taking a long-term view is emphasised in the apparently successful model of integration in the Canterbury Health District in New Zealand (Ham and Timmins, 2013). The outcomes are impressive, with low rates of acute medical admissions, reduced average length of stay, low readmissions rate, fewer cancelled admissions and an increase in elective work with reduced waiting times for elective surgery.

Before looking at how this has been achieved, it is worth noting that these measures of success are all acute care indicators because it is hospitalisation that is both the core of costs in the healthcare system and also the source of inefficiencies in the operation of the system. But addressing the outcomes this effectively would not happen without good liaison with primary care and social care.

In Canterbury, there were two particularly significant factors in the healthcare system – a programme of evidence-based seminars for GPs run by GPs about which medical tests to order and when, and an emphasis from new managers on lean systems to combat a yawning financial crisis. The concept of 'one system, one budget' was used to demonstrate the interconnectedness of a system with a wide range of contractors delivering social care and community nursing services and a medium-sized private sector. Building on this, a graphic design showing the patient at the heart of the joined-up system was used to reinforce the person-centredness of the new approach with a reduction in the time spent by patients waiting, whether for surgery, tests, or outpatient appointments.

Having created the vision, the task was to encourage and help staff and third-party contractors to develop the skills to innovate and to work out new models of contracting. The approach adopted was to engage clinicians, particularly hospital doctors and GPs, in developing health pathways for particular conditions. The pathways would identify the treatments that could be managed in the community and the tests required prior to a referral, as well as where and how GPs could find the resources to support community-based treatment. And the health district changed the basis of funding to budgets built from the base upwards and not contingent on a price and volume tariff. They developed a new model of alliance contracting where delivery on a contract was seen as a joint responsibility between commissioner and contractor and not an adversarial relationship.

Canterbury remains work in progress. The danger is that in the desperation to find a model that works, it will be transplanted wholesale to the very different climate in the UK. It does, however, contain valuable lessons.

It is essential to create a shared vision of change – and, to use Barack Obama's words, change we can believe in. The problem with NHS change is that it has almost invariably been seen in negative terms, involving the loss of buildings and services without any clear benefit to patients. Promoting change in terms of real tangible benefits in waiting times and access would be a powerful message. Second, change is a long-term process and thus unlikely to offer immediate benefits in terms of savings unless accompanied by a root and branch re-examination of budgets from the bottom up. Zero-base budgeting is not a new concept, but is rarely applied because vested interests find it too threatening. Third, in Canterbury the budget for social care was held by the health board, although there were many small providers funded from the budget. Achieving unity of purpose – one system, one budget – is easier in that context than in a system where health and social care are separately funded and separately organised. Fourth, the big gains in the changes in Canterbury came from securing integrated care at primary and secondary care levels. While integrating social care is important in a holistic approach, the significant productivity gains come from addressing the primary–secondary care divide.

So context is important. One important aspect not addressed in the north-west London pilot was the issue of access to primary care. Securing a GP appointment is critical if accident and emergency pressures are to be eased. Yet despite extended GP surgery opening hours, access remains difficult for a same-day appointment even when a caller has circumnavigated the intricacies of the telephone system (sometimes adding significantly to their bill). In these circumstances, many prefer the guarantee of being seen within four hours at accident and emergency. The lack of continuity in primary care with locums and group practices in urban areas means that who you see is no less of a lottery in a general practice than in a hospital.

The difficulties should not lead us to abandon the quest for the integration of care. It is a plea to recognise that this is not a simple or easy solution and is unlikely to lead to cost savings in the short to medium term. Successful partnership working to deliver quality care requires shared values and agreement about desired outcomes (which need to be modest and realistic). It requires a commitment to share confidential information across professional boundaries. It must involve patients from the outset, in securing both their consent and their understanding of the innovative aspects of the new approach.

AREAS FOR DISCUSSION

Have the policy goals within the Department of Health changed since joint finance was introduced?

Can you identify difficulties in achieving integration other than those listed in the text?

As a policymaker, what would you prioritise – the integration of health and social care, or of primary and secondary care? Describe what you would hope to achieve by integration.

FURTHER READING

The King's Fund is an invaluable source of current material on integrated care in Britain and elsewhere. It is realistic about the financial pressures driving integration and the limited evidence thus far that savings will result. It produces a regular bulletin on integrated care. The relevant materials, including a map of integrated care projects, can be found at www.kingsfund.org.uk/projects/integrated-care-making-it-happen.

The difficulty at an individual level in achieving even basic coordination is clearly described in Brand, D. (2012) 'Social and health care integration: the individual dimension', *Journal of Integrated Care*, vol 20, no 6, pp 371-8.

International perspectives are helpful. Goodwin, N., Dixon, A., Anderson, G. and Wodchis, W. (2014) *Providing integrated care for people with complex needs*, London: King's Fund, warns that integrated organisations do not necessarily lead to integrated care.

The final cautionary tale comes from the *National Evaluation of the Department of Health's Integrated Care Pilots* (2012) Rand Europe, Ernst and Young, for Department of Health, again demonstrating the difficulty of going beyond the rhetoric of joined-up care.

NINE

Social work and devolution

KEY LEARNING POINTS
»   Scotland has had a separate legislative and organisational framework for nearly 50 years
»   Northern Ireland has had an integrated health and social care system for over 40 years
»   Free personal care in Scotland has policy implications for the rest of the UK
»   Child protection issues have scarred each country in the UK

The separate identities of the four countries of the United Kingdom have become more distinctive with devolution. Scotland has always has its own legislative framework. Northern Ireland, partly because of its size and partly because of its long period of direct rule, has developed a distinctive model of integrated health and social care. The Northern Ireland form of integration differs from any on offer in the current discussion of integrated care. Wales, since the creation of the Assembly, has begun to develop its own institutions. It is alone among the four countries in having an organisational model in which social care is the responsibility of a number of very small authorities.

It is important to understand the reasons for these separate structures and the degree to which social work has been affected by devolution.

Scotland

Scotland owes its very different approach to children in trouble to the Kilbrandon report (1964) subsequently implemented in large measure in the 1968 Social Work (Scotland) Act. The Committee on Children and Young Persons, Scotland, chaired by Lord Kilbrandon, took a broad view of the topic, covering not only delinquency but also those in need of care and protection, persistent truants and those beyond parental control. The solution proposed was to remove all those under 16 from criminal proceedings and institute a system of children's hearings before a lay panel of three people. The hearings would be reasonably informal, would encourage the participation of young people and their families, and would look for a solution in the best interests of the young person. The reporter to the panel would play a key role in determining which cases went forward to the panel and which were dealt with elsewhere.

The system has been criticised by those who see it as a soft option. In 1980, proposals to introduce a more punitive element into the system were rejected. The lack of any entitlement to formal legal representation has also been criticised, but it is hard to see how the necessarily adversarial approach of legal representation would sit comfortably with the informality and participatory ethos of the hearings.

Despite various refinements, the basic structure of the children's hearings remains and is regarded a cornerstone of the progressive approach to social welfare in Scotland. It is curious that no other country in the UK has sought to experiment with such a system. This may reflect the influence in England of the tabloid press, where headlines about juvenile offenders out of control still carry potency.

The decisions taken in 1968 meant that criminal justice also came into the ambit of social work departments, so no separate probation service existed. In practice, courts became increasingly concerned about the resource pressures on criminal justice, with the introduction of new orders like community service and post-discharge supervision. In 1989, criminal justice services, while remaining located in social work departments, were directly funded from central government with the funding ring-fenced for criminal justice. National standards were introduced, with increasing emphasis on risk management, public protection and 'what works' paralleling developments in probation in England. With the exception of electronic tagging, services have not yet been outsourced to the private sector to the same degree, although the current proposals to outsource work to payment-by-results providers will also apply in Scotland.

The organisation of community care in Scotland was also reformed in the 1968 Social Work (Scotland) Act. The noteworthy feature here is the inclusion of the words 'social work' in the main title of the Act. In England, it was to be the 1970 Local Authority Social Services Act. Although the two pieces of legislation were broadly parallel in giving social care responsibilities to local authorities, Scotland had many small local authorities and there was an imbalance between the small local authorities on the one hand, and the two large ones (Edinburgh and Glasgow) on the other. The decision was made to move to regional authorities in 1975, creating in the process the largest social work authority in Europe – Strathclyde – serving two-and-a-half million people. These authorities lasted 21 years before another round of local government reorganisation.

Strathclyde's former director of social work, Fred Edwards, was a great leader of the massive new department. In 1984, he used powers under the Social Work (Scotland) Act to make direct payments in cash and kind to families of miners experiencing great hardship during the miners' strike. This was not popular with the Scottish Office and he was threatened with being personally surcharged for these payments. He persisted with the support of the council and survived without being surcharged.

The tensions between Westminster and Scotland illustrated by that episode and the rise of the Scottish National Party were eventually to lead to devolution and the creation of a Scottish Parliament in 1999. That change has had a profound impact on social care provision in Scotland through the introduction of free personal care for older people both in their own homes and in care homes. This was analysed in detail by the Joseph Rowntree Foundation (Bell and Bowes, 2006). While residents still had to meet the board and lodging element of care costs, the policy was popular, especially in relation to free home care. The provision of this care did not have the predicted impact on the level of support received from informal carers. It increased equity and fairness, especially for those of modest means, and further blurred the dividing line between health and social care that has so bedevilled policymaking in this area in England. But – and there always is a 'but' – the cost was greater than anticipated and has raised concern about the sustainability of the policy.

The cost of providing free personal and nursing care was estimated at 10% of total spending on care for older people by individuals, local authorities and the NHS. The review concluded that the model was an exemplar for the rest of the UK, but differences in funding social care costs meant that it was not easy to transplant directly.

The Scottish Government commissioned an independent review of the costs of long-term care, which drew on demographic projections and shifts in the balance of care and concluded that the costs of care were likely to increase by 4.4% a year, with the demographic pressures of the increasing number of those over 75 being the most significant factor in the increase. The £2.3 billion cost in 2005/06 was projected to rise to £3.3 billion in 2016 and £4.1 billion by 2021 (Sutherland, 2008).

The latest available figures show an interesting division between residential care and home care costs, with free personal care decreasing as a share of residential care costs from 20.3% to 17.3% between 2003/04 and 2010/11 but the element of home care costs increasing from 59.3% to 84.1% in the same period (Scottish Government, 2012). This clearly reflects public policy throughout the UK of seeking to care for people in their own homes for as long as possible. The question is whether the political will exists to meet the costs of that care and whether other parts of the UK will emulate the Scottish example.

These two distinctive features of social policy have had a major impact on the development of social work. The financial assessment that has been so important in England is less relevant when care is assessed exclusively on the basis of need. The children's hearings system, with its emphasis on participation, is more progressive than in England. But social work in Scotland has also been scarred by child protection issues. The Clyde report (1992) into the removal of children from the Orkney island of South Ronaldsay was highly critical of the way in which social workers had conducted interviews with the children. A decade later an inspection report into the abuse of three children in the Western Isles (SWIA, 2005) painted a grim picture of a lack of coordination and poor decision making between agencies. Both social work practitioners and managers and health professionals were criticised in the report.

A 21st-century review of social work (Scottish Government, 2006) was commissioned by ministers to take a fundamental look at social work to strengthen its contribution to the delivery of integrated services. The link with integration in the review's remit was a response to some criticism from health services about the commitment of social work services to integration – a reprise of the Berlin Wall and blocked beds arguments in England discussed in Chapter Eight. The review was specifically asked to consider whether social work was a single profession or whether it had become so specialised that it formed a number of similar but distinctive professions. On this the review was unequivocal: 'we concluded that it is, and should remain, a single generic profession, underpinned by a common body of knowledge skills and values' (Scottish Government, 2006, p 27). It addressed the issue of growing specialisation by arguing that the core skills were equally relevant in different settings. This conclusion is highly relevant to the debates in England about the creation of specialist training for children's services.

Research conducted specifically for the review in criminal justice and in work with older people identified three consistent elements in effective interventions – empathy, respect, warmth and therapeutic genuineness; establishing a relationship with agreement about the purpose of intervention; and a person-centred collaborative approach using the client's perspective and concepts. This is particularly interesting as the managerial emphasis on outcomes and processes in adult care in England is at odds with the emphasis on the therapeutic relationship so clearly endorsed here.

The review went on to recommend a tiered approach to the delivery of social work, with tier 1 being direct work with people and their families with complex unpredictable long-term needs and risks, tier 2 being early intervention with people where there was a high level of vulnerability and risk, tier 3 being advice and support to other professionals delivering targeted services, and tier 4 being prevention and community capacity building.

It recommended much greater professional autonomy but within a framework of clear accountability. It suggested that the reliance on tiers of management as a mechanism for quality control created only risk-averse practice. Once again, one can see a clear comparison with the recommendations of the Social Work Task Force and the Munro report in England, both calling for greater autonomy for practitioners.

The culture change sought by the review was for a more highly skilled and supported social work profession delivering personalised services, but one that embraced the need for change and accountability. The extent to which the changes envisaged by the review will be embedded into practice is still unclear, as the impatience to achieve integration, and the assumed savings flowing from that, have led to legislative solutions. The 2014 Public Bodies (Joint Working) (Scotland) Act was designed to drive the integration agenda. It required councils and health boards to set up an integration board with a budget managed by a chief officer accountable to both bodies. This has now been overtaken by plans to integrate adult health and social care through partnerships working towards nationally agreed outcomes.

The pressure on acute hospitals and the need for better community support are the drivers for change, but the evidence from England of joint appointments of directors of adult social services and chief executives of primary care trusts is not wholly encouraging, as few such appointments have been sustained for more than a couple of years. The criticism of the audit of community health partnerships – the existing delivery mechanism for integrated care – remains valid:

- a cluttered partnership landscape of overlapping partnership boards and collaborative arrangements;
- cultural differences between healthcare and local government in planning, performance measures and financial controls;
- a lack of understanding of the degree of change needed to achieve integration (Audit Scotland, 2011).

Responding to this critique, the Scottish Government decided to establish new bodies – health and social care partnerships – to achieve integrated health and social care, with a focus on prevention, anticipation and supported self-management. There was emphasis on ensuring that people got back into their home or community environment as soon as appropriate, with minimal risk of readmission. (This goal is similar to that espoused in England, but has a major advantage in delivery because of the provision of free personal care [Scottish Government, 2011a].) Scotland has contributed greatly to the development of social work from the days of Thomas Chalmers discussed in Chapter One. Its politicians often come through the ranks of local government and are familiar with the issues and tensions facing social work. Its brave endorsement of free personal care is a necessary first step in securing integrated health and social care. Although many of the instruments of regulation – the Scottish Social Services Council and the Care Inspectorate (formerly Social Care Social Work Improvement Scotland) – are similar to those in England, they have not attracted the same level of criticism that has led to the enforced departure of chief executives in England.

Size does matter. One benefit of devolution lies in the personal relationships built up over several years between the key players in the field. Being able to pick up the phone and say to a minister, "We have a problem here" is important in promoting a shared approach to resolution of difficulties. The issue of scale makes a difference. Until recently, both Northern Ireland and Wales had a disproportionate number of administrative units for their population in contrast to the regional administrations in Scotland.

Northern Ireland

In Chapter Eight, we noted that health and social services have been integrated in Northern Ireland since 1973. The initial decision was one of political expediency rather than high principle because local government had been tarnished by a long history of sectarianism. Between 1973 and 2009, health and social services were delivered by four area boards and a mix of acute hospitals and community health and social services (trusts from 1989).

Until 1990, there were separate management lines for health and social services, although social services were part of the area management team and of the management teams in the geographical units. Working there between 1985 and 1990 was a rich but sometimes puzzling experience. I found that my working assumptions about care close to home in smaller units for the mentally ill and mentally handicapped were not universally shared. The arguments had to be won all over again. I came to appreciate the importance of familiarity and location in the care of older people when attempting to close a home for older people located in a former workhouse with four residents to each room. I appreciated the intimacy of working in a small population where one knew the permanent secretary, the lord chief justice and all the key players in health and social services and could be invited to dinner at Stormont to discuss pending legislation with a government minister. Scale and the opportunity that gives for personal relationships are important factors, as observed earlier, in helping to resolve differences.

But what was very clear at that time was the historic over-reliance of the health and social care system on institutions retaining large psychiatric hospitals and learning disability hospitals long after the transition to community-based care in England. The dominance of the acute sector meant that transfer of resources was difficult when one was arguing for increased investment in home care against a new neonatal unit. And in healthcare, particularly, evidence-based decision making is always out-trumped by localism, so a small maternity unit dealing with 50 births a year will be fiercely defended in the face of professional opinion.

The troubled politics of Northern Ireland had one impact on health and social services. Despite the theoretical opportunity to try new models of service delivery through integration, Heenan notes that 'the default position was to copy English policy changes ... stability was the key priority and social and public policy reform was generally sidestepped by direct rule politicians' (Heenan, 2013, p 11).

This continued after the creation of the Northern Ireland Assembly, with the health and social services portfolio being little sought after despite its substantial budget. Sinn Fein was allocated the portfolio as the least desirable, creating the irony that the key social welfare services with the largest budgets – health, education and social services – were all administered by Sinn Fein ministers while the Unionists controlled the key economic portfolios. In a bid to streamline services, the board and trusts structure was replaced in 2009 by one health and social care board for Northern Ireland and five commissioning groups coterminous with five health and social care trusts responsible for service delivery. The board, through the commissioning groups, is responsible for commissioning services, but the trusts provide them on the ground, managing a mix of acute provision and community services. But the efficiencies resulting from the structure did not address the long-standing over-reliance on the acute sector.

The Compton review, commissioned by a new minister of health, sought to do that with a radical vision for the future (Compton, 2011). It called for a reduction in the number of acute hospitals from 10 to between five and seven, a shift of care from hospital to the community and a shift of funding from the acute sector, and the development of personalised care. The ministerial response was the creation of integrated care partnerships to be established in 17 areas and led by GPs responsible for planning and delivering integrated services across the range of community health and social care providers, hospital specialists, GPs and the independent and voluntary sector.

These partnerships seem difficult to justify, and it is unclear how they will relate to the commissioning function of the board. More worryingly, they threaten to undermine the shift in the model of care indicated by the Compton review by giving primacy to a model of care that looks to health indicators rather than a social model of care. Heenan notes that 'the plans may create a very unequal relationship between health and social care.…The Plans for the implementation of Transforming your Care pay little attention to the modernisation agendas for adult social care as developed in England, Scotland and Wales. The theme of user involvement and user control is largely ignored' (Heenan, 2013, p 12). Northern Ireland, then, is far from being a utopia of integrated care, despite its long history of nominal integration. It represents something of a missed opportunity to try different models but it is a salutary reminder that the search for integrated care has to go beyond structural change and has to embrace a social model of care if it is to deliver the gains anticipated.

Wales

Devolution has had a major impact on health and social care policy in Wales. The country has consistently been led by a Labour administration, either in coalition or ruling as a minority government. Unlike the Westminster parliament, which has endorsed market principles in healthcare even under Labour, the Welsh Labour Party has rejected quasi markets and competition in public services. Social services are delivered through 22 local authorities, several of which have populations under 100,000. Local health boards, initially coterminous with local authorities, were responsible for planning and delivery of health services but proved unable to deal effectively with with major secondary and tertiary care providers. They have now been reduced to seven boards responsible for planning and delivering services with no purchaser–provider split.

As a result of Welsh government policy social services have been partially protected against the impact of the cuts in local government expenditure. Together with the remodelled health boards, social services are seen as having a key role in the development of integrated care. A new legislative framework for social care is contained in the 2014 Social Services and Well-being (Wales) Act, which, in addition to duties in relation to direct payments and self-directed support, and to carers, is significant in the inclusion within the title of the Act of the word 'wellbeing'. It requires the government to establish a performance measurement framework for wellbeing. It requires local authorities 'to promote the integration of care and support with health and health-related provision with a view to improving wellbeing, prevention and raising quality'.

Wales, under different political control from the Westminster government, has been used in arguments about the NHS to demonstrate the superiority of the English reforms, with delays in patient discharge from Welsh hospitals being seen as evidence of its failure to adapt. Higher levels of expenditure in Wales are said to produce worse health outcomes. The paucity of comparative information, and different ways of measuring even something that sounds simple, such as delayed discharges, complicate the argument and obscure the truth. In addition, crude comparisons of a single indicator do not take into account the impact of deprivation.

Social work in Wales has suffered from the small size of many local authorities, and this is reflected in the dubious quality of management and supervision. The majority of authorities have remained providers of both adult and children's services unlike the legislative separation in England. Progress to cross-border provision of specific services has been patchy and the new Act includes provision for regional consortia in relation to adoption services. The chief inspector's annual report (CSSI, 2012) commented that inspections in 2011/12 showed 'a stark variability of performance' not altogether explicable in terms of different economic and social situations. For example, the number of looked-after children in Wales in 2011/12 was 50% higher than in England, despite the figures being similar in 1998.

As elsewhere, child protection concerns have cast a long shadow over social work in Wales. Child abuse in children's homes in north Wales has been the subject of numerous inquiries, such as the Jillings report, the Waterhouse inquiry, and more recently, Operation Pallial, launched by the police to investigate allegations of abuse at 18 different children's homes over a 30-year period. The Jillings report in 1994 was hampered by a complete lack of cooperation by North Wales Police and the reluctance of Clwyd council to cooperate under pressure from its insurers. It was finally published in redacted form in 2013 (Jillings, 2013). The Waterhouse inquiry, led by a high court judge, lasted three years and cost £12 million. It found evidence of widespread sexual abuse but no evidence of a 'widespread conspiracy involving prominent persons and others with the purpose of sexual activity with young people in care' (Waterhouse, 2000). These allegations of a well-connected paedophile ring continued to surface periodically and BBC's Newsnight programme subsequently repeated the allegations in the wake of the Jimmy Savile furore. The fall-out – and the naming on Twitter of an innocent Conservative former minister in connection with the allegations – cost the director general of the BBC, George Entwistle, his job. Operation Pallial was already under way and has led to a number of arrests.

What is striking about this episode is the length of time taken to bring perpetrators to justice, the ambivalent attitude of the police in the early stages of the Jillings inquiry, and the concern of the insurers and their bullying tactics to control the local authority response in relation to Jillings. Discerning the truth when powerful agencies are seeking to obscure it is a difficult task. The impact of these allegations is still being felt over 25 years after whistleblower Alison Taylor first reported child abuse allegations to North Wales Police.

One of the recommendations from Waterhouse was the appointment of a children's commissioner, an initiative subsequently followed by the other countries of the UK. The commissioners have used the UN Convention on the Rights of the Child as the basis for their work. In Wales, the government formally adopted the convention as a basis for policymaking for children and young people. In 2011, the Rights of Children and Young Persons (Wales) Measure placed a duty on all Welsh ministers to have due regard to the rights and obligations within the convention. Now ministers have to have due regard for the convention in respect of all their ministerial responsibilities.

Having established the Care Council for Wales, the Welsh government is moving ahead with plans for a National Institute for Care and Support, which will serve both as an improvement agency for social care services as well as regulator of the profession. This will involve a major reorganisation of existing responsibilities, with the former acting as regulator for social care professionals and the latter for service provision.

Wales has one other feature that differentiates it from other counties in the UK. The current health minister, Mark Drakeford, is a social worker and prior to his election to the Welsh Assembly was Professor of Social Policy and Applied Social Sciences at Cardiff University. While there are a number of former social workers in both the Scottish and English parliaments, no other has risen to a senior ministerial rank.

AREAS FOR DISCUSSION

Why has there been so little cross-fertilisation between social work and social care given the variation of practice within both fields?

What lessons from the other UK countries could usefully be applied in England?

Can you sketch a model of organisation from the four countries that would facilitate good social work?

TEN

Social work in a changing world

Thirty-five years ago the polemic by Brewer and Lait (1980) posed the question, 'Can social work survive?'. It has, and, despite a variety of assaults and criticism it has grown substantially, at least numerically, in the intervening period. But numbers tell only a partial story. The picture developed in the previous chapters is one of the progressive marginalisation of social work as a profession. The two case studies of mental health and probation in Chapter Seven show how swiftly social work can move from an established and recognised role to one on the margins of an occupational setting, or one redefined away from rehabilitation.

The challenge to social work

Although this move from a secure established position is at an earlier stage in other branches of social work than in probation, it would be rash to ignore the reality that there are a number of negative indicators. In both mental health and adult care, we have seen the development of a whole range of occupational groups taking on roles formerly fulfilled by social workers – support workers, social care workers, social work assistants and social service workers. While the designation varies, the aim is to use workers with a lower level of formal qualifications (or none) and thus at a lower pay grade to undertake some of the less complex work formerly undertaken by social workers.

Training, although now at degree level, is being challenged in two ways. First, there is a question mark over whether an integrated social work programme remains desirable in the light of the current specialist service model. This dilemma is exemplified by the appointment of separate chief social workers for adult care and for children's services, and in the separately commissioned reviews of social work education for children and adults. This goes to the heart of social work as an internationally recognised profession. Second, the adequacy of training was questioned by the Social Work Task Force (2009). Despite the changes in training since then, the issue of whether it is fit for purpose remains unresolved. Short cuts to competence like the Step up to Social Work programme and Frontline offer alternative models.

A more reductionist, checklist-based approach to practice has developed both in adult social care and in children's services. Such an approach was robustly criticised in the context of children's services by the Munro report, but her words are equally applicable to the assessment process in adult services:

> Too much prescription of practice, which diminishes professional responsibility for judgements and decisions, has an unintended

consequence of reducing the job satisfaction, self esteem and sense
of personal responsibility experienced by child protection workers.
(Munro, 2011, Appendix A, p 140)

Her report went on to associate this with increases in staff absence and sickness
rates, and increases in staff turnover rates, with the consequent increase in caseload
sizes further reinforcing the problems experienced by staff. The rigidity of the
integrated children's system and the use of time limits in assessment and now in
adoption show that these lessons have not yet been learned.

In adult care, thresholds are now so high that despite the rhetorical commitment,
prevention has little part to play unless as a justification for the withdrawal of
services. The organisational model of local authority departments is called into
question by the concept of social work practices organised like GP practices and
the increasing numbers of independent social workers. A more immediate threat
comes from the calls for integration with health, which are at present focused on
adult care rather than the poisoned chalice of child protection. The profession
itself is unable to speak with a clear voice, divided as it is by the respective claims
of the British Association of Social Workers (BASW) and the College of Social
Work. This is not a sound basis for progress.

A statement of confidence in the future of social work, given this unpromising
environment, requires justification. There are three main stands to this confidence
– the international nature of social work and its increasing influence at a global
level, the increasing recognition of the need for professional support and self-
development (shown in the membership growth of the two rival professional
bodies), and the resilience and innovation shown by social work practice at a time
of extreme organisational and financial pressure.

An international profession

Social work is not a peculiar Anglo-American invention drawing on a mix of
sociology, psychology, psychiatry to establish itself. It is a worldwide profession,
with over 90 national associations of social workers maintaining membership of
the International Federation of Social Workers (IFSW). It is strong and growing
in Latin and South America. It has developed rapidly in China, drawing heavily
on assistance initially from Australia and New Zealand and latterly from Southeast
Asia. As in the UK, social workers in other countries work in many different
settings. In Africa, much work that we might categorise as social development
work is undertaken by social workers operating with communities and groups
to secure food supplies, basic nutrition and environmental protection.

The European Union and the Council of Europe play significant roles in
promoting social development. The Technical Assistance to the Commonwealth
of Independent States programme has been an important funder of social
development projects in the emergent states in eastern Europe. The Russian
European Trust has been a valuable link between Russia and some English local

authorities, and has assisted in social services developments in several regions of Russia. These international links are an expression of how highly valued has been the experience of the UK and other western European countries in social work and social development elsewhere.

This process has been helped by the underlying values of social work. In particular, self-determination has been crucial because what applies at an individual level has also to apply at a national level. There is no one off-the-shelf model that can be transplanted on foreign soil. Each country has to adapt social work principles and practice in its own cultural context.

Yet there has been recent agreement at international level on a global agenda for social work and social development by three international bodies – the International Association of Schools of Social Work, the International Council of Social Welfare and IFSW. This global agenda sets the three organisations the task of promoting social and economic equalities through the United Nations and other international bodies, and promoting strong communities able to engage effectively with social development. Adopting the core ethical principle of the worth of each individual, it stresses diversity by emphasising the rights of migrants, the evils of human trafficking and the adoption of human rights principles. It talks of social integration and the importance of promoting wellbeing through sustainable human relationships.

At one level, this type of approach is vulnerable to the criticism levelled at many international documents of being one of motherhood and apple pie rather than one of engaging with the gritty realities of social workers' daily practice. However, securing the agreement of three autonomous international bodies is a considerable achievement in itself. More significantly, it establishes social work's role in development. With the Millennium Development Goals coming to an end in 2015, a new set of goals and targets is likely to be developed. Recognition of the part social work can play in addressing those targets is a step forward for the profession.

The international definition of social work has been widely adopted and is commendably brief. It is was sharply criticised by Narey in his review of social work training (Narey, 2014) as 'thoroughly inadequate'. The review went on to call for:

> ... a more satisfactory and relevant definition ... that concentrates on that work, generally carried out in the statutory sector, which is about protecting children. We need a definition which makes plain what Government, employers and the College of Social Work expect from children's social workers. (Narey, 2014, p 13)

A revised definition adopted in Melbourne after years of consultation in 2014 states:

Social work is a practice-based profession and an academic discipline that promotes social change and development, social cohesion, and the empowerment and liberation of people. Principles of social justice, human rights, collective responsibility and respect for diversities are central to social work. Underpinned by theories of social work, social sciences, humanities and indigenous knowledge, social work engages people and structures to address life challenges and enhance wellbeing.

This definition may be amplified at national and/or regional levels. (International Definition of Social Work [IFSW, 2014])

This too clearly fails the Narey test. Quite how an international definition can be expected to provide a job description for a small part of social work practice in one country is a task I suspect would be beyond even Sir Martin Narey. The narrowness of his viewpoint is exposed by his reference to protecting children, which is part, but should not be the only part, of social work with children. His alignment of the College of Social Work with employers and government is telling, since the thrust of his argument is hostile to anti-oppressive practice and to any social work engagement with social change and social justice.

The international dimension has not figured in the discussion of the proposed fast-track training programmes. Indeed, it is dismaying to see how little regard has been paid to the cross-border issues in the UK in developing such courses. It is uncertain whether the regulators in the other countries of the UK will recognise the fast-track qualifications such as Frontline and Step up to Social Work, although the mobility of social workers possessing a professional qualification has been one of the attractions of the profession. It is even more uncertain whether the qualifications will be recognised internationally.

The international credibility of social work will not in itself stop ministers from taking decisions that further fragment the profession in the UK – or at least in England, as the other countries of the UK may not follow. But it should give them pause before embarking on a policy of separate development and separate training for children's and adult services. Such a division would also pose major problems for the Health and Care Professions Council, the current regulator that governs recognition of overseas qualifications in England.

A divided profession

The row between the College of Social Work and BASW discussed in Chapter Three was damaging to social work. Two bodies that should have worked together in the interests of the profession engaged in a protracted slanging match. The task for the leaders of both organisations is now to find a way to complement their activities rather than to be competitive.

The position today is that the College exists only in England. It is heavily dependent on government funding provided to support the roll-out of the work of the Social Work Reform Board. Wales briefly flirted with the idea of merging its regulatory council with the responsibility for care improvement and designating the new body the College for Social Work and Social Care in Wales, but backed off because of the confusion this would cause. BASW, which many had assumed would be fatally weakened by the stand-off with the College, has forged ahead with the establishment of the Social Workers Union to safeguard its position in representing its members.

How can one take encouragement from this gloomy story? First, the increasing numbers joining BASW and the College – currently over 30,000 combined, even allowing for some who are members of both – indicates a growing professional identification among social workers. Whether motivated by professional self-protection in uncertain times or by the need for validation of academic courses, social workers are identifying themselves as professionals rather than by virtue of their setting. The fragmentation of social work employment with the growth of independent social workers and agency workers and the increasing volume of social work delivered by the private and voluntary sector has served to strengthen professional identity as social workers no longer see local authority employment as their natural home.

Second, after the angry words exchanged between BASW and College representatives at the time of the breakdown in 2012, a period of relative calm is welcome. This provides an opportunity for quiet reflection on the best way forward for social work. The two organisations have to find a *modus vivendi* if they are to survive as independent but complementary bodies.

Third, the pause allows the other three countries of the UK to consider their position and decide if the college model has any attractions for them, bearing in mind the substantial costs involved in setting up any new body. The Narey report (2014) suggested that the College might take on the role of regulator in England. In Wales, the government announced plans to establish the National Institute for Care and Support.

At a time of straitened resources, the working assumption is that cost savings may result from merging functions in this way. Working as an improvement agency is, however, a different task from that of regulation.

The one thing on which both reviews of social work education agree is the parlous state of some social work education with underqualified entrants and inadequate preparation for practice. The College is well placed to play an important role in quality control of courses and ensuring that best practice is incorporated into social work programmes. It is also well placed to develop thinking and offer guidance on the best use of professionals. Its recent paper (Allen, 2014) is a useful illustration of this role and secured high-level ministerial endorsement.

The College has, however, yet to establish itself as an independent body. Its membership growth has been as a result of corporate membership rather than individual subscribers. It has to demonstrate that it can champion the social work profession and be appropriately critical of government initiatives when they are not founded on solid evidence.

BASW too has a role to play in developing thinking about the profession. Its international links mean that it is best placed to lead work on the definition of social work and on ethical codes, both of which have been developed by the IFSW. It should do so in conjunction with the College. BASW has had a code of ethics for 40 years based on the IFSW code, yet the College decided to launch its own code of ethics. This decision was as misguided as the commissioning of two separate reviews of social work education by two separate government departments.

As an organisation dependent on the subscriptions of its members, BASW has greater freedom to be critical of government policy and its impact on the clients of social workers than does the College, which derives the bulk of its income from government grants. It needs to demonstrate that independence. As devolution becomes more significant with a divergence of policies and practice affecting social workers, BASW as a UK-wide body is able to draw out the strengths of different approaches and promote the cross-fertilisation of ideas in a way that eludes the governments of the four countries in the UK.

BASW's success in recruiting members has in part been driven by job insecurity. This has meant that membership services, including representation, have been the driver for the increase in membership rather than a wider interest in BASW's ability to develop professional practice or influence social policy. If it is to take on this role, BASW will need to raise its skill level, both in terms of policy analysis and political influence.

The way in which the College and BASW have moved on from the initial breakdown in relations suggests that the two organisations could fulfil complementary roles. That will require maturity from both and a willingness to see that working in concert will best serve the interests of social work.

Social work practice

The Munro review of child protection (Munro, 2011) was greeted with enthusiasm by social workers. It spoke for the profession in stressing the importance of the judgement of social workers and the discretion that they exercised. This was a contrast to the increasing bureaucratisation of social work dominated by checklists, procedures and protocols progressively reducing the task of social workers to an almost mechanistic exercise. It is important to understand that these procedures were not a malign attempt to strangle the profession in pursuit of a neoliberal agenda. They had developed over time in response to the childcare failures discussed in Chapter Three. Each inquiry report that followed these failures contained a litany of recommendations. The great majority were accepted. Some led to changes in legislation. Some were incorporated in guidance. Tim Loughton as children's minister noted that *Working together*, the Department for Education's guidance on inter-agency working in child protection had mushroomed from 72 pages in 1988 to 371 pages in 2010. The most recent iteration of the guidance on child protection has reversed the trend, producing guidance totalling 95 pages (DfE, 2013a).

In his report on the death of Victoria Climbié, Laming noted that 'the problem is less about the ability of staff to read and understand guidelines, and more about the huge and dense nature of material provided for them' (Laming, 2003, p 12). Brian Clough, the legendary football manager, was once asked for the secrets of his team's success and replied, 'Doing the simple things well'; Lord Laming similarly called for a social work practice that did relatively straightforward things well. While his recommendations for structural change were eagerly embraced, no changes in practice ensued. The government's enthusiasm for computer-based systems led to the integrated children's system, which was a major factor in creating a world in which social workers spent more time on the computer screen than engaging directly with clients. The deficiencies of this policy were devastatingly analysed by White and colleagues (2010).

As part of the consultation on the revisions to the Working together guidance, the Department of Health allowed a small number of local authorities to try out a more flexible approach, freed from the rigidities of the timetables governing initial and core assessments. Their orders giving these flexibilities had eight pages of conditions– eloquent testimony to how hard it is for the central government to relax its attempt to micro-manage the system.

The checklist approach criticised by Munro is also to be found in adult social care, where the rigid application of eligibility criteria has been used as a gatekeeping mechanism to control costs. It has become increasingly difficult to pinpoint the particular contribution social work can make in adult care. Various roles have been suggested, including support brokering, help with self-directed assessment, responsibility for adult safeguarding, and even (ironically, given what one might argue is the profession's raison d'être) direct practice with individuals. If the new model of care is about extending the choice and control available to service users, clients may wish to break free from the straitjacket of using local authority or – in the case of personal health budgets – NHS staff as their source of support in brokering a care plan. The shift from professional assessment of needs to user-directed assessment poses challenges to the traditional professional role. Adult safeguarding is an area where social work is seen as having a role partly because the safeguarding role in child protection is disproportionately ascribed to social workers. While there will be a limited number of individuals likely to benefit from social work help in maximising their potential, such a service is not readily available in the current configuration of services.

Service users prefer brokerage and advocacy systems independent of the local authority. They view social workers as divided in their responsibilities of support to the client and their gatekeeping role in relation to funding care (Leese and Leese, 2011). The future role of social work in adult care is far from clear. Already in pursuit of cost savings, some authorities are using care assistants in adult assessment and care management instead of social workers (*Professional Social Work*, April 2014, p 7).

Social work practices and reclaiming social work

There are two interesting examples of attempts to break out of this straightjacket of prescription. The first is the experiment with social work practices. The genesis of this idea was the replication for social workers of the model used for general practitioners – a group practice of social workers with complementary skills operating independently of statutory services. The pilots started in 2008 and in total 15 local authorities have participated in the scheme at some time. The evaluation of the pilots (DfE, 2012) indicated that they had failed to achieve the results originally anticipated and certain features – a round-the-clock service and payment by results – had been major obstacles to delivery. The positives, however, were increased satisfaction for those working in the pilots from the flattened hierarchy and greater participation in decision making, together with enhanced opportunities for direct work with children and young people. Stanley and colleagues conclude that a key feature for success was a satisfactory pre-existing relationship between the practice and the local authority (Stanley et al, 2014).

The original set of pilots were in children's work, but a further round in 2011 explored the concept of contracting out statutory adult social work functions to independent organisations. Only 14 local authorities expressed interest in the pilots. Early indications from the Social Care Institute for Excellence (SCIE, 2013) are that many of the same issues present in the children's services pilots were also an issue in adult care. There was evidence of increased job satisfaction and flexibility in practice. The gains to the local authority were less clear-cut. Independence from local authority systems was difficult to achieve in some areas where the local council sought to ensure that the pilots were integrated with council IT systems. These findings were confirmed in the final evaluation (Manthorpe et al, 2014) which was critical of the timescale, the lack of detail available when the pilots were set up, and the lack of consistency in measuring outcomes.

The results suggest that there are no easy gains to be had from practice pilots (but as we have seen in Chapter Eight, the same is true of integrated care). The issue is whether there are sufficient positives in the model to justify further experimentation. The correlation between levels of staff satisfaction and overall quality of service has been too little explored in the UK. Evidence elsewhere (Yee et al, 2008; Peltier et al, 2009), suggests that a well-motivated staff group, feeling themselves to be valued, deliver better-quality services. The pilots may therefore have been exploring the wrong questions in seeking evidence of savings. If improved quality can be secured at a comparable cost, with the savings coming from the progressive dismantling of the local authority superstructure rather than direct service costs, the projects will prove worthwhile.

The second area of experimentation with different models of service delivery took place in one local authority but has had considerable impact more widely. Reclaiming Social Work is the model developed in Hackney, with a multidisciplinary team headed by a consultant social worker, a social worker, a child practitioner, a clinical practitioner/systemic family therapist and a unit coordinator. The unit provides family support, therapy, practical help and the statutory social work function. It was supported by investment from children's mental health services funding of the therapist posts in the teams.

The formal evaluation of the model was very positive (Forrester et al, 2013). It contains a detailed description of the model in practice and compares it with data gathered from local authorities operating a more conventional service model. In its detail it conveys a vivid picture of the responsibilities, working methods and approach of social workers in children's services – a fine-grained approach resembling that undertaken by Parsloe and Stevenson (1977) in the early years of social services departments. It found that levels of job satisfaction were higher and stress levels lower in the authority adopting the systemic team approach of Reclaiming Social Work. Analysing the amount of time spent on direct contact, the evaluation noted that the senior members of the team – the consultant social worker and the clinician – were engaged significantly in direct client contact.

In terms of the quality of relationships between workers and clients, the findings were unequivocal in noting that in the systemic model 'practice was very consistent, and was of a consistently high standard. In general, workers were on time, relationships tended to be more positive with clients and workers tended to be consistently empathic with parents and children without – in our observations – losing an ability to raise concerns as appropriate' (Forrester et al, 2013, p 164).

The report noted seven key factors supporting high-quality practice that are of wider application than the systemic model being reviewed. These were practical organisational support such as desk space and good IT access; good administrative support; small teams; good ratio of supervisors to staff; high-quality staff; limited workload; and a clear value base for the work. While praising the systemic model, the evaluation concluded that the most significant element may be the opportunity to rethink the current hierarchical model of delivering children's services. In this it chimes with 'lean' models of management and the current delayering of management tiers being driven by budget reductions (unfortunately too often also stripping out the ready access to supervision that was identified as a strong positive factor in the evaluation).

The emphasis on relationships in the evaluation is echoed by Ray Jones in a plea to regain the remit and space for relationships:

> The danger is that the emphasis on eligibility criterias, FACs (Fair Access to Care) and Resource Allocation systems trump the human interaction which is important in discussing with people, often at a point of personal change and crisis, how they might want to choose to shape their lives. (Jones, 2014)

The politics of risk

Neoliberalism has also had an impact on services, not just in the proliferation of agencies engaged in what might once have been seen as the preserve of social workers, but also in the way in which risk is constructed. It assumes that individuals will make rational choices about their wellbeing when confronted with the evidence. Alcohol misuse, smoking and obesity are examples where personal choice influences outcomes. The responsibility is placed on the individual to make healthy choices and to mitigate risk. The responsibility for social maintenance falls to the individual. Those who fail to exclude risks are marginalised and stigmatised, with increasing calls for sanctions such as withdrawing gastric band surgery from obese people, or limiting high cost surgery for smokers and heavy drinkers.

Unemployment is viewed not as a failure of the economic and social conditions in the country but as a result of the lack of motivation and enterprise of the individual unwilling, in former Conservative Minister Norman Tebbitt's famous phrase 'to get on his bike' to find work. And in the division between the 'deserving' and the 'undeserving poor', social workers can be seen as apologists for those deemed undeserving of help, including teenage mothers, those young people not in education, training or employment, asylum seekers, those who are chronically sick or long-term unemployed people.

Yet as a society we are more conscious of risk than ever before. Furedi is critical of the dramatic growth of risk analysis and risk management. He argues that it institutionalises caution and results in the construction of new conditions, syndromes and addictions (from sex to video games). As a result, 'more and more social problems have become medicalised – that is, recast as medical problems over which people can have little or no control' (Furedi, 1997, p 11).

Webb develops this argument in the context of social work, noting the increasing dependence on rules and procedures militating against the development of judgement, ethical insight and holistic practice. He suggests that social work has moved from a preoccupation with need to a preoccupation with risk as the dominant paradigm. The development of self-governance in the promotion of choice in social care and the concept of user empowerment are 'the activation of the consumer service user under the thin veneer of leftist rights language' (Webb, 2006, p 57).

He develops a compelling argument that safety and security are key elements in social work practice, ranging from the place of safety order and the extensive procedures governing child protection to the risk assessments undertaken before an elderly person is discharged from hospital to their own home:

> Life planning becomes a crucial feature of front-line practice at precisely those fateful moments in people's lives when insecurity, risk and breakdown loom large. The strategy of life planning in social work is an attempt to manage and predict risk whilst alleviating uncertainty. (Webb, 2006, p 107)

Yet the attempt to regulate risk and deploy risk management schedules, while appealing to managers for its rationality and predictability, conflicts with 'practitioners valuing professional, individualised judgement for its flexibility and responsiveness to individual factors' (Kemshall, 2000). The shades of grey in which social workers operate do not lend themselves easily to schedules and protocols that often fail to capture the multi-faceted nature of the difficulties faced by clients.

Social work in a neoliberal age

Given the continuing squeeze on local authority funding, it is unrealistic to think that there will be a return to the monolithic departments that have dominated the 45 years since the Seebohm reforms. It is equally unrealistic to anticipate an expansion of public sector provision.

The search for cost savings leads to over-optimistic assumptions about reduced expenditure through integrating adult social care more closely with healthcare. The impact of the changes to the NHS driven by the Coalition government since the 2012 Health and Social Care Act is to fragment services as any qualified provider takes over services – diabetes services, musculoskeletal services – that are put out to tender. The danger with this is that the contract process assumes priority over the continued viability of the hospital, formerly seen as the universal provider of secondary care. Queen Mary's Hospital, Bexley, is an example where one provider manages the hospital but three different providers run services on the site.

The constraints on public spending that have been in place since 2010 are likely to continue after the election of 2015 regardless of the outcome. The differences between the two major political parties are slight. That means that further substantial reductions in public expenditure are inevitable. There are clear political attractions in taking money out of the infrastructure of government, central and local, rather than direct service delivery. That means that the role of local authorities – often jointly with health bodies – will become exclusively that of commissioning services from a range of providers. In the area of personal services – talking therapies in mental health, fostering and adoption services, family support for children in need, advice and assistance to those at risk in the community, and safeguarding services for both children and adults – those could be commissioned from groups of staff in local areas without the administrative superstructure and costs that accompany local authority-based services.

Social workers face a choice in their response to these changes in social policy and the organisational changes that flow from it. They are in daily contact with those who have suffered as a result of the changes. They have a duty to challenge the impact on their clients, to document their findings and to use them to promote change. It may be that they only succeed in minimising the most severe impacts of the changes, especially where reforms arise from national decisions that cannot easily be rescinded. Social work can criticise and campaign against the deepening inequalities that produce and exacerbate social problems. With its commitment to social justice and combating inequalities, it should do so as the impact of welfare reforms is felt most acutely by the most vulnerable. Social workers should be passionate about the injustice to which they are daily witnesses. But if that leads social work into an instinctive defence of the status quo in the organisational pattern of services, it would be a false step. It would be viewed as part of the innate conservatism of the public sector faced with change. The public sector model has not produced an environment in which social work can flourish. There is an opportunity to craft a different form of organisation and practice better fitted to a neoliberal era of decentralisation and better attuned to 21st-century technology.

The two models of practice described above – social work practices and the systemic model – have implications for future patterns of organisation. Small teams with social workers who are well supported administratively and have access to clinical support appear to offer more hope than the traditional local authority model. The issue is how we can get there from here. Is a wholly decentralised practice delivered by independent contractors or group practices a feasible model for social work?

Those writing from a critical social work perspective may view this suggestion with horror, yielding as it does to the neoliberal tide of choice and competition. Garrett has argued that these changes are designed to drive down costs and further neuter the voice of social workers (Garrett, 2008). I take a more robust view of the ability of social workers, freed from some of the constraints of public sector employment, to blend a commitment to good practice with a commitment to social justice. Social work practices do not have to be politically neutered. Operating locally, developing inquiry and research, they would be well placed to influence policy development.

Looking at the national picture, there is a marked change in the pattern of employment of social workers. In children's social work in a local authority setting in England, 14% of those employed are agency workers (DfE, 2014). In adult care in England, 72% of all jobs were in the independent sector. In both England and Scotland, only just over half of social workers work in local authorities, with the balance independently employed or working in the private or voluntary sector (CWI, 2012; SSSC, 2013). The professional roles – social worker, occupational therapists and nurses – constituted only 6% of the total employees in adult care (Skills for Care, 2013). There are two clear trends. First, the independent sector continues to grow. Second, social workers employed in adult social care are decreasing in number. The future pattern of employment is therefore likely to be more diversified and jobs more likely to be short-term contracts than secure, long-term public sector posts.

Social work practice pilots have shown the difficulties of this model. Some of them have been the result of complying with the requirements of local authorities seeking compatibility with their existing systems but the potential gains are real, in terms of both service quality (through improved morale of social workers and clear outcomes for service users) and reduced infrastructure costs. Such a devolved model does raise issues of quality assurance, but with the strengthened role of the Care Quality Commission, these are not insuperable.

If social work does not rise to the challenge, it is likely that the big corporates like Serco, Capita and G4S, notwithstanding their tarnished reputation, will bid successfully to run outsourced children's services. This externalisation of service is already being used as a sanction against poor local authority providers (*Community Care*, 2014). The consultation document published by the Department for Education on outsourcing children's services does not limit this to 'failing' authorities (DfE, 2014). It gives extensive powers to local authorities to transfer to third-party providers most of their children's services functions, with the exception of independent reviewing officer functions and adoption agency functions. Any outsourced services have to be under the direction or supervision of a social worker, but that is the lone safeguard.

The strong opposition led by social work academics including Professor Ray Jones and Professor Eileen Munro (*Guardian*, 2014) argued that 'the intention that private sector organisation like G4S, Serco, ATOS and others should be able to run child protection services causes us considerable concern'. As a result, assurances were given that private providers would be excluded from the delegation, with social worker-led mutuals, social enterprises and cooperatives being given the opportunity to run services. But there is nothing to stop private providers establishing a non-profit arm to move into this territory using their experience in legal frameworks, contracting, budgeting and performance management.

Even the proudest achievement of the post-war welfare state – the National Health Service – is under threat. Change is a given. Jordan and Parton (2004) argue that social work should not be afraid of change but should seek new opportunities in the space created by the curtailment of public sector provision and should not be seen as a predominantly public sector.

Croisdale-Appleby identified three roles for social workers – as practitioner, as professional, and as social scientist – which he defines as 'able to understand and apply to their social work practice the relevant principles methods and knowledge of social work; seeking to further the understanding of social work through evidence gathering and through research' (Croisdale-Appleby, 2014, p 15). The organisational model of small-scale practices may serve the first two of these roles better than current models. Achieving the evidence gathering and research would be challenging, although the record of existing local authority departments on developing locally based evidence and research is poor. Data tends to be sucked up into national data sets and then disaggregated. Practices would, however, have to demonstrate the success of the practice in achieving defined outcomes. Winning and retaining commissions for the provision of services will become contingent on demonstrating the collection and aggregation of data. That collection could include the identification of unmet needs in the community – part of the original remit for community care but largely unfulfilled.

It is instructive to look at general practice in medicine as an analogy. GPs and hospital consultants share a core training and a common value base before undertaking specialist training on completion of their medical degree. GPs operate as independent contractors, although there are an increasing number of salaried GPs, sometimes without the capital to buy into a practice and sometimes preferring the flexibility of part-time work. GP practices are being obliged to collaborate so that a full range of services, including extended surgery opening hours and out-of-hours care, can be offered in any given locality.

With a long tradition of continuous professional development, medicine offers many lessons to social work. But maintaining good professional practice standards is no longer enough. Doctors are required to meet outcome targets for their patient population. This combination of professional practice and outcome management is a model that could translate to social work delivery.

Passion and politics

This chapter has argued that social work needs to adapt to the neoliberal temper of the times and develop a model of practice that will deliver improved quality and outcomes at comparable cost. It is a suggestion that will be viewed with dismay from some social workers who see the pain and damage caused to vulnerable people by the policies pursued in the new era of austerity. The public sector has borne the brunt of the cuts, both in the numbers employed and the savings required, despite the situation being precipitated by a crisis of capitalism. The welfare reforms – the 'bedroom tax', the benefit cap, the punitive application of sanctions to those receiving Jobseeker's Allowance, the chaos of work capability assessments – are a betrayal of the values of the welfare state. They are driven by the same prejudices against the workless that animated the Poor Law for centuries. They even repeat much of the language used in previous generations.

The managerialism, bureaucracy and emphasis on procedures that has come to dominate social work practice have been accompanied by ruthless cost reductions. These have had an impact on the working conditions of social workers, including accommodation and access to administrative support. Hot-desking has become the norm in urban areas. This militates against a shared identity among practitioners and against the reflective practice essential to high quality.

As part of local government, social workers have been neutered in campaigning on political issues. They have had to resort to what Ferguson and Woodward termed 'guerilla warfare' (Ferguson and Woodward, 2009). Freedom from that constraint would enable them to be more active in campaigns demonstrating the passion that is an essential part of social work.

It would be foolish to underestimate the challenge facing social workers in integrating the personal and the political in their practice. William Butler Yeats in 1919 wrote that 'the best lack all conviction, the worst are full of passionate intensity' (Yeats, 1920).

The ideologues of the Right see virtue in the freedom of the market, are hostile to state provision and regulation, and have an exaggerated faith in the ability of the voluntary sector and 'active citizens' to fill the gap left. Their critique of the public sector is based on the need to return to Victorian values of self-reliance and thrift with the safety net of public assistance being accompanied by punitive sanctions. But ideologues come from the Left as well as the Right. Deep hostility to neoliberalism and the pursuit of the overthrow of capitalism can lead to the kneejerk reaction of 'public sector good, private sector bad'.

Social work needs to reclaim the spirit that drove its pioneers. It will best do so by liberating itself from large organisational structures so that it can pursue both the advancement of wellbeing individually and collectively, and the pursuit of social justice.

Rotherham and beyond

Just as the manuscript for this book was delivered, the report on child sexual exploitation in Rotherham (Jay, 2014) was published. It describes an appalling picture of sustained abuse and exploitation of young girls over a lengthy period:

> Our conservative estimate is that approximately 1400 children were sexually exploited over the full Inquiry period, from 1997 to 2013.... In just over a third of cases, children affected by sexual exploitation were previously known to services because of child protection and neglect. It is hard to describe the appalling nature of the abuse that child victims suffered. They were raped by multiple perpetrators, trafficked to other towns and cities in the north of England, abducted, beaten, and intimidated. There were examples of children who had been doused in petrol and threatened with being set alight, threatened with guns, made to witness brutally violent rapes and threatened they would be next if they told anyone. Girls as young as 11 were raped by large numbers of male perpetrators. (Jay, 2014, p 1)

The report has received huge media coverage. Not only is the story compelling, but the report itself was relatively unusual in being unequivocal in its criticism:

> The collective failures of political and officer leadership were blatant.... Within social care, the scale and seriousness of the problem was underplayed by senior managers.... At an operational level, the Police gave no priority to CSE [child sexual exploitation], regarding many child victims with contempt and failing to act on their abuse as a crime. (Jay, 2014, p 1)

The criticisms were given added weight by being placed on the first page of the executive summary of the report.

In the wake of publication of the report, the media turned its attention to finding people to blame. The leader of Rotherham council resigned on the day of publication. Shaun Wright, the former police and crime commissioner for South Yorkshire, who also held a senior position in child services during the Rotherham scandal, tried to withstand the firestorm but had eventually to stand down. Rotherham council's director of children's services also resigned, despite the many improvements in the preceding four years noted in the report, as did the chief executive.

Following this ritual bloodletting, it is important to put what happened in Rotherham in context if lessons are truly to be learned.

LSCBs, multi-agency leadership and accountability

Local safeguarding children boards (LSCBs) are responsible for coordinating local authority safeguarding work. They succeeded area child protection committees following the 2004 Children Act and the introduction of children's services departments. Their effectiveness is, however, open to question in the light of their composition and the limited authority they exercise.

LSCBs carry responsibility for the effectiveness of services designed to promote the welfare of children, for the development of multi-agency policies and procedures in relation to safeguarding children, and for serious case reviews in certain circumstances (DfE, 2013a). Their composition was prescribed in statutory guidance and consequently they can be very large groups, with up to 50 people in some counties. Jay notes that:

> As meetings become larger the more difficult it is for the Chair to give due weight to the varying interests represented, to encourage full and open debate and reach definitive conclusions which attract the agreement of all present…. Not only does this make the task difficult for a part-time Chair, but it also raises questions about the concept of accountability as applied to such a large, disparate group of people. (Jay, 2014, para 7.24)

Despite this acknowledgement, Jay is critical of the failure by Rotherham LSCB to monitor whether policies and procedures were being implemented:

> Over the years there appears to have been a failure to challenge policies, priorities and performance, especially those of statutory agencies. This judgement featured in the Ofsted report of 2012 and was cited by the Home Affairs Select Committee. One task of the Board is to 'ensure effectiveness', to question, to scrutinise, to demand and assess evidence. In the past this function does not seem to have been fully exercised. (Jay, 2014, para 7.35)

This criticism places a greater burden of responsibility on LSCBs than they are able to discharge, including in Rotherham. Boards comprise a part-time independent chair, usually working two to three days a month, a group of second- or third-tier officers representing children's social care, health services fragmented between commissioners and providers, probation, police and education, and representatives of schools, the voluntary sector and lay members. A designated doctor and nurse and a specialist in child protection provide the professional expertise supporting the board. The representatives of statutory agencies rarely have the authority to commit resources on behalf of their own agency or even to agree their agency's financial contribution to the work of the board. They do not have the capacity to interrogate decisions made by individual agencies and certainly not to overrule them, even if an agency reduces the level of resource devoted to safeguarding. With little support available to them – usually a board manager and a training resource – they do not have the ability to assess whether partner agencies are devoting an adequate level of resources to safeguarding.

Unable to direct their member agencies, LSCBs must work through influence and peer pressure. The more rigorous inspection regime of child protection adopted by the children's services inspection body Ofsted has highlighted weaknesses in the processes followed by LSCBs and their inability to hold to account any agencies falling short of their obligations.

LSCBs have achieved much in raising standards of training and audit. They serve a useful function for government in creating a mechanism for collaborative working, but they should not be expected to deliver overarching control of the safeguarding system in an area.

When it comes to a critique of shared accountability, Jay is on firmer ground. The shared accountability of the LSCB extends to those issues over which it has direct control – the quality and reach of training, the effectiveness of audit – both of single-agency practice and multi-agency working – and the clarity of procedures governing safeguarding. The quality of practice in agencies and compliance with procedures are matters for management within the individual agency.

What has been thrown into relief by the report is the structural weakness of LSCBs. Independent chairs have a shelf life resembling that of football managers, as they are caught between the sometimes conflicting expectations of elected members, directors of children's services and Ofsted. The chair of the Association of Independent LSCB Chairs David Jones has described the risks in the child protection system as greater than at any time in the past 40 years. He cited the constant changes in organisational structures and the turbulence which that creates in local partnerships that depend on good personal relationships. He pointed to the hollowing-out of middle management posts where much of the partnership work is sustained. While the Munro prescription of greater focus on individual responsibility was being followed, the support systems of supervision and discussion were not properly in place (Jones, 2014). Central government has been ambivalent about the role of LSCBs. This is most evident in relation to the requirement to publish serious case reviews in their entirety. This was a policy change introduced in the first month of the Coalition government by Tim Loughton, then children's minister. There have been a number of disputes where LSCBs have resisted calls from the Department for Education for full publication without any redactions. LSCBs have argued that full publication might cause serious emotional harm to some children, or might lead to identification of individual children.

One case in point is that of Child S, one of the victims of child sexual exploitation in Rotherham. The serious case review was published with redactions in 2012 because of the sensitive nature of the case, and led to accusations by *The Times* of a cover-up. Jay notes that Michael Gove, then Secretary of State for Education, became involved and demanded changes to the redactions: 'There followed an unedifying set of exchanges between the Department for Education (DfE) and the Chair of the Safeguarding Board. At one point, the DfE lost a copy of the Serious Case Review' (Jay, 2014, para 7.61). While recognising that some of the redactions concerning officials could have been reinstated, Jay is adamant that it was right that the interests of the children in the family concerned should have been paramount and that details of the children's lives should not have been placed in the public domain. In a barbed criticism of the Department for Education, Jay recommended that 'the Department of [sic] Education should not demand the removal of redactions without giving thought to the interests of the children concerned' (Jay, 2014, para 7.64).

The role of elected members

Delineating the boundary between the role of a local authority director of children's services and that of a cabinet member with responsibility for children's services is easier in theory than in practice. The statutory guidance (DfE, 2013b) states that the former has professional responsibility, including for operational matters, while the latter has political responsibility. There is much about shared responsibility, but this is dependent on the establishment of an effective working relationship between the two. That relationship is subject to a number of pressures. It can be threatened by personality clashes if a headstrong cabinet member is keen to put his or her stamp on services. It is vulnerable to political agendas following a change of control if the incoming party has been critical of aspects of policy or performance. Often it comes under strain because of the failure to negotiate the appropriate limits to the lead member's intervention in individual cases.

The Jay report is critical of the lack of leadership from elected members in response to an identified threat to children in Rotherham. Despite the numerous fora in which child sexual exploitation was discussed with members, it was not discussed in the ruling Labour group until 2012. The culture of the council was described as macho, sexist and bullying. Jay notes that 'the existence of such a culture is likely to have impeded the Council from providing an effective, corporate response on such a highly sensitive social problem as child sexual exploitation' (Jay, 2014, para 13.69).

The clear priorities of the majority group were the economic development of the area and education – both laudable objectives in a depressed area with high levels of unemployment. Councillors have to balance competing priorities but were reluctant to give the same priority to vulnerable children. This may in part be because the issue of child sexual exploitation threatened to raise tensions over ethnicity. In the macho culture so vividly described by Jay, the victims were largely seen as juvenile prostitutes and therefore the architects of their own problems.

Refreshingly, Jay devotes a chapter to workload pressures and budgetary resources – something absent from Lord Laming's reports on Victoria Climbié and Baby P discussed in Chapter Three:

> By 2016 Rotherham will have lost 33% of its spending power compared with 2010/11.... These figures highlight the extreme pressure that reductions in public spending are placing on Councils such as Rotherham, which is faced with high demands for vulnerable children and families' services, associated with significant levels of poverty and deprivation. (Jay, 2014, para 12.13)

Rotherham has made children's services a priority in recent years. But the scale of public expenditure reductions, and the further reductions presaged for the period 2016–20, have an inescapable impact on quality of provision and thus the protection we can afford to vulnerable children. The lessons to be learned are not for agencies alone but also for central government.

Stereotypes and stigma

The great majority of the victims of sexual exploitation in Rotherham were young, sexually active, troubled girls looking for affection and attention. Jay confirms that:

> … many of the children were already vulnerable when grooming began. The perpetrators targeted children's residential units and residential services for care leavers…. Many of the case files we read described children from troubled family backgrounds, with a history of domestic violence, parental addiction and in some cases serious mental health problems. A significant number of the victims had a history of child neglect and/or sexual abuse when they were younger. Some had a desperate need for attention and affection. (Jay, 2014, paras 5.15-5.16)

Despite accumulating evidence of the scale of the problem in Rotherham, with the Risky Business project aimed at combating child sexual exploitation at the forefront of the bid to raise awareness of the need for a coordinated response, the reaction of statutory agencies was piecemeal and individualised. The police in particular seem to have had a low opinion of the girls involved, regarding them as juvenile prostitutes, while ignoring the role of the men involved and allegations of violence. They were slow in responding to missing persons reports. Some young girls were threatened with prosecution for wasting police time. Victims were blamed for their own situation. And this response was not confined to the police. Within children's social care there was a similar attempt to minimise the scale of the issue and a reluctance to accept the evidence, which concerned many of the most difficult young people for whom they were responsible.

The ambiguity of society's response to sexuality is part of the problem. Advertising is directed at young teens to encourage them to make themselves attractive to the opposite sex. Prurient pictures of pubescent girls are carried on the web pages of national papers. Social media, Instagrams and 'sexting' have changed the nature of teenage interaction. All of these activities greatly increase vulnerability to grooming. But if under-age girls act on these cues, they are vulnerable to the description of 'slags' or 'sluts'.

The sense of stigma carried by the young girls in Rotherham even appears to have extended to the project working with child sexual exploitation, Risky Business, which was regarded by some in the police and children's social care as hyping up the problem in a bid to secure more resources.

The sanctions available to children's social care are limited in relation to persistent runaways from residential care or foster care. There is a slippery slope from regarding such youngsters as deeply troubled to viewing them as trouble. Under-age girls who stay out all night and engage in overtly sexualised behaviour pose severe problems in a residential environment for those responsible for their care. But trained workers should be able to look beyond the acting-out behaviour and the problems caused, seeing behind the bravado to the individual lost child.

The politics of ethnicity

The great majority of victims in the Rotherham case were white. The perpetrators were predominantly Pakistani, with some Kurds, Afghanis and Kosovans also reported to be involved. Child sexual exploitation was first identified as an issue in Rotherham in the late 1990s, with the launch of the Risky Business project. However, the sheer scale of the problem of child sexual exploitation was not reported until 2002, in the draft and never published Home Office report. Sensitivity on racial issues was acute at the time, as a result of the Oldham riots in May 2011 and lesser disturbances in Bradford and Burnley, two other northern towns with substantial Muslim populations, later that year.

In this context, one would expect political sensitivity in handling issues with a racial dimension, particularly with the anti-Muslim feeling generated by the September 2001 terrorist attacks in New York and Washington, DC. The 'Home Office' report was critical of the police response to the evidence to child sexual exploitation. It was severely criticised by senior officers and by the police and led to a complete breakdown of relationships. The report dealt with the topic of child sexual exploitation at a sensitive time with a politically inconvenient truth. But political sensitivity does not mean ignoring the problem and failing to address it. Sadly, while there were elements of openness, notably the briefing of all councillors on child sexual exploitation in 2005, there was no follow-through and no coordinated strategy agreed on an inter-agency basis.

In particular, Rotherham council did not engage with the Pakistani community other than through traditional channels of communication. Ethnic minority councillors saw the issue as an isolated problem and failed to recognise or act on the scale of the problem.

Social work practice in Rotherham

Overall, there was some good practice in Rotherham. There was positive engagement with children, with children being seen on their own and their views taken into account in the great majority of cases. A consistent theme of inspections, however, was the poor quality of assessments and care planning. Risk assessment and risk management in particular were found to be poor and these areas remained inadequate in nearly half the files reviewed by the inquiry team. Heavy workloads meant that staff gave priority to looked-after children and child protection. There was a concentration on short-term intervention when longer engagement was required. Echoing the findings of two serious case reviews published in 2013 in the wake of child sexual exploitation cases in Rochdale, Jay (2014) notes that social services' focus on very young children in Rotherham meant that older victims did not get the help they needed.

The national picture is unlikely to be very different. When resources are stretched, hard choices have to be made. Looked-after children and those in child protection procedures are two inescapable priorities. Preventive work and outreach work are vulnerable to budget cuts. Despite the focus on child sexual exploitation in Rotherham, Jay (2014) noted that some outreach services had been affected by budget reductions.

Social work after Rotherham

The pattern of the media coverage of the Rotherham case has differed from that of previous child abuse scandals. No individual social worker has been pilloried. The attack has been directed at councillors, senior managers and senior police officers, reflecting the organisational failures that Jay identified. Despite the lack of evidence to support claims of a cover-up, that narrative has underpinned the coverage.

Social work, however, has suffered what the military would term collateral damage. First, political correctness, already attached to social work, is seen as a contributory factor in the reluctance of senior figures in Rotherham to recognise the scale of exploitation and the communities in which it was located. There is no evidence of political correctness being applied in the case files examined by the inquiry team. Jay states that 'the inquiry team was confident that ethnic issues did not influence professional decision making in individual cases' (Jay, 2014, para 11.8).

Second, the impotence of children's services in dealing with absconders from residential care damaged belief in the effectiveness of intervention. Parents who felt that their children would be protected and secure in placements became disillusioned. This was mirrored by the victims themselves, who had no confidence in the ability of police or social workers to protect them against their abusers.

Every local authority will now have reviewed its policies and protocols in relation to child sexual exploitation. The level of awareness of grooming has been raised and agencies will collaborate to tackle emerging evidence of this method of entrapment. There will be a greater readiness to challenge unsympathetic attitudes to the victims of exploitation.

The danger, however, is that the attention and resources devoted to this topic will be at the expense of other priorities, and in particular the more prevalent familial child sexual abuse. And even in Rotherham, resource pressures mean that outreach work, so vital in the context of sexual exploitation, is being cut back. Scandals tend to set the social work agenda, from the blood tie debates of the Colwell case, through the merits (emerging from the Climbié case) of engaging with children without carers being present, to an awareness of strangers in the house in the wake of the Baby P case. The lesson is one of vigilance because the next issue will not mirror the circumstances of Rotherham.

References

Age UK (2013) *The 'Dilnot social care cap': Making sure it delivers for older people*, London: Age UK

Allen, R. (2014) *The role of the social worker in adult mental health services*, London: The College of Social Work

Andrews. C. (1974) *Social Work Today*, November

Attlee, C. (1920) *The social worker*, London: G Bell and Sons

Audit Scotland (2011) *Community health partnerships*, Edinburgh: Audit Scotland

Bailey, R. and Brake, M. (1975) *Radical social work*, London: Edward Arnold

Bailey, R. and Brake, M. (1980) *Radical social work and practice*, London: Edward Arnold

Bamford, T. (1990) *The future of social work*, Basingstoke: Macmillan

Bamford, T. (1997) 'Kenneth Brill', *Dictionary of national biography*, Oxford: Oxford University Press

Barclay, P. (1982) *Social workers: Their role and tasks*, London: National Institute for Social Work

Bartlett, H. (1970) *The common base of social work practice*, New York, NY: National Association of Social Workers

BASW (British Association of Social Workers) (1975) A Code of Ethics, Birmingham: BASW

BASW (1977) *The social work task*, Birmingham: BASW

BASW (2012) *Code of ethics for social work – values and ethical principles*, Birmingham: BASW

Beasley, J. (1986) *The social workers' strike and its aftermath*, London: Industrial Research and Information Services

Bell, D. and Bowes, A. (2006) *Lessons from the funding of long-term care in Scotland*, York: Joseph Rowntree Foundation

Beresford, P. (2013) *Beyond the usual suspects: Towards inclusive user involvement*, London: Shaping our Lives

Beveridge, W. (1942) *Report of the Interdepartmental Committee on Social Insurance and Allied Services*, Cmnd 6404, London; HMSO

Biestek, Father (1961) *The casework relationship*, London: George Allen and Unwin

Birrell, D. and Heenan, D. (2012) 'Implementing the Transforming Your Care agenda in Northern Ireland within integrated structures', *Journal of Integrated Care*, vol 20, no 6, pp 359-66

Blom-Cooper, L. (1984) *A child in trust: Report of the panel of inquiry into the circumstances surrounding the death of Jasmine Beckford*, London: London Borough of Brent

Board of Supervision Scotland (1893), *Annual Report*, Edinburgh: Board of Supervision

Board of Supervision, *System in Scotland of boarding pauper children in private dwellings: Report to the Board of Supervision 1893*, Edinburgh: Board of Supervision

Booth, C. (1903) *Life and labour of the people of London* (3rd edn, 17 vols), London: Macmillan

Bottomley, V. (1991) *Hansard*, 3 June

Boyer, G. (1990) *An economic history of the English Poor Law 1750–1850*, Cambridge: Cambridge University Press

Brand, D. (2012) 'Social and health care integration: the individual dimension', *Journal of Integrated Care*, vol 20, no 6, pp371-78

Branfield, F. and Beresford, P. (2006) *Making user involvement work*, York: Joseph Rowntree Foundation

Brewer, C. and Lait, J. (1980) *Can social work survive?*, London: Temple Smith

British Medical Journal (2012) 'Integrated care: a story of hard won success', vol 344: e3529

Brody, S.R. (1976) *The effectiveness of sentencing: A review of the literature*, London: HMSO

Bullock, R. et al (1995) *Child protection: Messages from research*, London: HMSO

Burns, T., Creed, E., Fahy, T. et al (1999) 'Intensive versus standard case management for severe psychotic illness: a randomised trial', *The Lancet*, vol 353, pp 2185-9

Burns, T., Rugkåsa, J., Molodynski, A., Dawson, J., Yeeles, K., Vazquez-Montes, M., Voysey, M., Sinclair, J. and Priebe, S. (2013) 'Community treatment orders for patients with psychosis (OCTET): a randomised controlled trial', *The Lancet*, 26 March

Butler, I. and Drakeford, M. (2005) *Scandal, social policy and social welfare*, Bristol: Policy Press

Butler-Sloss, Lord Justice E. (1988) *Report of the inquiry into child abuse in Cleveland 1987*, Cmnd 412, London: HMSO

Bywaters, P. (1986) 'Social work and the medical profession: arguments against unconditional collaboration', *British Journal of Social Work*, vol 16, no 6, p 670

Cannan, C. (1975) 'Welfare rights and wrongs' in R. Bailey and M. Brake (eds), *Radical Social Work*, London: Edward Arnold

Care and Social Services Inspectorate Wales (2012) *Improving care and social services in Wales: Chief Inspector's Annual Report 2011/12*, Wales Government

Carey, M. (2008) 'Everything must go: the privatisation of state social work', *British Journal of Social Work*, vol 38, no 5, pp918-935

Carter, P. (2003) *Managing offenders, reducing crime: A new approach*, London: Cabinet Office

Case Con (1975) 'Manifesto', www.radical.org.uk/barefoot/casecon.htm

Casey, L. (2013), www.bbc.co.uk/news/uk-politics-23158680

CCETSW (Council for Education and Training in Social Work) (1974) *Residential work is part of social work*, London: CCETSW

CCETSW (1989) *Rules and requirements for the Diploma in Social Work*, Paper 30, London: CCETSW

Challis, D. and Ferlie, E. (1987) 'Changing patterns of fieldwork organisation', *British Journal of Social Work*, vol 17, 2, April, pp 147-66

Challis, D., Chesterman, J., Darton, R. and Traske, K. (1993) 'Case management in the care of the aged', in Bornat, J., Pereira, C., Pilgrim, D. and Williams, F. (eds) *Community care: A reader*, Basingstoke: Macmillan

Chambon, I. and Epstein L. (1999) *Reading Foucault for social workers*, New York, NY: Columbia University Press

Cheetham, J. (ed) (1982) *Social work and ethnicity*, London: George Allen and Unwin

Chief Secretary to the Treasury (2003) *Every Child Matters*, Cmnd 5860, London: TSO

Clifton, J. and Thirley, C. (2014) *Think Ahead: Meeting the workforce challenge in mental health social work*, London: Institute of Public Policy Research

Clyde, J. (1992) *Report of the inquiry into the removal of children from Orkney in February 1991*, London: HMSO

College of Social Work (2014) *Role and functions of social workers*, London: College of Social Work

Colwell Report, Committee of Inquiry into the Care and Supervision provided in relation to Maria Colwell (1974), London: HMSO

Community Care (2014) 'Government tells "inadequate" Slough to outsource its children's services', 25 April, www.communitycare.co.uk

Compton, J. (2011) *Transforming your care: A review of health and social care in Northern Ireland*, Belfast: Department of Health, Social Services and Public Safety

Cooper, T. (2012) 'Easier said than done', *Professional Social Work*, October

Corrigan, P. and Leonard, P. (1978) *Social work practice under capitalism: A Marxist approach*, Basingstoke: Macmillan

COS (Charity Organisation Society) (1879) *Cooperation of district committees of the Charity Organisation Society with Boards of Guardians, Relief of Cases of Permanent Distress June 1879,* London: Spottiswoode

COS (1895) *Annual report*, London: COS

COS (1895b), Occasional Paper first series no 46, reprinted from the Charity Organisation Review, Jan 1895

COS (1908) *Social service handbook*, London: Charity Organisation Society

CQC (Care Quality Commission) (2010) *Market profile. Quality of provision and commissioning of adult social care services*, London: CQC

CQC (2012) *State of care 2011/12*, London: CQC

CQC (2013) *CQC announces Chief Inspector of Adult Social Care*, www.cqc.org.uk/content/cqc-announces-chief-inspector-adult-social-care, 19 July

Croisdale-Appleby, D. (2014) *Re-visioning social work education, an independent review*, London: Department of Health

Crossman, R. (1977) *The diaries of a cabinet minister. Volume 3, Secretary of State for Social Services, 1968–1970,* London: Hamish Hamilton and Jonathan Cape

CSCI (Commission for Social Care Inspection) (2008) *Cutting the cake fairly: CSCI review of eligibility criteria for social care*, Newcastle upon Tyne: Commission for Social Care Inspection

Cullen, L. (2013) 'The first lady almoner; the appointment, position and findings of Miss Mary Stewart at the Royal Free Hospital 1895–99', *Journal of the History of Medicine and Allied Sciences*, vol 68, no 4, pp 551-582

Curry, C., Harris, M., Gunn, L., Pappas, Y., Blunt, I., Soljak, M., Mastellos, M., Holder, H., Smith, J., Majeed, A., Ignatowicz, A., Greaves, F., Belsi, A., Costin-Davis, N., Jones Nielsen, J., Greenfield, G., Cecil, E., Patterson, S., Car, J. and Bardsley, M. (2013) 'Integrated care pilot in north west London: a mixed methods evaluation', *International Journal of Integrated Care*, vol 13, July-Sept

Curtis, M. (1946) *Report of the Care of Children Committee*, Cmnd 6922, London: HMSO

CWI (Centre for Workforce Intelligence) (2012) *Workforce risks and opportunities: Social workers*, London: CWI

Daily Telegraph (2009), www.telegraph.co.uk/news/uknews/baby-p/4334287/Take-more-children-into-care-says-Barnardos-chief-Martin-Narey.html

Daily Telegraph (2012) 'Speed up adoption processes, Cameron tells councils', 9 March.

Darley, G. (1990) *Octavia Hill*, London: Constable

Davies, B. (1992) *Case management, equity and efficiency*, Canterbury: Personal Social Services Research Unit, University of Kent

Davies, B., Bebbington, A. and Charnley, K. (1990) *Resources, needs and outcomes in community-based care*, London: Gower

DCSF (Department for Children, Schools and Families) (2009) *The protection of children in England: Action plan. The government's response to Lord Laming*, Cmnd 7589, London: DCSF

DCSF (2009a) *Facing up to the task*, Interim report of Social Work Task Force, London: DCSF

DCSF (2009b) *Building a safe, confident future*, Final report of the Social Work Task Force, London: DCSF

DCLG (Department for Communities and Local Government) (2013a), E. Pickles quoted in '14000 troubled families' lives turned round', Press Release, 10 September, London: DCLG

DCLG (2013b) *Troubled Families: Progress as at the end of September 2013 and Families turned round as at the end of October 2013,* London: DCLG

DCLG (2014) *Troubled Families programme: Progress information and families turned around*, London: DCLG

De Schweinitz, K. (1943) *England's road to social security*, Philadelphia, University of Pennsylvania Press

DfE (Department for Education) (2010) *Building a safe, confident future: progress report from the Social Work Reform Board,* London: DfE

DfE (2011) *Monitoring and evaluation of family intervention services and projects between February 2007 and March 2011*, London: DfE

DfE (2012a) *Building a safe and confident future: Maintaining momentum. Progress report from the Social Work Reform Board*, London: Department for Education

DfE (2012b) *Evaluation of social work practice pilots*, London: DfE

DfE (2013a) *Working together*, London: DfE

DfE (2013b) *Statutory guidance on the role and responsibilities of the director of children's services and the lead member for children's services*, London: DfE

DfE (2013c) *Step Up to Social Work Programme Evaluation: the Regional Partnerships and Employers Perspectives*, London: DfE

DfE (2014a) *Children's social work workforce*, London: DfE

DfE (2014b) *The views of Step Up to Social Work Trainees Cohorts 1 and 2* (auths M. Baginsky and J. Manthorpe), London: DfE

DfES (Department for Education and Skills) (2004) *Every Child Matters: Change for children*, Nottingham: DfES

DfES (2006) *Working to Prevent the Social Exclusion of Children and Young People, Final Lessons from the National Evaluation of the Children's Fund*, Department for Education and Skills Research Report 734, Birmingham: University of Birmingham

DH (Department of Health) (1989) *Caring for people: Community care in the next decade and beyond*, London: HMSO

DH (1991) *The Patient's Charter*, London: DH

DH (1996) *The spectrum of care: A summary of comprehensive local services for people with mental health problems*, London: DH

DH (1998a) *Caring for children who live away from home: Messages from research*, London:

DH (1998b) *Modernising social services*, London: DH

DH (1999a) *Patient and public involvement in the new NHS*, London: DH

DH (1999b) *Reform of the Mental Health Act 1983: Proposals for consultation*, London: DH

DH (1999c) *Report of the expert committee: Review of the Mental Health Act 1983*, London: DH

DH (2000a) *Reforming the Mental Health Act*, London: DH

DH (2000b) *A quality strategy for social care*, London: DH

DH (2003) *Fair Access to Care Services: Guidance on eligibility criteria for adult social care services*, London: The Stationery Office

DH (2007a) *Putting people first*, London: DH

DH (2007b) *Mental health: New ways of working for everyone*, London: DH

DH (2007c) *Valuing People Now*, London: Department of Health

DH (2008a) *Real involvement: Working with people to improve health*, London: DH

DH (2008b) *Refocussing the care programme approach*, London: DH

DH (2008c) *National carers strategy*, London: Department of Health

DH (2009) *Shaping the future of care together*, London: DH

DH (2010a) *Equity and excellence: Liberating the NHS*, London: DH

DH (2010b) *A vision for adult social care: Capable communities and active citizens*, London: DH

DH (2010c) *Prioritising need in the context of putting people first: A whole system approach to eligibility for social care. Guidance on eligibility for adult social care*, London: The Stationery Office

DH (2011) *No health without mental health: Delivering better mental health outcomes for people of all ages*, London: DH

DH (2012) *Caring for our future: Reforming care and support*, London: DH

DH (2013) *Integrated care: Our shared commitment*, London: DH

DHSS (Department of Health and Social Security) (1974) *Non-accidental injury to children*, LASSL 9 (74) 13, London: DHSS

DHSS (1975) *Better services for the mentally ill*, London: HMSO

DHSS (1976) *Manpower and training for the personal social services* (the Birch Report) London: DHSS

DHSS (1980) *An investigation into the effect on clients of industrial action by social workers in the London Borough of Tower Hamlets*, London: DHSS

Dilnot, A. (2011) *Fairer care funding for all: The report of the Commission on Funding of Care and Support,* London: Commission on Funding of Care and Support

Dominelli, L. (1988) *Anti-racist social work*, Basingstoke: BASW/Macmillan

Dominelli, L. (1996) 'Deprofessionalising social work: anti-oppressive practice, competencies and postmodernism', *British Journal of Social Work*, vol 26, no 2, pp 153-175

Driver, F. (1993) *Power and pauperism: The workhouse system 1834–1884*, Cambridge: Cambridge University Press

Easton. C., Hetherington, M., Smith, R., Wade, P., Aston, H. and Gee, G. (2012) *Local authorities' approaches to children's trust arrangements*, Slough: National Foundation for Education Research

Economist, The (2006) 'Milton Friedman – a giant among economists', 23 November

Featherstone, B. (2001) 'Where to for feminist social work?', *Critical Social Work*, vol 2, no 1

Ferguson, H. (2001) 'Social work, individualisation and life politics', *British Journal of Social Work*, vol 31, no 1, pp 41-56

Ferguson, H. (2003) 'In defence (and celebration) of individualisation and life politics for social work', *British Journal of Social Work*, vol 33, no 5, pp 699-707

Ferguson, I. (2008) *Reclaiming social work*, Bristol: Policy Press

Ferguson, I. and Woodward, R. (2009) *Radical social work in practice: Making a difference*, Bristol: Policy Press

Fitzgibbon, W. (2011) *Probation and social work on trial: Violent offenders and child abusers* Basingstoke: Palgrave Macmillan

Folkard, S., Lyon, K., Carver, M.M. and O'Leary, E. (1976) *Intensive matched probation and after care treatment. Volume 2: The result of the experiment*, Home Office Research Study 36, London: HMSO

Forder, J., Jones, K., Glendinning, C., Caiels, J., Welch, E., Baxter, K., Davidson, J., Windle, K., Irvine, A., King, D. and Dolan, P. (2012) *Evaluation of the personal health budget pilot programme*, London: Department of Health

Forrester, D., Westlake, D., McCann, M., Thurnham, A., Shefer, G., Glynn, G. and Killian, M. (2013) *Reclaiming social work? An evaluation of systemic units as an approach to delivering children's services*, Luton: Tilda Goldberg Centre, University of Bedfordshire

Fowler, N. (1984) Speech at Association of Directors of Social Services conference, Buxton

Fraser, D. (1973) *The evolution of the welfare state*, Basingstoke: Macmillan

Furedi, F. (1997) *Culture of fear*, London: Cassell

Garrett, P.M. (2003) 'The trouble with Harry: why the "new agenda of life politics" fails to convince', *British Journal of Social Work*, vol 33, no 3, pp 381-97

Garrett, P.M. (2004) 'More trouble with Harry: a rejoinder to the life politics "debate"', *British Journal of Social Work*, vol 34, no 4, pp 577-89

Garrett, P.M. (2008) 'Social work practices: silences and elisions in the plan to transform the lives of children looked after in England', *Child and Family Social Work*, vol 13, no 3, pp311-318

Garrett, P.M. (2009) *'Transforming' children's services? Social work, neoliberalism and the 'modern' world*, Maidenhead: McGraw Hill/Open University Press

Giddens, A. (1992) *The transformation of intimacy: Sexuality, love and eroticism in modern societies*, Cambridge: Polity Press

Glasby, J. and Dickinson, H. (2008) *Partnership working in health and social care*, Bristol: Policy Press

Glasgow Digital Library (nd) 'Scotland in the nineteenth century: 14. Poverty and relief measures', http://gdl.cdlr.strath.ac.uk/haynin/haynin1401.htm

Glendinning, C., Challis, D., Fernandez, J.L., Jacobs, S., Jones, K., Knapp, M., Manthorpe, J., Moran, N. and Netten, A. (2008), *Evaluation of individual budgets pilot programme*, York: Social Policy Research Unit, University of York

Glover-Thomas, N. (2012) 'Community treatment orders in England and Wales: are these the way forward in reducing perceived risk of harm?', in B. McSherry and I. Frackelton (eds) *Coercive care: Rights, law and policy*, Abingdon: Routledge pp157-171

GMC (General Medical Council) (2009) *Tomorrow's doctors*, London: GMC

GMC (2013) *Good medical practice*, London: GMC

Goodwin, N. et al (2012) *Integrated care for patients and populations: Improving outcomes by working together*, London: King's Fund and Nuffield Trust

Goodwin, N., Dixon, A., Anderson, G. and Wodchis, W. (2014) *Providing integrated care for older people with complex needs*, London: King's Fund

Gove, M. (2013), Speech to the NSPCC, 12 November, www.gov.uk

Gray, M. and Webb, S. (2013) *The new politics of social work*, Basingstoke: Palgrave Macmillan

Griffiths, R. (1983) *NHS management inquiry*, London: London: DHSS

Griffiths, R. (1988) *Community care: Agenda for action*, London: HMSO

Griggs, J. with Walker, R. (2008) *The costs of child poverty for individuals and society: A literature review*, York: Joseph Rowntree Foundation

Grounds, A. (2001) 'Reforming the Mental Health Act', *British Journal of Psychiatry*, vol 179, no 5, pp 378-9

GSCC (General Social Care Council) (2012) *Annual report and accounts, 2011–12*, London: GSCC

Guardian (2014) Letter from R. Jones and others, 17 May

Hall, P. (1976) *Reforming the welfare*, London: Heinemann

Ham, C. and Timmins, N. (2013) *The quest for integrated health and social care: A case study in Canterbury, New Zealand*, London: King's Fund

Handbook (1601) *An ease for overseers of the poore abstracted from the statutes*, Cambridge

Harris, J. (1997) *William Beveridge: A biography*, Oxford: Clarendon Press

Harris, J. and McDonald, C. (2000) 'Post-Fordism, the welfare state and the personal social services: a comparison of Australia and Britain', *British Journal of Social Work*, vol 30, no 1, pp 51-70

Hastings, S. and Jay, P. (1965) *The family and the social services*, London: Fabian Society

Hawksley, H. (1869) *Charities of London and some errors in their administration with suggestions for an improved system of relief*, London: John Churchill and Sons

Hayek, F. (1944) *The road to serfdom*, London: Routledge

HCPC (Health and Care Professions Council) (2012a) *Standards of proficiency for social workers in England*, London: HCPC

HCPC (2012b) 'Mapping of standards of proficiency against the PCF', www. hpc-uk.org/publications/standards/index.asp?id=569

Health and Social Care Information Centre (2013) *Personal social services expenditure and unit costs 2011/12*, Leeds: Health and Social Care Information Centre

Health Development Agency (2004) *Lessons from Health Action Zones*, HDA Briefing No 9

Heenan, D. (2013) *Northern Ireland,* in C. Ham, D. Heenan, M. Longley and D. Steel, *Integrated care in Northern Ireland, Scotland and Wales: Lessons for England*, London: King's Fund

Her Majesty's Commissioners (1834) *Report from Her Majesty's Commissioners for inquiring into the administration and practical operation of the Poor Laws*, London: B Fellowes

Heller, J (1979) *Good as Gold*, New York: Simon and Schuster

Hill, F. (1894) *Children of the state*, London: Macmillan

Hindle, S. (2004) *On the parish? The micro-politics of poor relief in rural England c1550–1750*, Oxford: Clarendon Press

Hollis, F. (1964) *Casework: A psychosocial therapy*, New York, NY: Random House

Home Office (1968) *Children in trouble*, London: HMSO

Home Office (1984) *Statement of national objectives and priorities for the probation service*, London: Home Office

Home Office (1988) *Punishment, custody and the community*, London: Home Office

Home Office (1990a) *Crime, justice and protecting the public*, London: Home Office

Home Office (1990b) *Supervision and punishment in the community: A framework for action*, London: Home Office

Home Office (1995) *Strengthening punishment in the community*, London: Home Office

Home Office (1996) *Protecting the public*, London: Home Office

Horner, N. (2003) *What is social work? Contexts and perspectives*, Exeter: Learning Matters

House of Commons Committee of Public Accounts (2014) *Probation: Landscape review*, London: The Stationery Office

House of Commons Health Committee (2003) *The Victoria Climbié inquiry report*, London: The Stationery Office

House of Commons Health Committee (2009) *Health inequalities: Third Report of Session 2008–09*, HC 286-I, London: The Stationery Office

House of Commons Justice Committee (2010) *Cutting crime: The case for justice reinvestment. First report of session 2009-10*, HC 94-I, London: The Stationery Office

Hudson, A. (1999) 'Changing perspectives: Feminism, gender and social work', in M. Langan and P. Lee (eds) *Radical social work today*, London: Unwin Hyman pp 70-96

Imperial College London (2013), www3.imperial.ac.uk/newsandeventspggrp/imperialcollege/newssummary/news_17-5-2013-13-41-52

IFSW (International Federation of Social Workers) and IASW (International Association of Schools of Social Work) (2014) *International Definition of Social Work*, www.ifsw.org/policies

Ismail, S., Thorlby, R. and Holder, H. (2014) *Focus on: Social care for older people*, London: Health Foundation and Nuffield Trust

Jackson, S. (1987) *Education of children in care*, Bristol: School of Applied Social Studies, University of Bristol

Jay, A. (2014) *Independent inquiry into child sexual exploitation in Rotherham (1997–2013)*, Rotherham: Rotherham Metropolitan Borough Council

JM Consulting (1999) *Review of the Diploma in Social Work*, London: Department of Health

Jillings, J. (2013) *Child abuse: An independent investigation commissioned by Clwyd County Council* (redacted), released by successor councils Conwy County Borough Council, Denbighshire County Council, Flintshire County Council, and Wrexham County Borough Council

Jones, O. (2011) *Chavs: The demonization of the working class*, London: Verso

Jones, D. (2014), quoted in *Professional Social Work*, October 2014

Jones, R. (2014) 'The best of times, the worst of times: social work and its moment', *British Journal of Social Work*, vol 44, no 3, pp 485-502g

Jordan, W. and Parton, N. (2004) 'Social work, the public sphere and civil society', in R. Lovelock, K. Lyons and J. Powell (eds) *Reflecting on social work: Discipline and profession*, Aldershot: Ashgate

JRF (Joseph Rowntree Foundation) (2013) *Tough on people in poverty*, York: JRF

Kemshall, H. (2000) 'Conflicting knowledges on risk: the case of risk knowledge in the probation service', *Health, Risk and Society*, vol 2, no 2 pp 143-58

Killapsy, H., Bebbington, P., Blizard, R. et al (2006) 'The REACT study: randomised evaluation of assertive community treatment in North London', *British Medical Journal*, vol 332, pp 815-19

Laing and Buisson (2013) *Care of elderly people market survey 2012/13*, London: Laing and Buisson

Laming, Lord H. (2003) *The Victoria Climbié inquiry: Report of an inquiry by Lord Laming*, Cmnd 5730, London: HMSO

Laming, Lord H. (2009) *The protection of children in England: A progress report*, London: Department for Children, Schools and Families

Langan, M. and Lee, P. (1999) *Radical social work today*, London: Unwin Hyman

Lavalette, M. (2011) *Radical social work today*, Bristol: Policy Press

Lawton-Smith, S., Dawson, J. and Burns, T. (2008) 'Community treatment orders are not a good thing', *British Journal of Psychiatry*, vol 193, no 2, pp 96-100

Leese, J. and Leese, D. (2011) 'Personalisation: perceptions of social workers in a world of brokers and budgets', *British Journal of Social Work*, vol 41, no 2, pp 204-23

Leonard, P. (1975) 'A paradigm for radical practice', in R. Bailey and M. Brake (eds) *Radical social work*, London: Edward Arnold

Levy, A. and Kahan, B. (1991) *The pindown experience and the protection of children: The report of the Staffordshire child care inquiry 1990*, Stafford: Staffordshire County Council

Lieveley, N. and Crosby, G. with Bowman, C. (2011) *The changing face of care homes*, London: Centre for Policy on Ageing and BUPA

LGA (Local Government Association) (1895) *24th Annual Report 1894–5*, Local Government Board

LGA (1906) *Inquiry into the general condition of the Poplar Union*

LGA (2012) *A-Z guide to the Children's Improvement Board*, London: Local Government Association

LGA (2013) *Towards Excellence in Social Care: progress with adult social care priorities 2012/13*, London: LGA

LGA (2014) 'Improvement and support', www.local.gov.uk/cyp-improvement-and-support

Littlejohn, R. (2013) 'The not-me-guv culture that failed poor Daniel', *Daily Mail*, 1 August

Lloyd George, D. (1929) *Slings and arrows: Speeches of David Lloyd George*, London: Cassell and Sons

Lloyd, C., Wollny, I., White, C., Gowland, S. and Purdon, S. (2011) *Monitoring and evaluation of family intervention services and projects between February 2007 and March 2011*, London: Department for Education

London Borough of Greenwich (1987) *A child in mind: The protection of children in a responsible society. Report of the commission of inquiry into the circumstances surrounding the death of Kimberley Carlile,* London: London Borough of Greenwich

London Borough of Lambeth (1987) *Report of the panel of inquiry into the death of Tyra Henry*, London: London Borough of Lambeth

Longford, F. (1964) *Crime – a challenge to us all*, Labour Party Study Group

Lymbery, M. (2001) 'Social work at the crossroads', *British Journal of Social Work*, vol 31, no 3, pp 369-84

Macpherson, W. (1998) *The Stephen Lawrence inquiry*, Cm 4262-1, London: Home Office

Malone, C. (2008) 'Baby P: they're all guilty', *News of the World*, 16 November

Manley, I. (2010) *Stab proof scarecrows*, Leicester: Troubadour Publishing

Manthorpe, J., Harris, J., Hussein, S., Cornes, M. and Moriarty, J. (2014), *Evaluation of the Social Work Practices with Adults Pilots*, Kings College London, Social Care Workforce Research Unit

Marquand, D. (2004) *The decline of the public: The hollowing out of citizenship*, Cambridge: Polity Press

Mayo, M (1975) 'Community development: a radical alternative' in R. Bailey and M. Brake (eds), *Radical social work*, London: Edward Arnold

Mays, J. (1954) *Growing up in the city*, Liverpool: Liverpool University Press

McDonald, C. (2007) 'Wizards of Oz? The radical tradition in Australian social work (and what we can learn from Aotearoa New Zealand)', in M. Lavalette and I. Ferguson (eds) *International social work and the radical tradition*, Birmingham: Venture Press

McLaughlin, K. (2008) *Social work, politics and society*, Bristol: Policy Press

Midwinter, E. (2011) in Lieveley, N. and Crosby, G. with Bowman, C, (2011) *The changing face of care homes*, London: Centre for Policy on Ageing and BUPA

Ministry of Justice (2010) *Breaking the cycle: Effective punishment, rehabilitation and sentencing of offenders*, London: TSO

Moberly Bell, E. (1961) *The story of hospital almoners*, London: Faber and Faber

Monckton, W. (1945) *Report on the circumstances leading to the boarding out of Dennis and Terence O'Neill*, London: Home Office

Monger, M. (1964) *Casework in probation*, London: Butterworths

Monitor (2013) *A fair playing field for the benefit of NHS patients*, London: Monitor

Morgan, C., Dazzan, P., Morgan, K., Jones, P., Harrison, G., Leff, J., Murray, R. and Fearon, P. (2006) 'First episode psychoses and ethnicity: initial findings from the AESOP study', *World Psychiatry*, vol 5, no 1

Morison, R. (1962) *Report of Departmental Committee on the Probation Service*, London: HMSO

Munro, E. (2011) *The Munro review of child protection: Final report – a child-centred system*, Cmnd 8062, London: TSO

Murphy, S., Irving, C.B., Adams, C.E. and Driver, R. (2012) 'Crisis intervention for people with severe mental illness', *Cochrane Database Systematic Review*, May 16:5

NAO (National Audit Office) (2011) *Oversight of user choice and provider competition in care markets*, London: NAO

Naqvi, S, (2013) 'The highs lows and potential of the ASYEs', *Professional Social Work*, July/August

Narey, M. (2011) 'A blueprint for the nation's lost children', *The Times*, 5 July

Narey, M. (2014) *Making the education of social workers consistently effective*, London: Department for Education

National Probation Service (2001) *A new choreography*, London: National Probation Service/Home Office

Newman, J., Glendinning, C. and Hughes, J. (2008) 'Beyond modernisation: social care and the transformation of welfare governance', *Journal of Social Policy*, vol 37, no 4, p 250

NMC (Nursing and Midwifery Council) (2008) *The code: Standards of performance, conduct and ethics for nurses and midwives*, London: Nursing and Midwifery Council

Oliver, M. (1983) *Social work with disabled people*, Basingstoke: Macmillan

Oliver, M. (ed) (1991) *Social work: Disabled people and disabling environments*, London: Jessica Kingsley

Onyett, S. (1997) 'Collaboration and the community health team', *Journal of Interprofessional Care*, vol 11 no 3, pp 257-65

Panorama, BBC (2009) 'Britain's home care scandal', Panorama programme, www. bbc.co.uk/programmes/b00jnknl

Parker, R. (1990) *Safeguarding standards*, London: National Institute for Social Work

Parliament (2010) *Key issues for the new Parliament,* www.parliament.uk/business/ publications/research/key-issues-for-the-new-parliament/value-for-money-in-public-services/the-ageing-population/

Parsloe, P. and Stevenson, O. (1977) *Social services teams: The practitioner's view*, London: HMSO

Payne, M. (2013) 'Social work', in A. Worsley, T. Mann, A. Olsen and E. Mason-Whitehead (eds) *Key concepts in social work practice*, London: Sage Publications

Pease, R. (2013) 'A history of critical and radical social work', in M. Gray and S. Webb (eds) *The new politics of social work*, Basingstoke: Palgrave Macmillan

Peltier, J., Dahl, A. and Mulhern, F. (2009) *The relationship between employee satisfaction and hospital patient experiences*, Chicago, IL: Forum for People Performance Management and Measurement, Northwestern University

Perlman, H. (1957) *Casework: A problem solving process*, Chicago, IL: Chicago University Press

Phillips, M. (2008) 'The barbarism of ideologues', *Daily Mail*, 17 November

Pickles, E. (2013) Speech, 25 November, www.dclg.gov.uk

Pierson, J. (2011) *Understanding social work: History and context*, Maidenhead: McGraw Hill/Open University Press

Piketty, T. (2014) *Capital in the twenty-first century*, Cambridge, MA: Harvard University Press

Pinker, R. (1982) 'Appendix B: An alternative view', in P. Barclay (ed) *Social workers: Their role and tasks*, London: National Institute for Social Work, Bedford Square Press

Pinker, R. (1990) *Social work in an enterprise society*, London: Routledge

Pinker, R. (1993) 'How the race commissars brainwash our social workers', *Daily Mail*, 2 August

Prior, P. (1992) 'The approved social worker: reflection on origins', *British Journal of Social Work*, vol 22, no 2, April, pp 105-119

Professional Social Work (2014) April

RAND Europe/Ernst and Young LLP (2012) *National evaluation of the Department of Health's integrated care pilots*, Cambridge: RAND Europe

Rankin, G. (1971) 'Professional social work and the campaign against poverty', *Social Work Today*, vol 1, no 10, pp 19-21

Right Care (2013), www.rightcare.nhs.uk/index.php/2013/05/findings-from-the-evaluation-of-the-inner-north-west-london-integrated-care-pilot/

Ritchie, J., Dick, D. and Lingham, R. (1994) *The report of the inquiry into the care and treatment of Christopher Clunis*, London: HMSO

Rogowski, S. (2010) *Social work: The rise and fall of a profession*, Bristol: Policy Press

Rooff, M. (1972) *A hundred years of family welfare*, London: Michael Joseph

Rose, M.E. (1971) *The English Poor Laws 1780–1930*, Newton Abbot: David and Charles

Rose, M.E. (1972) *The relief of poverty 1834–1914*, London: Macmillan

Rowe, J. and Lambert, L. (1973) *Children who wait*, London: Association of British Adoption Agencies

Rowntree, S. (1901) *Poverty: A study of town life*, London: Macmillan

Royal Commission (1909) *Report of the Royal Commission on the Poor Laws and the relief of distress*, Cd 4499, Appendix, Volume 1, Minutes of evidence, Question 2230

Royal Commission on the National Health Service (1979) *Report of the Merrison Commission*, Cmnd 7615, London: HMSO

Royal Commission on the Funding of Long Term Care (1999) *With respect to old age: Long term care? Rights and responsibilities*, Cmnd 4192-1, London: The Stationery Office

Rummery, K. and Glendinning, C. (2000) *Primary care and social services: Developing new partnerships for older people*, Abingdon: Radcliffe

Sayle, A. (1985), www.youtube.com/watch?v=vmlJFykua_0

Scarman, Lord (1982) *The Scarman report: The Brixton disorders 10-12 April 1981*, London: Penguin Books

SCIE (Social Care Institute for Excellence) (2011) *Factors that promote and hinder integrated working between health and social care services*, Research Briefing 41, London: SCIE

SCIE (2013) *Social work practice pilots and pioneers in social work with adults*, London: SCIE

Scott, D. (2010) 'Who's protecting who?', *Probation Journal*, vol 57, no 3, pp 291-5

Scottish Education and Scottish Home and Health Departments (1966) *Social work in the community*, Edinburgh: Scottish Education and Scottish Home and Health Departments.

Scottish Government (2006) *Changing lives: Report of the 21st century social work review*, Edinburgh: Scottish Executive

Scottish Government (2011a) *Achieving sustainable quality in Scotland's healthcare: A '20:20' vision*, Edinburgh: Scottish Government

Scottish Government (2012a) *Free personal and nursing care, Scotland, 2010-11*, Edinburgh: Scottish Government, www.scotland.gov.uk/Resource/0039/00399515.pdf

Scottish Government (2012b) 'Integration of health and social care', press release, 12 December

Scottish Home and Health Department/Scottish Education Department (1964) *The Kilbrandon report: Children and young persons, Scotland*, Edinburgh: HMSO

Seebohm, F. (1968) *The report of the Committee on Local Authority and Allied Personal Social Services* (Seebohm report), Cmnd 3703: London: HMSO

Select Committee of the House of Commons (1846) *Report of the Select Committee of the House of Commons, the Andover Union*

Shaw, S., Rosen, R. and Rumbold, B. (2011) *What is integrated care?*, London: Nuffield Trust

Silverman, J. (2011) *Crime, policy and the media*, London: Routledge

Skills for Care (2013) *The size and structure of the adult social care workforce in England in 2013*, Leeds: Skills for Care

Slasberg, C., Beresford, P. and Schofield, C. (2013) 'The increasing evidence of how self-directed support is failing to deliver personal budgets and personalisation', *Research Policy and Planning*, vol 30, no 2

Smith, J. (2002) Department of Health press release, 22 May

Society Guardian (2011) 27 July

Solly, H. (1868) *A few suggestions on how to deal with the unemployed poor of London, and with its 'roughs' and criminal classes*, London: National Association for the Promotion of Social Science

Spearing, H. (2013), www.radical.org.uk/barefoot/students.htm

SSSC (Scottish Social Services Council) (2013) *2012 Scottish social services workforce data*, Dundee: Scottish Social Services Council

Stanley, N., Austerberry, H., Bilson, A., Farrelly, N., Hargreave, S.K., Hussein, S., Ingold, I., Manthorpe, J., Ridley, J. and Strange V. (2012) *Social work practices: Report of the national evaluation*, DfE

Stanley, N., Austerberry, H., Bilson, A., Farrelly, N., Hargreave, S.K., Hussein, S., Ingold, I., Manthorpe, J., Ridley, J. and Strange V (2014) 'Establishing social work practices in England: the early evidence', *British Journal of Social Work*, vol 44, no 2, pp 367-83

Stein, M. and Carey, K. (1986) *Leaving care*, Oxford: Blackwell

Stevens, M. and Wilberforce, M. (2008) *The IBSEN project: National evaluation of the individual budgets pilot projects*, York: Social Policy Research Unit, University of York

Sutherland, Lord (2008) *Independent review of free personal and nursing care in Scotland*, Edinburgh: Scottish Government

SWAN (Social Work Action Network) (nd) 'Manifesto', www.socialworkfuture.org/attachments/article/56/SWAN%20Social%20Work%20Manifesto.pdf

SWIA (Social Work Inspection Agency) (2005) *A report into the care and protection of childen in Eilean Slar*, Edinburgh: Scottish Executive

Taylor, M. (2013), 'Probation PBR - a lot more questions than answers', 9 May, www.matthewtaylorsblog.com/public-policy/probation-pbr-a-lot-more-questions-than-answers

Tew, J. (2011) *Social approaches to mental distress*, Basingstoke: Palgrave Macmillan

Think Local Act, Personal (2010) *Next steps for transforming adult social care*, London: Department of Health and others

Thoburn, J. (2013) '"Troubled families", "troublesome families" and the trouble with payment by results', *Families, Relationships and Societies*, vol 2, no 3, pp 471-475

Thompson, N. (2012) *Anti-discriminatory practice* (5th edn), Basingstoke: Palgrave Macmillan

The Times (1973) 'Social worker booed and shouted at', 6 November

The Times (2012) 'Bed blocking costs NHS £200m a year', 24 September

Titmuss R. (1966) 'A challenge for local government', *The Journal of the Royal Society for the Promotion of Health*, vol 86, no 1, Jan-Feb

Titmuss, R. (1970) *The gift relationship: from human blood to social policy*, London: George Allen and Unwin

Today programme, Radio 4, 18 July 2013

TOPPS (2000) *Modernising the social care workforce*, Leeds: TOPPS

Townsend, P. (1959) *The last refuge*, London: Routledge and Kegan Paul

Townsend, P. and Wedderburn, D. (1965) *The aged in the welfare state*, London: G Bell and sons

Utting, W. (1991) *Children in the public care: A review of residential child care*, London: HMSO

Utting, W. (1997) *People like us: The report of the review of the safeguards for children living away from home*, London: Department of Health

Vanstone, M. (2004) *Supervising offenders in the community: A history of probation theory and practice*, Aldershot: Ashgate

Waterhouse, R. (2000) *Lost in care: Report of the tribunal of inquiry into the abuse of children in care in the former county council areas of Gwynedd and Clwyd since 1974*, London: The Stationery Office

Webb, A. and Wistow, G. (1987) *Social work, social care and social planning*, Harlow: Longman

Webb, S. (1910) *English Poor Law policy*, London: Longman Green and Co

Webb, S. (2006) *Social work in a risk society*, Basingstoke: Palgrave Macmillan

Weinstein, J. (2011) *Social Work Action Network, Newsletter 4*, Autumn

Welsh Government (2013) *Social Services and Wellbeing (Wales) Bill Explanatory Memorandum*, Cardiff: Welsh Government

West, K. (2013) 'The grip of personalisation on adult social care: between managerial domination and fantasy', *Critical Social Policy*, vol 33, no 4, pp 638-657

White, C., Warrener, M., Reeves, A. and La Valle, I. (2008) *Family Intervention Projects: An evaluation of their design, set-up and early outcomes*, London: National Centre for Social Research

White, S., Wastell, D., Broadhurst, K. and Hall, C. (2010) 'When policy o'er leaps itself: the "tragic tale" of the integrated children's system', *Critical Social Policy*, vol 30, no 3, August

Whitehead, P. and Statham, R. (2006) *The history of probation: Politics, power and cultural change 1876–2005*, Crayford: Shaw and Sons

Wilson E, (1980) 'Feminism and social work' in M. Brake and R. Bailey (eds) *Radical social work and practice*, London: Edward Arnold

Wilson, G. and Campbell, A. (2013) 'Developing social work education: academic perspectives', *British Journal of Social Work*, July, pp 1005-24

Winter, J.M. (1980) 'Military fitness and civilian health in Britain during the First World War', *Journal of Contemporary History*, vol 15, no 2, p 211

Woolham, J. and Benton, C. (2013) 'The costs and benefits of personal budgets for older people: evidence from a single local authority', *British Journal of Social Work*, vol 43, no 8, pp 1472-1491

Wootton, B. (1959) *Social science and social pathology*, London: Allen and Unwin

Yeats, W.B. (1920) *The Second Coming*, Dublin: the Dial

Yee, Y., Cheung, A. and Cheng, T. (2008) 'The impact of employee satisfaction on quality and profitability in high-contact service industries', *Journal of Operations Management*, September, pp 651-68

Young, A.F. and Ashton, E.T. (1956) *British social work in the nineteenth century*, London: Routledge and Kegan Paul

Young, G. (1936) *Victorian England: Portrait of an age*, London: Oxford University Press

Young, M. and Willmott, P. (1959) *Family and kinship in East London*, London: Routledge and Kegan Paul

Younghusband, E. (1947) *The employment and training of social workers*, Dunfermline: Carnegie UK Trust

Younghusband, E. (1951) *Social Work in Britain*, Dunfermline: Carnegie UK Trust

Younghusband, E. (1959) *Report of the working party on social workers in local authority health and selfare services*, London: HMSO

Younghusband, E. (1964) *Social work and social change*, London: Allen and Unwin

Younghusband, E. (1978) *Social work in Britain 1950–75*, London: Allen and Unwin

Index